Divine Action

This book is an expanded version of the Teape Lectures, given at St Stephen's College, Delhi, Bishop's College, Calcutta and the United Theological College, Bangalore in 1989.

I am very grateful to the Teape Committee of the University of Cambridge for their invitation to deliver these lectures.

Divine Action

Keith Ward

Collins

First published in Great Britain in 1990 by Flame.

Flame is an imprint of
Collins Religious Publishing
part of the Collins Publishing Group
8 Grafton Street, London W1X 3LA

© 1990 Keith Ward
ISBN 0 00 599205 2

Typographical design by Ann Hewitt
Typesetting by The Bath Press
Made and printed in Great Britain by Bell & Bain Ltd, Glasgow

CONDITIONS OF SALE

Contents

1

The Abyss of Reason

The Christian faith is committed to the belief that there is a God who acts in history. In the Old Testament God liberates the Hebrews from Egypt by acts of mighty and terrible power. He guides them through the wilderness in a pillar of cloud and fire. He gives them victory over their enemies by sending plagues, earthquakes and inducing supernatural panic. He allows his people to be taken into exile because of their sins, and helps them to return to the promised land at the time he has foretold. The core of the New Testament is a record of the acts of God in the life, death and resurrection of Jesus. It is by the power of God that Jesus heals, exorcizes demons and is raised from the dead in vindication of his prophetic ministry. In the daily life of the churches, Christians pray, by their Lord's command, for God's help and guidance; and believe that God can and will act to heal, convert and empower human lives. There can be little doubt that the historic faith of Christianity is a continuing testimony to the existence of a living God, who works out his purposes in the world and acts to judge evil and redeem his people.

   Yet the idea that God acts in the world has become peculiarly problematic, even for those firmly committed to the truth of Christianity. There are many reasons for this; but among intellectual reasons is the astounding success of the post-seventeenth-century scientific world-view; and among moral reasons is a reluctance to see the catastrophes and disasters of the world as reconcilable with the existence of a God who has the power to prevent them. The scientific world-view seems to leave no room for God to act, since everything that happens is determined by scientific laws. "Man has learnt to deal with himself in all questions of importance without recourse to the 'working' hypothesis called 'God'. In questions of science, art and ethics this has become an

1

understood thing" (Bonhoeffer 1979:348–9). There is no place in our world-view for a real God who makes a difference to human life. That concept belongs to an archaic, superstitious world-view, for which spirits and demons battle in the world for supremacy, and can be called up and propitiated by suitably trained "holy men". Now God has gone, and his passing has not even left a gap where he used to be. There are no God-shaped gaps in the world; there is not even a trace of where he was. As Bonhoeffer says, "If in fact the frontiers of knowledge are being pushed further and further back (and that is bound to be the case), then God is being pushed back with them, and is therefore continually in retreat" (ibid.:311).

Modern moral awareness, too, finds difficulty with the idea of Divine action. Sensitive to the amount and degree of apparently unavoidable suffering in the world, it tends to accuse God both of acting too little, in failing to stop earthquakes and disasters; and of acting unfairly when he does act, by healing some people and not others, and generally by being too arbitrary and partial in his interferences in nature. A particularly clear account of these problems is given by Maurice Wiles, who writes, "If the direct action of God ... is an intelligible concept, then it would appear to have been sparingly and strangely used ... it would seem strange that no miraculous intervention prevented Auschwitz or Hiroshima ... Thus to acknowledge even the possibility of miracle raises acute problems for theodicy" (Wiles 1986:66). Wiles finds the problems so acute that he abandons the idea of particular Divine action in the world; though it is worth noting that he also protests that if God did act in such ways, that would imply "a manipulative control of human action that is wholly unacceptable" (ibid.:63). It often seems that we can neither stand the thought of God acting often (since that would infringe our freedom), nor the thought of him acting rarely (since that makes him responsible for our suffering). This does not allow God much leeway; and Wiles' bold and carefully argued conclusion is that "If we think of the whole continuing creation of the world as God's one act, an act in which he allows radical freedom to his human creation ... (this is) incompatible with the assertion of further particular divinely initiated acts within the developing history of the world" (ibid.:93). Moral considerations lead us to prefer to deny that God can act at all, rather than to say that he either acts arbitrarily or manipulatively.

Many people in the West, and among them eminent Christian theologians, have simply lost any sense of the world as the sphere of particular Divine action. They find it hard to interpret what happens in terms of acts that God performs. Perhaps, as Nietzsche suggested, God is dead (Nietzsche 1972:41); that idea has no use now that we have accepted full responsibility for how the world goes. We have almost conquered nature, in theory. We have taken morality out of the hands of religious dogma. What happens in our world is either too much under human control, or too arbitrary and random, to be ascribed to God any longer. So the sense of God as a real agent, making a difference to the world in ways we might at least sometimes identify, has evaporated. It has become embarrassing to hear simple believers ascribing the good things that happen to them to God, when this same God seemingly destroys thousands in earthquakes and fires. It has become embarrassing to hear people ascribing remote disasters to Divine judgment, when their own lives seem often to be so sheltered, so unaware of their selfishness and so self-righteous in their moral complacency.

As if this was not enough, further blows to the edifice of faith come from Biblical critics and philosophical theologians. The critics claim that many, perhaps most, of the Biblical records of God's acts are legends; that, for instance, there is little evidence the exodus ever happened; that Jericho ever had any walls at all; or that Canaan was conquered in the way the Bible records (for a representative scholarly account of the problems, see Alberto Soggin, *A History of Israel*, 1985). So even the historical records of God's mighty acts are thrown into doubt. The philosophers complete the confusion by querying whether the word "God" can refer to anything; whether metaphysics has any meaning; whether we do not use religious language to express attitudes and policies of life rather than to describe objective realities (a view enthusiastically canvassed by Don Cupitt in a number of works). After all that, one might well come to think that there is no objective

God who could act; so that talk of Divine action must be just a poetic way of seeing meaning and value in one's experience.

It is not at all clear, then, that the notion of Divine action makes any sense, or what sort of sense it makes. If it makes no sense, the Christian faith may for a while cling on to a tenuous and marginal existence as a set of legends outlining an optional policy of life. But it will eventually evaporate to take its place with the great legends of Greek and Roman mythology, its policy of life at last becoming as quaint and archaic as that of ancient Athens. It is therefore a matter of vital importance to examine the idea of Divine action, starting again from first principles, to discover what may be said of it in view of the many difficulties raised in the modern age.

Where should one start? The Christian theologian or philosopher must start from the belief that forms the life of the church community in which he lives, from the idea of God as one who reveals his nature in the life of the man Jesus, who has acted to redeem the world, not in visible power and majesty, but in a life of humility, healing, forgiving and self-renouncing love. At the same time, this God must be recognizably the God of the people of Israel and Judah, who delivered the Hebrews from Egypt, gave the Torah to Moses and raised up the prophets to declare his judgment and forgiveness. Whatever is said of Divine action must constantly be referred back to this idea; it must be an intelligible development of this idea for the contemporary world.

One indisputable characteristic of the God of Abraham, Isaac and Jacob, the Father of the Lord Jesus Christ, is that he is the creator of all things in heaven and earth ("The Lord is the everlasting God, the creator of the ends of the earth", Isaiah 40:28). If one is exploring the idea of Divine action, this is where one must begin, for creation is the first act of God in relation to all other things, without which no further acts would be possible. There may, in the history of religion, be many gods who are not creators, who act in a material universe which they do not wholly cause. In the speculations of philosophers, Plato's god, the *Demi-urgos* who does the best he can with an everlastingly existent matter, is such a

God ("Intelligence controlled necessity by persuading it for the most part to bring about the best result", Plato 1971:65). So is the God of A.N. Whitehead, father of process thought, who does not bring all things into being as their sole cause, but is more like the all-including spectator of an everlasting cosmic process, ultimately constituted by an infinity of actual occasions which are the real basis of all causal change ("God ... does not create the world, he saves it: or, more accurately, he is the poet of the world, with tender patience leading it by his vision of truth, beauty and goodness", Whitehead, 1929:490).

Against all such views, the doctrine of creation *ex nihilo* asserts that God is the sole originating cause of everything other than himself. Nothing exists apart from God that he has not brought into being and in some sense willed to be. So, if God has not created, there would be no finite beings to act upon. It is in that sense that without creation no further Divine acts would be possible, at least with regard to beings other than God himself. The doctrine of creation *ex nihilo* is not explicitly formulated in the Bible. The Genesis account of creation can be, and is even quite naturally, interpreted as the shaping action of God upon a primal stuff or chaotic matter, the "great deep" (Genesis 1:2). Nor is a doctrine of creation out of nothing (i.e. not by shaping already existing matter) easy to establish theoretically – for how can we be sure that nothing does or could exist independently of God or beyond the range of his causal power? Even if the prophets had experience of a being of immense power, how could they know that nothing was beyond his power?

It is clear that such a belief could not be established by observation. Yet it is not different in kind from many beliefs that modern scientists have – for example, that every event has a cause; or that the laws of physics will apply everywhere in the physical universe. We might call these postulates that are implicit in the practice of science; that can never be conclusively established; but which are increasingly confirmed, and never disconfirmed, by continued scientific investigation. A cautious sceptic might say that scientists should confine themselves to saying that the laws have applied so far, and that they might apply in future. But in practice scientists have to assume, and act on the assumption, that these basic postulates are true even despite some apparent evidence to the contrary. Their beliefs go far beyond the evidence, although they are falsifiable if enough evidence resists all attempts to fit them into the assumed postulates (arguably, quantum theory has done this to classical physics).

It seems that the Biblical writers developed the idea of God as creator of all things relatively late in their history. Beginning with the compelling experience of a God whose power was known in acts of liberation and judgment, they gradually came to see that he must be the Lord of all history; that nothing could be beyond his power, or be able to defeat his purposes. The primitive experience was of a god who set one group of tribes apart to keep his law of justice and mercy; to worship him. In return, he promised them a homeland and a unique destiny among the nations. Reflection on this idea soon led to belief that he must be powerful above all other gods; and that the values embodied in his law were supreme above all others. By the time of the later prophets, God was seen as a being of unsurpassable value and power, worthy of unconditional worship and absolute faith in his ability to fulfil his promises.

The idea of God as unconditionally valuable and powerful is a presupposition of worship, of unconditional faith and loyalty. It became clear that the worship of any finite "god" would be idolatry, the sin of giving unconditional obedience to what was only of limited reality and value. The possession of unsurpassable power entails the idea of creation *ex nihilo*, since otherwise something (and perhaps anything) could exist independently of God; and it might then oppose or limit his power. It is therefore correct to see this doctrine of creation as implicit in the Biblical doctrine that God is the creator of heaven and earth, that he can do all things, that nothing is beyond his power ("I know that you can do all things" Job 42:2).

So the idea of creation out of nothing is contained in Biblical revelation, and it is a presupposition of true worship and unconditional obedience. But is it true? Only God himself could know with absolute theoretical certainty that nothing exists, or could exist, without his bringing it about. Humans could only know it if God told them (and if they knew that he had done so), or if they framed it as a conjecture, a theoretical postulate acceptable because of its elegance, fruitfulness, adequacy to experience and integrating power. That conjecture, however, is not a merely theoretical one. If I am to put my confidence totally in God, I must believe that absolutely nothing could defeat his purposes. So I must believe that everything is in his power, that nothing can exist without his willing it, in some sense, to be. So this postulate is the foundation of a way of life which embodies total faith.

I accept the postulate, without having theoretical certainty (realizing that such certainty is in principle unobtainable), not on wholly theoretical grounds, but primarily because of my assent of unconditional trust to the self-disclosure of a being of unconditional reality and value. As I reflect upon what is involved in giving unconditional trust, and upon what is involved in the idea of unconditional value, I may realize that only a being of unsurpassable power, of power that could never in principle be defeated or even resisted, could be the adequate object of faith. And so I come to the idea of the sole creator of everything other than itself as the only adequate conceptualization of the One who is revealed to the patriarchs and prophets. A good exposition of this process of reflection is briefly given by J. N. Findlay, in his essay, "Can God's Existence be Disproved?" (Flew and MacIntyre 1955). In that essay, Findlay argues that the idea of worship leads one to an idea of a God of such perfection that it could not possibly exist. It is worth noting that Findlay retracted his claim that such a God is impossible, and came to affirm the existence of an all-perfect God in his later work. The God of the philosophers is not different from the God of Abraham, Isaac and Jacob. It is the ultimate reflective formulation of the presupposition of absolute faith; and that faith is evoked by the revelation of the Divine nature through the prophets and in the person of Jesus.

What the theologian needs to do, as part of the reflection on revelation, is to explore what is involved in this idea of creation *ex nihilo*. One aspect of it is that nothing can possibly exist without God willing it. But if one asks, "Why not?", it is quite difficult to give a satisfactory theoretical answer.

7

David Hume, the urbane and acute scourge of theists everywhere, supposes that anything at all might exist, or nothing.
Nothing is essentially connected to anything else, so there
can very easily be a world without God, just existing for no
reason at all. "I can imagine such a thing", says Hume, "so
it is obviously possible" (Hume 1935:Part 9). And indeed,
if one says, "Things cannot exist without God", it is hard
to see in what this "cannot" might consist.

There are a number of philosophical theologians who have
argued that God is what they call an "ultimate brute fact".
John Hick, for instance, takes this view, arguing that to call
God "necessary" is to say that he is without beginning or
end and without dependence. But, he says, "this does not
imply ... a logically necessary being" (Hick 1970:86). And
Richard Swinburne concurs: "It must be held that God is
a logically contingent being" (Swinburne 1979:76). God does
exist; he may even in fact be self-existent; but he might not
have been. Nothing compels him to be; his existence is contingent, like the real existence of anything else. Indeed, it is
a dogma of empiricism to add to the two popularized by Quine
that all existential propositions are contingent. One can deny
any assertion of existence, including "God exists", without
any inconsistency. Therefore God might not exist, or might
never have existed.

These assertions may seem harmless, but in fact they are
deeply inimical to theism. If anything might or might not
exist, then there could be a world without God; there could
come into being something as powerful as God; or there could
exist many things beyond God's power to control. The dependence of things upon God cannot, it seems, be a logical dependence, one that is true by definition of terms. So it is not
surprising that we can *assert* "X does not depend upon God"
without contradiction. Yet it must be impossible for X so
to exist, whatever X may be. For this to make any sense,
something must make it impossible for X to exist without
God. Things which might or might not exist, for no reason,
must actually be prevented from coming into existence by
something with the power so to prevent them. We have to
say, then, that in every possible world there exists a being
with the power to prevent anything existing which it does

equivocation between logical + factual necessity?

not will to exist. That is to say, the necessary dependence of all things upon God – the fact that nothing can exist without God – logically depends upon the existence of God being necessary – actual in every possible world. (This formulation of necessary existence has been popularized by Plantinga, especially in *God, Freedom and Evil*, 1977:111–12.)

This can be formulated with precision. If no world can exist without God, then it is not the case that there can be a world and not be a God. A world is a set of states of affairs; so it is true that, if any state of affairs exists, then God exists. It immediately follows that, if God does not exist, then no state of affairs exists. A possible world is one which can possibly exist. But no world can exist unless God also exists; so no world is possible unless it includes the existence of God. Therefore God exists in every possible world. A being which could not fail to exist in every possible world is a necessary being – there is no possible alternative to its existence, as just the being it is. It is bound to be true that God cannot fail to exist, and he cannot be other than he is, in his essentially Divine properties.

If God is creator *ex nihilo*, nothing can exist unless he wills it. Thus God is such that he cannot fail to exist; he is an "absolutely necessary being", and he necessarily possesses the property of omnipotence, at least in the sense of having the power to create or destroy all possible creatable and destructible (all contingent) things. The presupposition of Biblical theism is that there exists a necessary being which necessarily possesses the power to create or destroy all contingent things. This principle of Divine necessity is a significant principle, for it shows that God is not an ultimately contingent being, who happens to have the nature he has. He is not just the greatest or most powerful thing that exists. His mode of existence is different in kind from that of all contingent things. It is necessary, and independent of all other things. The classical formulation of this view is found, appropriately, in the form of a prayer, reflecting upon the character of the supreme object of worship, in Anselm's *Proslogion* (Anselm 1965).

Immanuel Kant pointed out that this idea of "unconditioned necessity, which we do indispensably require as the last bearer of all things, is for human reason the veritable

abyss" (Kant 1952:A.613). We cannot, he said, think the existence of anything as necessary – for we can imagine anything
to be non-existent. In one sense he is right; in another, wrong.
He is right, in that the mode of existence of such a being
is quite beyond our capacity to comprehend. We cannot
imagine what it is like to exist in that way. We have not the
remotest conception of what can make something incapable
of non-existence. In this respect, the being of God is a mystery
beyond human comprehension. "I am that I am", said God
to Moses (Exodus 3:14). Only God can comprehend the manner of his own existence. In a significant sense, his being is
beyond all analogies and images, wholly *sui generis*, unique.
Yet in another way Kant is wrong. For we can form the concept of a being which is unable not to exist. We can contrast
it with the notion of a contingent being, which may not exist,
or may exist differently. Human imagination is a wholly unreliable guide to what may really be, and the fact that we seem
to be able to imagine God's non-existence merely shows that
we are unable to imagine God. So it is quite possible to conceive that God exists necessarily, while confessing, and indeed
requiring, that we are quite unable to comprehend the nature
of necessary existence.

May the notion of necessary existence not be vacuous? We
think we are conceiving something, but there is really nothing
that we are conceiving at all. Since this concept is at the very
edge of human thought, we have to confess that we cannot
prove it to be non-vacuous. Yet it is entailed (if I am right)
by concepts that are not vacuous – like the concept of creation
ex nihilo. And it seems to be, at least syntactically, a well-
formed expression. It cannot be proved to be vacuous, either.
So the balance of probability is that it has content, that it
points towards a form of being which is beyond the capacity
of any finite mind to comprehend. It is, then, perfectly permiss-
ible to adopt the concept, as one presupposed to the revealed
ideal of God, and to take one's stand on revelation as the
source and justification of one's belief.

These considerations help us to see, however, why this belief
in God's necessary existence does not, as Kant mistakenly
thought, commit one to the validity of the ontological argument (Kant 1952:A.629). From the fact that one believes God

to exist by necessity, it does not follow that one can establish that God exists by simply analysing the concept of God. The concept of God may be – and I have held that it is – the concept of a being which exists by necessity. But it does not follow that this concept is instantiated. On the other hand, I can believe that God exists by necessity, without believing that anyone has, or could have, a clear enough concept of God to be able to see how that necessity flows from the concept itself. Thus, while my concept of God is of a being which exists by necessity, I may deny that I can prove that there is a God just by analysing a concept. If we could comprehend the concept of God, then and only then might we be able to establish that there really must be, and therefore is, such a God. This is the burden of Aquinas' short but telling treatment of Anselm's reflections, in *Summa Theologiae*, 1a,2,1, *Responsio* ("The proposition, 'God exists' is self-evident in itself . . . (but) the proposition is not self-evident to us").

A number of recent philosophers have argued that the sense in which God is said to be necessary, in the classical Christian tradition, is significantly different from the sense of "logical necessity". God, they suggest, exists eternally and with complete independence from anything else. He is not liable to corruption, dissolution or decay. It is in these senses that Aquinas, for example, speaks of God as necessary, according to Geach and Anscombe (1961:115). Now it is true that "God exists" is not necessarily true, in the same sense in which "A bachelor is an unmarried man" is necessarily true. The latter is true by definition. As Kant put it, the meaning of the predicate is contained in the meaning of the subject. We can know that such propositions are true as long as we know the meaning of the terms used in framing the proposition.

We can make "God exists" true in this sense, if we define "God" as "a being who cannot fail to exist". It is true by definition that a being who cannot fail to exist, exists. But that goes no way to settling the question of whether there is such a being. Perhaps I must think of God as a being who exists in a quite unique way, such that there is no alternative to his being what he is. This may lead me to the thought that God is a unique being who has control over the complete range of possibilities, since he excludes the possibility of his own non-existence, and therefore excludes the possibility of anything existing without his determining will. This is an important thought, but it hardly establishes that there really exists such a being. It does not even establish that such a being is really possible, rather than being a vacuous figment of human imagination.

Thus the sense in which "God exists" is true by logical necessity is in one way a trivial sense, an uninformative sense as to what really exists. Many philosophers have held that it does not make sense to suppose that some being could not fail to exist. Consequently, one must mean something else by speaking of necessary existence. One may mean that God's existence is a necessary condition of the existence of anything else, or that God's existence is not dependent upon the existence of anything else, or that God's existence, though it might not have been instantiated, is not subject to change or destruction if it is instantiated – probably because it is timeless, and thus not subject to change in any respect. This is the account Anthony Kenny gives as an interpretation of Aquinas (Kenny 1969:48), but it seems to me to be radically deficient.

Although one cannot establish that there is a God by defining God as necessarily existent, it is far from trivial to say that the concept of God is the concept of a being which cannot fail to exist, and which renders it impossible for anything to exist without dependence on it. Indeed, I have tried to show that one cannot assert that any possible world depends upon the existence of God without asserting that God cannot fail to exist (i.e. that he exists in all possible worlds). Nor can one assert complete Divine independence from all other things without ruling out the possibility of anything existing which could prevent God from existing. And that brings us back to the concept of God as excluding all possible beings which could cause his nature to be different, and thus as existing in every possible world. Finally, it is not enough to say that God just happens to exist timelessly, and that is why he is not contingent, in the sense that he may change or cease to exist. For such a being still might not have existed. Then there could have been a world, even a world otherwise exactly like this one, without God – unless, of course, one goes back to the argument that no world can exist without God, and we are back to necessary existence, in a fuller sense.

I conclude that "God exists" is after all a logically necessary truth, in the sense that it cannot be denied without contradiction. Of course, many people deny it. But that is either because they do not see that God is a necessary being, or because they think such a concept is senseless. In other words, "God exists" is either true by logical necessity, or false by logical necessity (being senseless, it could not possibly be true). It has the peculiarity that we do not know for certain which; making it very different from easier necessary truths, like "2+2=4", which we know with certainty to be true. But there are many examples of propositions of that sort – such as Goldbach's Conjecture, that every even number is the sum of two primes, which has never been proved, and so could conceivably be false, though if it is true, it is necessarily true. The proposition asserting God's existence is similarly either necessarily true or necessarily false, though perhaps it is beyond human capacity to establish conclusively by argument which it is.

The theist would really expect the concept of God to be incomprehensible (not inconceivable); for, as Baron von Hügel said, any God that we could comprehend would not be God. But if the concept of God is incomprehensible, does it have any meaning? Can it refer to anything in objective reality? It is quite clear that the idea is meant to refer to an objectively existing being, a being upon which all other things depend for their existence. It is extremely strange that some modern theists have rejected the possibility of this most real of all beings and insisted that the idea of God is a mere construct of the human imagination (e.g. Don Cupitt, in *Taking Leave of God* 1980). But here again, there are some distinctions to be made. The concept of God is, of course, a human construct, in that we invent the word and give it a meaning in our language. That does not imply that it has no possible reference. We may construct it exactly in order to refer to something. But, it may be asked, how can the concept refer, when God cannot be pointed to or identified in experience? God is not an object we might come across, since he is the creator of everything whatsoever. How, then, could I ever know that the concept, "God', referred to anything? The straightforward reply is that the concept "God" refers by giving a unique description. God is the one and only creator of everything other than himself. That reference is absolutely precise and uniquely identifying. It is not possible to refer to the wrong God by mistake, although of course it is possible that I could misdescribe the God to whom I am referring.

But can I know that my attempted reference succeeds? That there is such a God? Of course not; at least, not in the sense of achieving total theoretical certainty. Only God can have that. But I can have good reasons for thinking there is such a God – the whole history of claimed revelation to Israel gives me such reasons. Of course my concept pushes the idea of the Lord of all to its ultimate conclusion, and I cannot be theoretically certain that it can be pushed so far. There may exist a god who is limited in power, and who just happens to find himself existing. It may just be true that there exists no being more powerful than God, though there might have been. God might then say to me, "Luckily, as it happens, I am powerful enough to achieve my purposes. Trust Me." God would then be a cosmic super-person, the greatest being around – though at any moment he may cease to exist, or a more powerful being may simply pop into existence.

None of this shows that the idea of a necessarily existing, necessarily omnipotent being does not make sense. But it does suggest that we cannot be justified in believing there is such a being, since we could never get sufficient evidence for it. We may be able, then, to settle for less. And we might remove some of the disadvantages of having a contingent and limited God by suggesting, as Kenny does, that God happens to be timeless. Then, though he might not have existed, if he exists at all he cannot cease to exist, since a timeless being must be changeless. Nor can another timeless being come into existence, since that would be a change, which would presuppose time. One might think that a timeless God is as difficult a concept as a necessary God, and just as liable to be vacuous. But it offers the possibility of a contingent universe which just happens to depend upon a contingently omnipotent being, which does exist, even though it might not have done.

Is there anything to choose between these concepts of God?

There is a clear difference between them, since a contingent God is one whose own existence is unaccountable. There is no reason why it should be as it is. It could just as easily have been different, but it just happens to be the way it is. A necessary God, however, is the way it is because there is no alternative. There is a reason, an utterly conclusive reason, for its existence (even though human beings are incapable of understanding that reason, which only God can comprehend). The reason is that nothing else is even logically possible. Without God, nothing at all would be possible; but something is always possible. Even a supposed "null world", in which nothing is possible, is a possible world. So God cannot fail to be, as the ground of all possible existence, as what Boethius called "the unlimited ocean of being".

We have here two different pictures of the ultimate origin of things. On the one hand, we have the idea of a world "derived from night", as Aristotle put it – a world springing into being from nothing. One may say that a timeless being does not spring into being, since it must always be or not be. But its being has no cause or reason. On the other hand, we have the idea of a finite world as springing from an unconditioned infinite reality, a fullness of being which cannot fail to be, which is in itself wholly intelligible and which gives intelligibility and value to all things. Given that both pictures are at the extreme limit of human conceivability, neither is intrinsically more puzzling than the other. There is no advantage in terms of clarity or evident coherence. It may be thought that we should just leave the question alone, as unprofitable speculation.

I believe that the thesis of total contingency does have theological defects, however, which can be brought out by analysis. If God just happens to exist, then there might have been a world without God, or there might have been a different, more limited, even malign god. God might not be uniquely independent in existence, or timeless in his being, even if he is thought to be. In a word, anything is really possible, although of course if there is a timeless independent being on whom all else depends, the world will look very much as it does. Still, there might very easily not have been a God; and even now, very powerful finite beings may simply spring into existence, as God might have done; they might even be more powerful than God. Total contingency, in other words, puts God, and God's power over the world, constantly at risk. Such a risk can only be avoided if God is the most powerful *possible* being, not just the most powerful actual being. But that entails that God can prevent more powerful beings coming to be, that he has actual power over all possibles. No possible being is beyond God's power, so he must exist in all possible worlds, as the origin of all possible things. That is precisely the doctrine of Divine necessity.

It is the total contingency of all things which is the dizzying abyss of thought, throwing the mind into the stupor of realizing that nothing is secure, that even God may change or die, that the world is constantly threatened by annihilation and darkness. In such a world there is no spiritual security; even the Divine is subject to time and fate, or to the ultimate power of irrationality. The sense of Divine necessity has thus a firm root in human feeling, in the sense that there is a firm and unshakable foundation of being, that all things are wisely ordered, that the power of non-being can be defeated and good purposes will be achieved. This basic religious sense is supported by the self-disclosure of being as able to fulfil its purposes and bring all to good. So the sense of Divine necessity is not merely an abstract concept: it is an apprehension of the faithfulness of being, of unlimited power, rooted in the experience of worship and confirmed by revelation. Worship is thus seen as the deepest possibility of human apprehension, as it reflects on what it is to be. Of course this apprehension cannot be neutrally confirmed, as it were by observation. But it can be seen to be rooted in deep human feelings, to be implicit in the ultimate rational postulate of intelligibility, and to be presupposed by a total commitment of the will to a being unconditioned in value and reality. Divine necessity is the ultimate ideal, uniting affective, rational and volitional aspects of human life. To assert the reality of that ideal is to commit one's life to the unconquerable faithfulness of unconditioned being. And out of such commitment may come, occasionally and fitfully at first, but later perhaps forming a continuing apprehension underlying all one's experience of this changing, fading world, a faint glimpse of God, of that unlimited power which cannot fail to be.

If that sense comes, one will no longer ask if God is real. One will see the reality of this sensory world as only half-real by comparison with the unrestricted infinity of the Divine being, as only existing as a faint and dependent reflection, a fractured image, of substantial eternity. It is that perception which the abstract concepts of the philosophical theologian seek to evoke, a view of the traditional "proofs" of God which has been helpfully developed by E.L. Mascall, who writes, "The classical arguments lead us not merely to intellectual acquiescence in a proposition but to a genuine apprehension of God as present by immensity at the ontological root of finite beings" (Mascall 1966:197). These words are means to what lies beyond all words; to what, one may say, may be found in the silence beyond the storms of thought, in confession of the dependence of the contingent upon that which must be.

2

Divine Freedom and Necessity

(t)

The doctrine of creation does not assert, as is sometimes thought, that a very powerful unembodied person, God, brought the first state of the universe into being at some time, and then, perhaps, left it to go on its own way. It affirms that there is one and only one being that cannot fail to be, that possesses its essential properties by necessity. All other beings whatsoever, including every part of space and every moment of time, derive wholly from this being and depend upon it in every respect for their existence and nature. Moreover, all dependent beings derive from the self-existent being, God, by way of knowledge and intention. They do not arise unconsciously or by total necessity. God knows or conceives what could possibly be. He intends to bring about some of these possible states, to make them actual. And his so intending brings them about. It is in this sense that creation is a Divine act, not just a process or event. As an act, it is the bringing about of some state of affairs through knowledge and intention.

At least in the case of God, the agent is necessarily aware of whatever he brings about, and he brings things about precisely in virtue of his knowledge of what they are or will be. In saying that he does so through intention, it is not supposed that "intention" is a prior event by means of which God brings about some state. As A. I. Melden points out (Melden, in White 1968:77), "to say that one moves certain muscles by willing them to move is not to give any causal account at all ... it means simply that one moves a muscle". God has the power to bring things about. There is no possible answer to the question "How does he do so?", any more than there is a possible answer to the question "How does one raise one's arm?" One just does!

But of course God brings states about, meaning to do so. The exercise of his powers is intentional. As Professor Anscombe expresses it, it is such that a certain sense of the question "why" has application to it: the sense which requires as an answer the giving of a reason for acting (Anscombe 1957:28–30). In saying that a state of affairs is brought about through intention, one means to assert that there is a reason for the existence of the state of affairs, it realizes a purpose. That is to say, God brings about states for a purpose, or rationally. The intention is not a prior causal event or act, but part of what makes the event an "action", its *raison d'être*. God does not first perform an act of intending, which causes a further state of affairs to exist. He simply brings a state into being, in virtue of his knowledge of its nature and for a reason.

"God's intending to do something in future" must, however, be taken as characterizing a state of God prior to the act itself. In this sense, "forming the intention to do something" is one of the class of basic actions, in Arthur Danto's phrase (Danto, in White 1968:57), ones "which do not really require any other action as cause", which one simply has the power to do. No infinite regress is generated, since it is not being said that all acts must be preceded by prior acts of intention-forming or "volition". It is only being said that all intentional acts must be such that a reason can be given for their performance – and if God now forms the intention to do x tomorrow, a reason can be given, for example, that x is a good thing to do.

God can, but need not, plan out his reasons in advance. Then there would be an act of intending to create a certain universe, followed by the act of creation itself. In this case, the intention-forming is not an act which causes the later act of creation to come about; it is an act which provides the reason why God creates. "Forming an intention to do x" is an act, but not a cause. Both it and "creation in accordance with a prior intention" are thus basic acts. So God could simply create a universe without forming a prior intention to do so, since that is in his power, and he may have good reason to do it. It is conceivable that God forms many intentions in advance, especially ones of a rather general nature (e.g. ensuring that all the good that can be saved in a created universe, will be), but also often acts without having previously formulated a precise intention (i.e. creatively). In general, to say that God brings about states through knowledge and intention is to say that he has the power to do so, he knows what he is doing and has good reason to do so.

A number of problems are raised by this account. It is not clear whether creation is best conceived as one act – a bringing-about of the universe as a whole – or as a series of acts, of bringing about particular space-time segments, one by one. Either way, creation cannot be properly thought of as just the first moment in the existence of a space-time universe. Every moment will stand in the immediate relation of "being created" to God. Nor is it clear how a necessary being can act, or at least act freely, in any meaningful sense. Even if it can bring about states of affairs through knowledge and intention, can it really bring about contingent states of affairs, if it is wholly necessary? The classical tradition of Christian theism, as found in Augustine and Aquinas, opts (with some vacillation) for the view that God brings about the whole universe, in the totality of its spatio-temporal existence, in one act, which is directly rooted in the necessity of the Divine being itself. Thus Augustine: "All that ever God created was in his unchanged fixed will eternally one and the same" (Augustine 1945:Book 11, ch.17). However, this is not a view which is explicitly found in the Bible and an alternative account is provided by the notion of creation as a continuous series of Divine acts, which are contingent in detail, though they contain important elements of necessity. This is the notion I now wish to explore.

If creation is viewed as a series of intentional acts which are contingent in at least some senses, then it is natural to ask what reasons there are for God to perform these acts. If they are not simply inevitable outflowings of the Divine nature, but freely performed acts, then there is presumably some reason for deciding to perform them. But God is a self-existent being, who has usually been thought to be complete and perfect in himself, not needing anything other than himself to complete his self-sufficient reality. So what reason could such a God have for creating contingent spatio-temporal processes?

One good reason for bringing things about is that they possess intrinsic value or goodness. Could God bring things about out of a sense of disinterested benevolence, simply because they are of value to themselves or to others? Perhaps he could, but have we any reason to think that he would? Can we be sure that God is benevolent in this way? The gods have not always been seen as benevolent. Thomas Hardy saw them as sporting with human lives – playing with them and then discarding them. And the gods of the Greek and Roman pantheons also seem to take pleasure in seeing the struggles of human beings, and in bringing their plans to nothing. These Olympian gods are, of course, human persons writ large, with all the foibles, jealousies and defects of human persons. May the one God in whom Christians believe not be a malevolent or arbitrary creator, making things for his sport, delighting in their miseries?

Classical theism rejected this possibility by holding that God is impassible. He cannot be affected by creatures in any way. He cannot be made happy or sad by what happens to creatures. So he is logically unable to take pleasure in the misery of creatures. If such a god brings any world into existence, he will do so not for the pleasure it gives him, whether that pleasure comes from the happiness or misery of creatures. The price paid by this doctrine is that God cannot be made happy by creatures at all, he cannot really relate to them in any interactive personal way. In fact, such a God can hardly be said to relate to creatures in any positive way. As Aquinas clearly puts it, "Being related to God is a reality in creatures, but being related to creatures is not a reality in God" (1964:3, 75). The impassible God is clearly not malevolent, since he does not create for any pleasure it gives him. But it is quite hard to see him as benevolent either, or at least as entering into any sort of loving relationship with creatures. That God assorts oddly with the Biblical idea of a God whose essential nature is Love (1 John 4,16).

There is an important truth in the doctrine of impassibility, however. It is that God does not depend for his happiness and perfection upon any created world. His essential nature cannot be destroyed or impaired by anything that happens in any created world. Divine omnipotence requires that nothing happens contrary to the Divine will (we shall soon see, however, a need to qualify this blunt statement). Still, how can one know what God may will? God's creative action cannot be governed by desires which God just happens to have. God exists by necessity, and his desires cannot be other than they are. But what sort of desires could exist in this being who is the fullness of reality, the most real of beings? Obviously there cannot be the sorts of physical desires human beings have – desires for physical satisfaction. Nor can God have any unfulfilled desires since, being omnipotent, he can fulfil them all. So God will not have the sort of desire which is a lack of something good. His desire will be wholly fulfilled simply by his awareness of his own fullness of being. "In thy presence is the fullness of joy", says the Psalmist (Psalm 16,11), and that joy lies in the full appreciation of perfect goodness. When the choirs of angels surrounding the throne of God sing, "Holy, holy, holy", they acknowledge the wholeness of the Divine being, the plenitude which allows of no defect, since it is the fully actualized fountainhead of all possibilities. Our desires are perfectly fulfilled by the full and entire possession of their objects. So God, and he alone, possessing his being in full awareness and without the possibility of loss or impairment, is the fulfilment of desire, the endless possession of unlimited joy. This concept in its philosophically explicit form is due to Aristotle (1960:section 12) rather than to the Bible; but it does seem to spell out what is involved in the Biblical notion of God as supremely great. God is the final ideal of human reason as well as the one true object of unreserved worship. It is clear that such a God cannot create because he needs something which he lacks.

But it may still be possible for God to create another, distinct subject of awareness, which is capable of its own finite sort of happiness. God's happiness may not be greater; but there will in one sense be more happiness in the universe, since there will be another subject which is happy, which otherwise would not have existed. So a reason for creation could be to increase the sum total of happiness – or, more generally, of value – in existence. God may create a world if it contains values which otherwise would not exist. What are these values? David Pailin suggests that they will be "novel forms of aesthetic value" (Pailin 1989:112). But the restriction to aesthetic value seems unduly parsimonious. A value is any state which is worthwhile for its own sake. There may be an infinite number of kinds and degrees of such values, from mountain walking to hearing music, from discovering a molecular structure to lying in the sun. It is impossible to say that all values are of just one sort. But perhaps one could say that they must be enjoyable states of consciousness. It is intelligible to say that such a state is a state worth having; it is better for it to exist than not. But one can extend the idea of an intrinsically valuable state much further than this. Ideally, one can suppose that the highest value will consist of the richest set of the maximal degree of the most diverse sorts of worthwhile state. This ideal may be asymptotic, in that an infinite set of sorts or degrees of desirable states is not completable in fact. There will not be a "best possible" set, precisely because one could always add more to any finite set, and all actual sets must be finite. Further, different sorts of value are incommensurable – such that it makes no sense to compare one with another (say, fishing with reading poetry) on any objective or common scale. This is a point that Leibniz failed to take into account when he supposed that God would morally have to create the best of all possible worlds – the world, he said, "is determined in such a way that its contrary would imply imperfection or moral absurdity" (Leibniz 1973:139).

Where there is no such possible world, no one can have an obligation to create it. It follows from this that God could always create a better world in some respects than he has done. Yet he is not to blame for not having done so. There is no actual maximum value. So there is no one optimum creation. Any creation will be good which realizes a good range of values to a fairly high degree. But where a very valuable state already exists, there can be no obligation to produce more. So there is no *obligation* on God to create a world. It is good for God to create any world which realizes a large range of values, precisely for the sake of the unique values it realizes.

So one reason for the creation of a world will be that subjects capable of valuing their own existence come into being, in addition to the infinite subject of God. This is a good reason for distinguishing the being of creatures, as finite subjects of consciousness, from the being of God; and for saying that, while they depend wholly on God for their existence, they are not identical with or parts of God. They have an independent existence, and can, by sin and ignorance, become alienated from God. However, the Christian doctrine of incarnation suggests that there is not a total opposition between Divine and human nature, but that they can be united, human persons being the free and conscious finite vehicles of the Divine nature, members of the visible body of the invisible God. Still their consciousness remains ineluctably their own, perceiving and valuing the world from a unique finite point of view. In this sense, any created world increases the sum total of value. However, it does not follow that a good God must create the greatest possible number of worlds, or the best of all possible worlds. The argument that it does follow has been termed "Leibniz's Lapse" by Alvin Plantinga (1974:173). For there is no such greatest number, the number of possible worlds being infinite. Any such possible world will be a world that it is good to create, but none will be such that God is obliged to create it.

 Another reason for the creation of a world is that the sorts of values which can be realized in a world of finite beings will be values that otherwise would not have existed at all. It is not only that more valuing subjects exist, but also that sorts of valued objects exist, which would not exist without creation. For instance, the value of taking a good walk could not exist without a physical world. However infinitely blissful God may be, he cannot enjoy a tiring walk, since he has no body and is logically incapable of getting tired. If a finite world exists, new sorts of values will then exist, and the sorts of values will depend on the particular world which is created. God's decision as to which world to create will thus depend on what sorts of values he chooses to be realized. If he creates a world, it will be because of the unique sorts of values which can only come to be in that world.

This consideration leads to a qualification of the statement that God's happiness cannot be increased by creation. The happiness he enjoys by the contemplation of his own unlimited being cannot be increased or decreased. It is supreme and unqualified bliss, unpierced by evil or sorrow of any sort. But we have not yet fully faced the problem of whether God might be a cosmic sadist, who enjoys causing worlds of pain and sorrow. Clearly, if God is not affected by creation in any way, it is senseless to regard him as a sadist. But it is odd to say that an omniscient God can create new sorts of finite values, while not having his awareness changed in any respect by their existence. An omniscient being will have complete knowledge of everything that exists, in its particularity and uniqueness. If that is so, God will have total empathy with the feelings of creatures. If a creature feels pain, God will know by total empathy what the creature feels. He will not only register intellectually that pain is occurring, he will know that pain by acquaintance, though he will not feel it as *his* pain.

Process theologians put this by speaking of all finite experiences as "included in" God. Thus Charles Hartshorne says that God is "world-inclusive, having all things as constituents" (Hartshorne 1953:16). Whereas classical theologians supposed that God had a complete intellectual knowledge of all things but no feelings, process thinkers argue that an omniscient being must also have knowledge by acquaintance with all things. He must in some sense experience my experiences. This point is persuasive, although one needs to emphasize that "my" experience remains the experience of an active self which is distinct from God; it is not just part of God's experience. There remains an important element of "otherness", which means that God cannot experience things just as I do. He can be acquainted with my experiences in a total and inward way, but he cannot acknowledge them as his own, or experience them exactly as I do (with all my selfish partiality and ignorance). In other words, God will not have my toothache, but he will know and appreciate exactly what it is like for me to have toothache. That knowledge will change the character of God's experience, by causing a resonant and wholly empathetic feeling in God. Thus it is not so much that God includes my feelings as part of himself, but that he has a total empathetic responsiveness to and uniquely inward acquaintance with my feelings. It follows that God will not choose the pain of any creature. On the contrary, since he will also feel the happiness of creatures with total empathy, God will always choose the happiness of creatures. That will, in a sense, increase his own happiness, by giving him different sorts and degrees of happiness. They will not impair or affect the bliss of his eternal being, but they will add sorts of happiness to the Divine being which otherwise would not have existed, and which it is good to have. This is a third sort of reason for creation – not only that additional subjects of value exist, and that new and distinctive sorts of values will exist, but also that God himself will experience new sorts of value, as he comes to know as actual those finite values which he chooses to create.

The reason God cannot be a cosmic sadist, then, is that his complete knowledge enables him to share in the sorrow and happiness of creatures, not in some external way, but as from within. Since no being will choose pain for itself, God cannot choose to make creatures feel pain, for its own sake. An omnipotent and omniscient being must create, if he creates at all, for the sake of the goodness, the sorts of value, that a world will realize. God is necessarily good, in creating all things for their goodness. But if God is necessarily good, can it be appropriate to thank him for his goodness? After all, we do not thank people for what they cannot help. However, even if whatever world God creates must be good, in the sense outlined, God did not have to create the particular world in which we exist. In this way, the world we live in is an unmerited gift, for which we can properly thank God. It is not some necessary outflowing of the Divine being, which he cannot help – which might have made gratitude less appropriate.

The trouble with this argument is that it seems to have proved too much. If God creates the world for its goodness it seems impossible to account for the vast amount of evil and pain that actually exists. Surely he would have created a universe of exceedingly happy beings, who never or only rarely felt any pain? The proper treatment of this subject is reserved for the following chapter, but a general reply can be made in the following way: God, being necessarily what he is, cannot choose his own nature, nor is there any alternative to it, in any possible world. Even for God, there is something "given", which is unchangeable. Sometimes theists have wanted to give God such complete power that he could even decree his own nature. Austin Farrer at one point proposed a view of God as one "who is all he wills to be, and wills to be all he is: for his act is himself, and his act is free" (Farrer 1967:118). Taken in one way, this statement is misleading, since it can suggest that God might will himself to be absolutely anything. But it makes no sense to speak of God as "pure will", without any given, antecedent nature. Such a will would be wholly contentless and arbitrary. God must have a given nature. What is unique about it is that it alone is what it is by absolute, unconditional necessity. There is no sense in complaining about the Divine nature, once one sees it to be absolutely necessary (I take this to be the teaching of the Book of Job). No being, not even God, can properly be held responsible for what it is, or what it causes or wills, of necessity.

Now part of the Divine nature is the array of possible worlds which are contained in his being, from which he has the power to actualize some of his choice. God does not choose that array; it is necessarily what it is. Clearly, suffering and conflict and destruction are possible states of many possible worlds. It is even possible that they are parts of any possible world which is rich and complex enough to contain free rational agents. Plantinga has argued the hypothesis of what he calls transworld depravity – the idea that certain possible individuals would sin in any possible world of which they were members; so that, if God creates them, he necessarily creates a world containing sin (Plantinga 1974:173–89). And I think it is true that many individuals could not be the individuals they are if they were not involved in conflict and suffering. They would not just be the same people in different circumstances, their basic individuality would be different. The possibility of pain exists necessarily in God, as essentially part of many possible worlds. God does not choose that possibility. Even he cannot eliminate it. What we cannot understand, with our finite comprehension, is just how that necessity is grounded. But we can see that it may be so, and accordingly that the creation of many actual worlds (and perhaps any of them that could have beings like us in them) will entail at least the possibility of some sorts of suffering and destruction. Even the omnipotent God cannot create those worlds without actualizing at least the possibility of suffering in them.

If he creates those worlds, he will create them for their unique forms of goodness, but the consequence will be that he must create the possibilities of suffering which they entail as well, and he must permit those possibilities to be actualized if they are consequences of the exercise of forms of freedom which are of great value in themselves, or are the necessary conditions of realizing states of great value, like the state of freely giving and accepting mutual love. Now one may say that God should not create such worlds, even if their forms of goodness are quite unique, intense and enduring, at the price of a great deal of suffering and destruction. At the very least, he should have created a world with much more happiness in it than this, at the price of much less suffering. This assumes, as I have been assuming, that God has a free choice between all possible worlds. So he could always choose a better one, or none at all. But this assumption stands in need of further examination.

If God's being is necessary, must it not follow that he necessarily does whatever he does? And therefore that he necessarily brings this universe into existence, just as it is? That is a conclusion that Spinoza felt driven to, and that even theologians like Augustine and Aquinas found it extremely difficult to avoid. Aquinas, for instance, says that "as the divine existing is essentially necessary, so also is the divine knowing and the divine willing" (1964:1a,19,3). In what sense, then, is the world contingent? It may be contingent only in the sense that the denial of its existence is not self-contradictory. That is the sense in which Aquinas holds that the existence of the universe is not logically necessary. Aquinas holds that God is immutable and simple, so that his will is identical with his essence, which is incapable of change. It follows that whatever

God wills, he wills changelessly and essentially. Being what he is, he cannot will other than he does. In this sense, the world necessarily follows from the existence of God, even though I can always *say*, "This world logically could be different, or might not exist". If we could comprehend God's nature fully, we would see that, given the existence and essential nature of God, the whole world could not have been other than it is.

At first sight, this seems to resolve at least one of our problems. For if God had to create this world, we can no longer complain that he *should* not have done so. Yet the resolution is not ultimately satisfactory. For is there not an infinite array of possible worlds, a great many of which must instantiate quite distinctive sorts of value? Why should just this world be necessary? Does this not open up an area of arbitrariness in the Divine will? As Pailin puts it, "If God were to have such a choice (between different cosmic structures), it must be arbitrary since there could be no reasons for choosing one structure rather than any other" (1989:129). This is because, either the options are equally good, or, more subtly, because there is no best option, so that any choice is better than some but less good than others – which is not a reason for choosing any particular world. We thus have the hypothesis that some world necessarily follows from the changeless will of God, but there seems to be no reason why any particular world should so follow. The combination of necessity and arbitrariness is a very uneasy one. We say that God must create some good world. But how good must that world be? And what determines which one is to come into existence?

In fact, if we posit that there are alternative possible worlds, we have already opened up an area of contingency in the Divine being. For, if it is possible that any, but not all of worlds a–n exists (not all, for the array of possible worlds will necessarily contain states which contradict one another. Some will contain p, and others contain –p; thus only some possible worlds can be actualized simultaneously), then it is necessarily possible. If God is omnipotent, he can do whatever is possible, compatibly with his own nature. So, necessarily, God must be able to create any, but not all of a–n. That is to say, he must be able to perform some contingent act, to create something to which there are alternatives. That act of creating must itself be contingent, for it cannot both be necessary that God creates a, and also that he is able to create any (not just one, but any one), but not all, of a–n. It follows that God's creation of any specific contingent world is itself contingent. By necessity of his nature, then, God can perform contingent acts. If God lacked that ability, in a universe in which truly contingent states of affairs are possible, then he would lack some ability which is necessarily possessed by any omnipotent being. Accordingly, God's being cannot be necessary in all respects. It will still be necessary in many respects, though since we cannot comprehend the Divine nature, we cannot know in detail what they are.

This means that there may be many elements of necessity in the way the world is, that God is not wholly free to do anything at any time in any world. Yet there will also be elements of contingency, and one of those elements, it seems, will be the choice of one specific contingent world out of a possibly infinite array. The God who exists of necessity, and necessarily possesses many properties such as omni-potence, omniscience and goodness, will necessarily possess the capacity to act contingently, to bring some, but not all, of an array of contingent states of affairs into being. This follows from the logical possibility of there being contingent states of affairs. It explains how God can be a necessary being many elements of whose will are contingent, although human beings are in no position to know exactly what those are.

The possibility that God may be necessary in some respects and contingent in others is a perfectly coherent one, and was first clearly formulated in Whitehead's philosophy of organism (Whitehead 1929: esp. pps. 484 ff.), as the doctrine of the dipolar nature of God. In Whitehead's view, however, one pole of the Divine nature, the necessary, primordial aspect of God is abstract, unconscious and "deficiently actual"; while the other pole, the contingent aspect, is the all-inclusive multiplicity of "the individual, fluent satisfactions of finite fact", forever remembered in the endless process of actual occasions which is the consequential nature of God. Whitehead's view does not allow substantial existence to God, as the prime cause of all and a distinct subject of omniscient awareness, with a proper fullness of Divine life in himself, and a responsive personal relation to finite and created consciousnesses other than himself. Nor does it permit the idea of God contingently choosing to actualize some universe from the array of possibles in its eternal being, since Whitehead's "ultimate metaphysical truth" of atomism gives existential and causal priority to the beginningless series of actual occasions, which God may "persuade" or "lure", but which he does not bring into being by knowledge and intention. The stress on Divine temporality and dipolarity, developed from aspects of the Hegelian philosophy, is a very helpful expansion of classical Christian views of God. But it does not entail, and need not be restricted to, the metaphysical pan-psychism of the philosophy of organism, with its rather passive and abstract interpretation of the primordial nature of God.

If we conceive God as the creator, free to choose to actualize one of many worlds, we still wish to know why a creator God should choose to create one particular world, instead of all the others he might have created. The dilemma the theist is apt to be faced with is, that either God's acts are necessary, or they are arbitrary. For what reasons could determine a truly contingent act of God? This is a question that will crop up time and again, as we consider God's providential and miraculous acts. Some light may be thrown on the question of Divine creation by considering the nature of creativity in general. Consider the case of a composer writing a piece of music. It makes no sense to speak of a "best possible" symphony. Some are better than others, but they are better in different ways, they display different sorts of value, in style, harmony and configuration. If you ask a composer why he writes the piece he does, the answer will be that it expresses his imaginative creativity in one particular way out of a great number of alternative possibilities. If he is going to compose at all, he has to choose a particular form, for particular instruments. The reason for choosing to write some piece is that thereby his imagination is expressed. The reason for writing a particular piece is not that it is the best possible, but that it is a progressive working-out of unique themes which develop a pattern and style of their own.

One might see the universe as God's composition, a particu-

lar expression of Divine imagination, progressively working
out a pattern and style of its own. The starting-point may
be fairly arbitrary, but the development takes on a form and
beauty unique to itself. In this context, it is perhaps better
not to consider, in a quasi-Augustinian way, the array of possible worlds as consisting of a disjunctive set of completely
specified world-states, one of which God must choose as a
whole. On that model, God must choose either world A as
a whole, with all its details fixed from beginning to end, or
world B as a whole, and so on. Most classical Christian theologians have thought of creation in this way, as the realization
of some universe as a completed whole. But that model leads
to intractable difficulties about the place of free creative action
within a natural order which is already in some sense wholly
determinate. There is no compelling reason to use that model.
One might think, instead, of God bringing some initial state
into existence, which has a future development not entirely
determinate, but which he can help to determine by the exercise of his supremely imaginative creativity. This would give
us an intelligible reason why God should act within a created
universe, as well as creating it as a whole and simply sustaining
it in being. He will act within it to shape and guide it to
new and original forms of beauty and goodness.

 If this consideration is plausible, it adds a fourth reason
for creation to the three already considered. It is true that
God is not obliged to create any universe, because of its goodness. Yet it may be that it is essential to God to be an imaginative creator. If the First Letter of John is right in characterizing
God as "Love", and if this is an essential characteristic of
God, then we may indeed see the creation of some world
as necessary to God – not that he needs it, but that his essential
creativity naturally overflows into a created expression of his
unlimited potency. As Aquinas puts it, "It befits the divine
goodness that others also should partake of it" (1964:Q.19,
art.2). Then God, by his unlimited creativity, will bring some
world into being, and, because of his unlimited love, he will
ensure that its unique values are brought to final consummation and fulfilment.

In the creation of such a world, God foreknows that he
will bring creatures to fulfilment, unless they resist his will

utterly. So the writer of the letter to the Ephesians can say, "He chose us in him [Christ] before the creation of the world ... in love he predestined us to be adopted as his sons through Jesus Christ" (Ephesians 1:4,5). I do not think one should take this as meaning that God chooses some specific individuals and determines them, apart from any exercise of their wills, to achieve glory. It is rather that, in setting out on the adventure and risk of creation, God's intention is that creatures should be brought to glory. Even before the world's beginning, God foreknows that there is a fulfilment of all things, which he will bring about by his power. If we achieve this fulfilment, then our achievement is properly seen as a response to God's preceding choice and determination, which we make our own. This is a strong statement of God's power to bring about what he purposes. But the dark possibility seems to exist that we may impede or resist his will. I can say, "God has chosen you for glory; he has so ordered things that you may attain glory". And yet creatures may turn from God and his foreknown and predestinating purpose, by the freedom that he himself has given them. God's final purpose cannot be defeated, though the precise form the fulfilment of all things takes will be determined both by the free acts of creatures and by the creative activity of God.

But does this not mean that God's will can be thwarted? We must be quite clear that his antecedent will, to create a universe of free moral agents, can never be thwarted. All the same, may not all free creatures reject God? Then his final purpose of overwhelming good for the universe will never be realized. Is that conceivable? It would be a very uncomfortable conclusion. Is it true that, if any creature can ever reject God, then it can always do so? And that, if any can, then all can? We know that a creature can reject God, disobeying him and choosing selfish desire. We have some reason to think that almost every human being has chosen self to a great extent ("There is no one righteous, not even one", Romans 3:10). It seems possible that all, or at least the majority of persons, may harden into a state of final corruption, when there is no longer any real possibility of repentance for them. Many Christian theologians have taken this view. And the postulate of radical freedom seems to entail its possibility.

A rational creature can finally choose against God. Hell, in at least one sense, is a possibility.

But this would seem to entail that all could choose Hell, and would that not mean that the existence of rational creatures was not, in the end, worthwhile? It would be better for humans never to have been born, if they all choose Hell. Having said that, the strongest reason for thinking that not all will choose Hell has come to light. It is irrational to choose a course of life which it is better not to live. And it is supremely rational to choose a life which is overwhelmingly worthwhile, since it offers endless bliss. Seeing this, one might come to see that selfishness, though terribly attractive, is deeply irrational and leads to terrible suffering. Perhaps I can only really learn this through the experience of it. But if I do, then I will return, however slowly, to find the way to eternal bliss. After all, rational creatures are made for relationship with God, that is their true nature. And it may be thought that a creature can fight against its true nature only for so long, but is likely to come to the discovery of it if given time and experience enough. If one adds to all this the thought that God shares in the feelings of all creatures, it becomes unbearable to suppose that he will permit endless suffering in any universe he creates.

Taking these factors into account, we have good reason to think that all evil and suffering will be eliminated from God's creation, as it reaches its final consummation. And there is good reason to hope that many creatures will discover their true natures and find the way to eternal bliss, thus entering into that consummation of all things. One may indeed hope, with Origen and Gregory of Nyssa, that all rational creatures will come to endless bliss at last – but after very different life-experiences and periods and forms of suffering. Then we could say that God's final purpose of an overwhelming good for all creatures will be realized. His persuasive and co-operative actions will finally be fully effective, when all finite selves allow themselves to be attracted and empowered by the one supremely desirable goal of all things.

As far as Christian revelation is concerned, Jesus warns of uncompromising judgment on human evil; though at the same time he proclaims the full forgiveness of sin to all who turn to God in penitence and faith. He is prepared to die on a cross in order to take away the sins of the world, and stand in the place of all who will accept his sacrifice. The only firm conclusion to be drawn from Jesus" teaching and life is that the impenitent will find God to be a consuming fire, and, if finally impenitent, may be destroyed by that fire ("At that time I will tell the harvesters: first collect the weeds and tie them in bundles to be burned, then gather the wheat and bring it into my barn" (Matthew 13:30). But all who are penitent will be saved from judgment and from evil, and God will do all he can, without infringing their freedom, to bring them to fullness of life ("Your Father in heaven is not willing that any of these little ones should be lost", Matthew 18:14). I doubt if human reasoning can confidently decide whether all will eventually be penitent or not. But we can hope and even pray that all will be. And we can say that, even if they are not, God will achieve his purpose in creation by using even the rebellion of the impenitent for some good purposes, and by bringing all who freely turn to him to a unique fulfilment of their distinctive form of existence.

So we can see this universe as a particular contingent expression of the imaginative creativity of God. If, in addition, we take seriously the character of God as love, which Christ reveals, we may see this, not as a sole determining creativity, like a composer writing an inert piece of music, but as an interactive co-creativity with created subjects which are themselves creatively free. Maurice Wiles suggests the analogy of an improvised drama, in which God sets the plot-outline, but then leaves the actors free to improvise their parts (Wiles 1986:37–8). This model leaves God as an absentee playwright, and we may well want the playwright to come on stage and take a more active part in the drama, or at least to direct things, rather firmly at times, from the wings. Some such model, however qualified, guarantees that what happens in the history of this world is at least partly dependent upon the choices of creatures. God must decide what choices are to be open to creatures, but if he grants them freedom, his actions in regard to them will be largely responsive and interactive, not just despotically determining. The possibility that God should enter into a personal form of relationship with

(E)

creatures, and that this is itself an essential part of his nature as love, is a fifth consideration helping to show why a necessary and infinite creator should create a universe, and what sort of universe he might create.

God could perhaps create a different universe than this. But if he is the infinitely dynamic creator and the eternal lover, he must create some finite world of persons. Consequently, there must always be some such world, or perhaps an endless succession of such worlds, as Augustine proposed in the *City of God*, Book 12, Chapter 19. Each world can contain a distinctive and unique set of values, and, in all of them, the sorts of values that exist will necessarily contain the possibility of sorts of disvalue that freely creative action entails. So each world will contain many features which are necessarily what they are, but also some points of alternative potentiality. If we ask why God creates the world we are in, the answer is given partly by his sheer imaginative creativity, which shapes this as an original world of unique values; partly by the necessary connections between possible states which changelessly exist in the Divine being; and partly by consideration of the way in which the distinctive values and disvalues of this world are bound together in one integral whole, and realized largely by free creaturely actions.

If God is free, and freely loving, we might expect this to be a universe open at many points to the influence of free and rational agents – both God himself and finite creatures. At the same time, it will be bounded and defined in its nature by necessities rooted in the eternal being of God. Since we have no hope of knowing what these are, lacking any direct insight into the Divine nature, it will be impossible for us to know (except by guesswork or revelation) just where free Divine action modifies the necessary determination of the laws of the natural order. God's primal act of creation is the positing of a universe of a distinctive sort, for the sake of the values it contains, and with the general structural necessities which determine its general nature. Far from excluding the possibility of further Divine actions, such a universe invites the possibility of particular Divine acts at those points of contingent process, unknown in detail to us, which are allowed and defined by the structure of the world. It follows that it would be wrong either to think of God as excluded wholly from particular action within the world; or to think of him as doing absolutely anything he wants at any particular moment of the world's history. He brings into being a total system, allowing the realization of certain sorts of value. But then he continues to work, imaginatively and lovingly, to develop those values in particular ways – and always in co-operation with the creative (or in opposition to the destructive) acts of creatures. The created universe is a system – so it has fixed elements of general structure; but it is an open and developing system – so it is open at many points to creative change. It is in that interplay of freedom and necessity that God's purpose for the world is worked out towards its final consummation.

3

The Origins of Suffering

God creates this world for its goodness. Theoretically, that may seem a plausible supposition. And it is securely based upon the statement of Gen. 1:31 that, when God created the world, "he saw all that he had made, and it was very good". Yet it is plain to all that there is an enormous amount of pain and suffering in the world, which threatens the apparent complacency of this belief. To many contemporary Christians, the problem of evil seems hopeless. People tend to throw up their hands and say that there is simply no way of accounting for the massive amounts of pain and suffering in the world. It has even been suggested by Kenneth Surin (Surin 1986:3) that any attempt to find a theoretical solution is an expression of bad faith. Suffering, he says, is simply to be overcome, any attempt to justify its existence leads to an acceptance of the *status quo*, and is thus morally obtuse. Of course, some attempts to deal with the problem are naive, and some strike many of us morally offensive. If it is said that pain is good for us, or that we all deserve to suffer extreme torment for ever for our sins, few will feel that we have here an acceptable solution.

It may seem that I am speaking rather too easily of a problem and a solution, and it is important to say exactly what the problem is and what sort of solution might be expected of it. The problem is capable of succinct expression: a perfectly good and omnipotent God would not wish to create suffering, and he would be able to prevent any suffering. But there is suffering, and an immense amount of it, in this world. Therefore there is no good and omnipotent creator (Hume 1935: pt.10). The formulation is precise and it seems clear and decisive. One looks at the suffering and death of thousands of children in war, by famine and earthquake, and one says, "How could a good God create this?"

It is important to distinguish a cry of agony in the face of what we cannot comprehend from the recognition of contradiction at the heart of theistic belief. We might feel the terrible force of pain in our own lives, we might weep at the pain of others which we are forced to confront, we might confess that we have no idea why such pain exists or what its point might be in a larger scheme of things. We might do all this and still believe in God, for there is much in his nature which we do not understand. But if the existence of suffering is actually incompatible with the existence of a good and all-powerful God, then, whether we weep or not, we must simply give up belief in such a God. The view that there is no way out of the contradiction (that is what a "solution" to the problem would be) is not compatible with rational belief in God. If a theist says such a thing, he is therefore not deserving of intellectual respect. There is no merit whatsoever in saying, "The problem can never be solved", and carrying on with the practices of theistic faith. A quite different view would be that, while we are unlikely to understand in detail how the apparent contradiction is to be resolved, there is a resolution to be found. That is the only decent view a theist can take.

It is not enough for the theist to say that there may be a resolution of what clearly seems to be a contradiction, though no one has ever thought it. The lack of any hints of a solution would constitute an enormously strong argument against the probability of there being a God. One has at the very least to show how some of the ideas involved in the statement of the contradiction which constitutes the problem may be susceptible of reformulation, or have some inherent weakness or uncertainty about them. It would be much better if they could actually be reformulated, at least in outline, so that we could see how the contradiction might disappear, when its terms were more fully understood. This, I think, can be done. A solution to the problem of evil can be offered, in the sense that the basic and precise apparently contradictory triad of perfect goodness, omnipotence and undesirable suffering can be reformulated so that the contradiction disappears. It goes without saying that such a solution will not take away the agony of pain for those who suffer and encounter it. But it may place the occurrence of pain in a context in which some sense can be made of it in a God-created universe.

Any such solution is unlikely to be wholly new. Theists have not been irrational until the moment of its appearance. As a matter of fact, the problem of evil has not traditionally been thought to be of tremendous significance. It takes little space in the great *Summae* of Thomas Aquinas, and does not delay any of the great classical Christian theologians for very long. The problem has assumed immensely greater significance today for a number of reasons. One is the disappearance of a real belief in life after death among many religious believers. Another is the rejection of the literal Biblical accounts of the "Fall" of Adam and of an angelic fall by Satan and his cohorts, which brought the earth under the dominion of a destructively evil will. A third is the growth of much more anthropomorphic ideas of God than were common among the Christian Fathers. Many people today see God as so like a loving human father that they cannot any longer think of him as a fearful judge, and so cannot reconcile his existence with the suffering he allows his children. A fourth is a widespread rejection of ideas of retributive punishment, which enabled theologians like Augustine to regard everlasting Hell as a just recompense for evil. And a fifth is a greater emphasis on freedom of choice in both God and creatures, which deprives us of the defence of inevitability which is implicit in the accounts by Augustine and Aquinas. If we now have an idea of a loving God, who will not willingly harm or punish anyone, and who could really have chosen to make a better world; if we believe that our animal impulses of lust and aggression are built up in the course of evolution, and are not particularly sinful, or freely chosen by us; and if we cannot look forward to endless bliss after death, then it is indeed very hard to reconcile the observed course of the world with the existence of God.

One can see how, in earlier ages, when God was seen as a stern judge and an implacable will, when mankind was seen to be, by its own fault, under the destructive rule of Satan, and when all who accepted Christ were offered endless happiness after just a few years of suffering, things could look very different. But we cannot go back. If we cannot recover the world-view of the early Fathers, can we construct another, more in keeping with modern science and our wider knowledge of the universe, which may perform a similar function in placing suffering in a context where it can to some extent be understood?

There are a number of directions in which one could look for a solution. In many ways, the most interesting is that canvassed by Process Theology, which generally restricts the omnipotence of God and stresses the freedom of finite beings to a great degree ("The nature of evil is that the characters of things are mutually obstructive"; and this is not due to some sheer *fiat* by God, it is metaphysically necessary to the basic structure of any universe: Whitehead 1929:482). But that is not the only possibility, and though what I have to say is influenced by some Process thinkers (and more by the German philosopher Hegel and the Indian philosopher Ramanuja), it works with a rather different view of the nature of the world. The view I shall expound is a development of the view of God as the necessary creator of all things, unrestricted in eternal intelligence and bliss, without end or beginning in his imaginative, co-operative and unitive creativity.

It should be quite clear that this is a very non-anthropomorphic view of God. It agrees with the classical Christian tradition in saying that God in himself is ineffable, that he is in many respects necessarily what he is, and that his goodness primarily consists in his possession of maximal perfection. Talk of God as a loving Father has an important place in Christian tradition, and is based upon the authoritative teaching of Christ. But it must be balanced by a recognition of the mystery and necessity of the Divine being, so powerfully conveyed in the Old Testament ("Where were you when I laid the earth's foundations? Tell me, if you understand", Job 38:4). Otherwise, not only will the problem of evil prove insoluble, but one may be in danger of giving absolute worship to what is something much less than the truly perfect God.

This may sound suspiciously like the beginning of an attempt to win by definition – to bring in the mystery of God wherever one is stuck for a rational response to objections. Is is not that. It is primarily a rejection of attempts to conceive of God as too much like a human person, to remember his majesty, his fearfulness and glory. But of course it does mean that we shall not speak of such a God as "good" and as "powerful" in just the same sense as we might speak of a human person in such terms. They will have some sense, and an intelligible one, which I shall try to spell out. It is not, as J. S. Mill feared, that one can make them mean anything one wants (Mill 1969:ch.2). But when we see their uniqueness as applied to the Divine being, we shall see that some of the inferences we might draw if God were a human person will simply not apply. That is the first move in defusing the apparent contradiction between Divine power and goodness and the existence of finite suffering.

Divine power is not rightly thought of as the ability to do absolutely anything at all. Some people misguidedly think that they magnify God by giving him such power, but all they do is to saddle him with impossible contradictions. God cannot make himself not exist, he cannot create an uncreated world, and he cannot suddenly decide to kill everyone for no reason (this point is clearly made in A. Kenny, *The God of the Philosophers* 1979:96). Why "cannot"? Because God does not just *happen* to exist, with certain attributes. He necessarily exists, as the exemplar and origin of all perfections. It has been noted that the theologians of the classical tradition took this doctrine to such an extent that they were compelled to say that God was necessary in every respect. Indeed, since he is simple in being, there are no respects in God which differ from one another in any way ("There is no way in which God is composite, and he must be altogether simple", Aquinas 1964:1a, 3, 7). It is hard to see how this view is consistent with belief in a Trinity of distinct persons within the unity of God, or with belief that God assumed human nature to himself in Jesus. So I, in common with many theologians in the last hundred years, suggest that God may be contingent in some respects, though he will be necessary in his possession of all immutable perfections.

Such a God is, so far as we can think it, "that than which no greater can be conceived" (Anselm 1965:ch.2); and it seems to me that a God who can create new contingent beings is greater than one who cannot do other than he does in any respect. Nevertheless, fundamental necessities remain in the

Divine being. Such a being, the most perfect there could possibly be, cannot do anything which is incompatible with his own necessary nature. This is no failure of power in God; it is precisely a consequence of his perfection. What we need to ask is what things are incompatible with the necessity of the Divine nature. God cannot do anything which might be described in an apparently consistent proposition, if it contradicts a necessity of his nature.

As I suggested in the previous chapter, among such necessities must be included the array of possible worlds and states which God could create. All possibles, being as such immutable, are necessarily in the mind of God, so he has no choice over what sorts of things are possible. I have argued elsewhere (Ward 1982:154f.) that this statement may need qualification, to allow the creative origination of radically original facts. But they must be derivative from an original matrix of possibles, which lay down their parameters and general structures. Otherwise one would have generation without preconception or knowledge, and the perfection of the Divine being would be compromised. So at least the array of archetypal possibilities must exist necessarily in the Divine being. Accordingly, if suffering and destruction are ever possible in any world, they are necessarily included in God, not freely chosen by him. Thus God is not free to eliminate the possibility of suffering. Suffering is necessarily possible in many forms of creation. If anyone argues that an all-powerful God should not let suffering be even a possibility, they have failed to consider the respects in which necessity must enter into any adequate account of the nature of the Divine being.

But surely God could prevent these possibilities being actualized? This is not necessarily true. Suppose, as suggested in the previous chapter, that God necessarily creates some world or other. This supposition may seem to go against the tendency of much Christian thinking, which holds that God was free to create the world or not. However, classical theologians effectively denied this tendency in any case, by rooting creation in the Divine will, which was identified with a changeless and necessary Divine essence (see, for instance, Augustine's statement that "The will of God belongs to his very substance" (Augustine 1876:ch.11). We can agree with them by suggesting that God freely creates some world, in the sense that he does not make a world out of any inner lack. He necessarily creates a world out of his goodness, and also, I have suggested, out of his naturally creative imagination, his necessarily possessing the attribute of being a God of self-giving love. If this is the case, God cannot prevent *every* possibility being realized, that is to say, some are necessarily realized.

But could he not actualize a world wherein suffering is not a possibility? He could not, if any world complex and diverse enough to include rational and moral agents must necessarily include the possibility of suffering, as well as happiness. If, for example, I can make you happy by caring for you, then I can make you unhappy by neglecting you. It seems plausible to suppose that any world in which finite agents can make each other happy will be one in which they can make each other unhappy. If so, the possibility of some suffering (even if it is never actualized) will be implicit in any such world.

There are other considerations which amplify this point. Buddhists generally hold that transient existence as such has the nature of suffering, for it gives rise to desires which can either not be fulfilled or which will pall as they are attained. Any world of action and desire will be a world which entails at least the possibility of failure, frustration and loss. There is no sense in speaking of an attempt to get something which is logically bound to succeed. The notion of "trying" carries the possibility of failing as well as of succeeding. For Buddhists, this is true even of the Paradisal worlds to which most ordinary believers hope to go after death.

Christians have usually been less pessimistic about Paradise, and thought that a state of individual personal existence is compatible with the enjoyment of perfect felicity. Yet they have also said that Paradise is hard to attain; or, if it was easily attained by Adam, it was easy to lose unless the will has been united irreversibly to the Divine will by a voluntary act of free obedience. For traditional Christians, Paradise is possible, but the possibility of a fall is necessarily present in it, unless and until the finite will has renounced pride of self and given itself freely to God. Moreover, it belongs to the nature of a free and distinct finite will that it can fall as well as rise. It cannot freely give itself unless it can freely refuse, and choose the darker possibilities which are associated in its understanding with independence, adventure, pleasure and the desire of knowledge of all possibilities.

A world with the sorts of success and happiness in it that we occasionally experience is a world that necessarily contains the possibility of failure and misery. It may be, as Buddhists have thought, that any finite realm in which desire and will exist must contain possibilities of suffering. It is hard for us to be very sure of this, but it certainly seems to be possible, and it would go a good way to explaining why there is suffering in this world, or in any world at all. The only way to transcend suffering would be to transcend desire. Or, as Christians might prefer to put it, to centre one's desires on God alone.

We may call in aid here, too, the Vedantic perception that Brahman, perfect and blissful in being, yet contains in itself the seeds of finitude and suffering. As Brahman breathes out its being, like a spider spinning its web, in universe after universe without beginning or end, it appears, at least through the veil of ignorance, to unfold into a diversity of finite selves, entering into the realm of unknowing, bound to the wheel of the cosmic law of desire and suffering, until it has played out all the possibilities inherent in its limiting adjuncts, and all returns to the oneness of infinite consciousness and bliss. Thus the *Prasna Upanishad*, 1, 4 says: "Prajapati, wishing offspring, mortified himself. When he had done this, he produced a couple – matter and the breath of life (prana) ... so arises this universal life-breath which has every form". Prajapati, who seems to be Brahman personified, produces out of the sacrifice or self-limitation of himself all beings of finite name and form.

There is here the picture of the Ultimately Real, source of all possibilities, unfolding those possibilities, which seem, as it were, to press into existence by an inner dynamic, both for good and ill. "Essence in itself tends towards existence", as Leibniz put it (Leibniz 1973:137). Perhaps, after all, everything that can be will be, and the notion of the possible is identical with the notion of the potential, awaiting actualization at the appropriate time. That idea, however, seems too extravagant, since it would require the actual existence of an infinity of worlds, differing only in the minutest respects from many other worlds. It would seem to deprive the notion of choice of meaning, since if I choose x, then in some parallel possible universe someone exactly like me in every other respect chooses not–x. Cosmologists have toyed with this idea, but it is as alarming, in its way, as the myth of eternal recurrence, and as destructive of the notion of contingency and freedom.

We cannot then think that all possibles must become actual. But it may be the case that there is something in the Divine being which drives, by inner necessity, towards an unfolding of sets of possibilities which include many varieties of suffering and injury. Not only must the Divine create some world; he must create a world containing at least a subset of the darker possibilities inherent in his own being. Or, to put the point in another way, perhaps every really possible world contains possibilities of suffering. As Isaiah 40 puts it, "I create light and dark; I wound and I make alive". In so far as God's creation is the necessary unfolding of the general sorts of possibilities inherent in him, darkness will issue from God inevitably with light. At this point, we see a decisive respect in which God is unlike loving human persons, and in which too sentimental a view of God's love makes one unable to sense the overpowering reality of the Divine being.

If this necessary origination of suffering is a limitation on Divine power, it is a limitation which is necessary to the most perfect of all possible beings. It is one that cannot be overcome, in any possible world. The issuing forth of suffering from God will not be something of which we can say that it should not have been. Once we see that it is necessarily so, terms of moral disapprobation (and approbation too) are inappropriate. It may be said, then, that we should not praise God for his goodness, if we should not blame him for the suffering that flows from him. It is true that we should not *morally* praise him, as though he did well against great odds. But "praise" is simply awe, reverence and admiration of Divine perfection. That remains in order, even though we fear and seek to avoid the suffering which belongs to the finite realm.

Nor should the recognition that much suffering is necessary in any finite world lead us simply to accept suffering as inevitable, much less to welcome it as Divinely willed. Much suffering is necessarily possible, but its actualization depends in large part on evil wills, which must be opposed. And, while much suffering may be inevitable, it is also part of Divine providence to give us the means to eliminate much of it. That some suffering occurs may be inevitable, but that we can, and should, eliminate it when we can is also inevitable. Whether we do so or not is largely up to us, but it is not true that this view leads to any acceptance of suffering as something we can never do anything about, and must passively accept. It does not "justify" suffering in the sense that Surin fears, of leading us to accept it complacently as part of the Divine plan.

In many ways the early Biblical idea of God as sending plagues and death, as being dangerous and unpredictable, is truer to the nature of things than the rather sentimental idea of a God of indulgent love that figures in some Christian writing. God is the destroyer as well as the creator (this insight is nowhere better put in religious literature than in the great vision of the Divine being in the *Bhagavad Gita*, section 11: "I see them all rushing headlong into thy mouths, with terrible tusks, horrible to behold. Some are mangled between thy jaws, with their heads crushed to atoms"); and the possibilities that unfold from the depths of his necessity are terrible as well as gentle and delightful. It is appropriate to fear God as well as to love him, to receive all things from his hand whether for our good or ill, for on him all things depend, from him all things come and to him all things return.

But should we receive all with gratitude? If things arise of necessity, and if many of them are destructive of our good, how can we be grateful for them? We might accept that God, when the internal necessities of his nature are comprehended, could be the most powerful possible being and yet be unable to prevent the existence of a world wherein suffering is a real possibility. But can he be good? Here again we may err in taking "goodness" to be too much like cases of human goodness, where it is plausible to say that, as J.L. Mackie puts it, "a being who is wholly good eliminates evil as far as he can" (Mackie 1982:150). It is a mark of human goodness to eliminate suffering where one can, for suffering has arisen against one's will, and is a challenge and obstacle to be over-come, in the search for life and health. But God is the source of all possibilities, and he contains in himself the supreme case of all logically compossible perfections. Finite suffering cannot be to him an obstacle, as something which arises from some external source, and opposes or frustrates him. But does that mean that he desires creatures to suffer?

It is true that nothing exists except by God's power. So it may be thought that he desires everything to be just as it is, that he wants me to have cancer or be tortured to death. That may seem to be the implication of the statement that nothing exists without God willing it. How can we avoid the dilemma that if he does not desire my suffering, something happens that he does not want, even though everything is supposed to exist by the will of God?

A distinction needs to be made, following Aquinas and the classical tradition, between antecedent and consequent willing. Suppose I antecedently will to take part in a game of chance, that is what I want to spend the next hour or so doing. If it is a game where dice are thrown, for instance, I want the throws to be random. It would not be a game of chance otherwise. But at every specific throw of the dice, what I want is that sixes should be thrown, if that is the highest score. Thus a paradox is generated – I want each throw to be random, so I want this throw to be random. If the result of the throw is threes, and that happens at random, then that is the result I want. Yet I also want this throw to produce sixes, that is, not to produce threes. Are those wants not incompatible?

The paradox is easily resolved by distinguishing between antecedent and consequent wants. I antecedently want throws to be random, because of my ultimate purpose in playing the game. But I consequently want each throw to be sixes. If I always got what I consequently wanted, there would be no point in playing the game. That would really contradict my antecedent want. So it is that I may want this game to be played as it is, but I do not want some of the events in it to happen as they do. Nevertheless, I must accept them, if I will the game. In a similar way, I may antecedently want a democratic society, but not want the results of a particular election. I will have to accept the result, nonetheless, because it follows from my antecedent decision quite inevitably.

We can suppose that God antecedently wants there to be a world-system with many possibilities in it, many of which are contingent and dependent upon the choices of rational creatures. If so, many things may happen that he does not consequently want, since he may have wished that creatures chose otherwise. But even God will have to accept an outcome he does not (consequently) want, if it follows from a system which he does (antecedently) want. If God knows, desires and brings about the unique goods of a specific world-system, it does not follow that he desires or intends the ills which may be a necessary part of that system. He may nevertheless be the cause of such ills, and know that they must exist. He cannot eliminate them without eliminating the goods as well. In that sense, and in that sense alone, God wills suffering to occur, though he would never intend it for its own sake, and would always desire its elimination wherever possible.

But does God have to will such a system? Could he not change the rules? Not if, as I have supposed, some such system necessarily is created by God. The point of this analogy is to show that God could originate a world through desire and will, and yet be bound to accept many events in it that he does not desire. This could be either because of the free choices of rational creatures which he would have willed them to make otherwise, or because of particular consequences, which he does not desire for themselves, which flow from the nature of the system as a whole, which he does desire. Since he cannot change the nature of the system (it is necessarily rooted in his immutable nature), he can properly be said to desire the existence of a world containing many particular events that he does not desire. Some world necessarily originates from God. In so far as this origination is necessary, God cannot be held responsible for it, as though he could have avoided it. This particular world originates by his freely creative choice, and is neither markedly better nor worse in its possibilities than any other possible world, though it will possess distinctive goods and evils which other possible worlds do not contain. God can be held responsible for the creation of this particular universe. For it originates through free Divine choice, and for the sake of the good it contains, even though there are necessarily many evil parts of it which God does not (consequently) desire or will. These are necessary consequential features of any world-system that God may freely desire, and, by the necessity of his nature, he desires and therefore must create some such system.

It is a natural first thought that if God freely creates a world, so that everything in it arises from and is wholly dependent upon God, he must intend and be responsible for everything that happens in that world. But a much more subtle account of Divine action is needed than this. One needs to distinguish a number of ways in which God is actively related to events that occur in the created universe. First, God may bring a set of objects into being and give them powers to act in specific ways. At every successive time, God causes these objects and their powers to exist, and this act of "sustaining in being" is a basic action – the objects are brought about, not by means of any other act as their cause. J.R. Lucas says, "Both as creator of the world and as non-intervener in particular cases, God's will is an essential part of every cause in the wide sense" (Lucas 1976:9). Of course, each event in the world has many preceding causes, many regularities of succession by which it is connected to preceding events. So a distinction is required between the basic Divine act of making the powers of things exist at every time, and the particular states which are caused by the exercise of those powers at particular times.

For example, God creates and holds in being all the fundamental particles of the physical universe, together with the powers – of electro-magnetic, gravitational and nuclear force – which constitute their existence. That is a basic Divine action. When a stone falls to earth, it does so as a result of the exercise of these forces. Does God make the stone fall? He certainly does not do so as a basic action, for the stone's fall is caused by the powers of other existing objects, which powers exist by a basic Divine action. So this event has a prior cause which is itself existent by an action of God, it is not something which God simply does. On the other hand, the stone's fall is clearly causally dependent upon God, God must take ultimate responsibility for its falling, since all its natural causes and their powers as well as its actual continuation in being, exist by Divine action.

However, there are various conscious relations God can have to an event like this. He can desire it and intend it, and in this case we may be happy to speak of it as an act of God, even though it is a non-basic action, brought about by previous states and powers of the natural order. Here we have what Austin Farrer called the "paradox of double agency", when a state is both brought about by natural causes and by the agency of God. This is not really a paradox, however, if one spells out the way in which particular states are brought about by natural causes, while the whole system of causal powers is held in being by God's action. Naturally caused states like beautiful sunsets and foliage may be ascribed to Divine activity, since it is for the sake of states like that (states exhibiting beauty, truth and goodness) that God creates the system of nature. States like "stones falling" will be less easily thought of as acts of God, since they do not seem to realize any goal or purpose. They do not occur in order to bring about some desirable state, and are therefore more easily regarded, not as acts, but as non-purposive processes of nature.

If God creates a deterministic system of nature, then he intends specific goods, which inevitably follow from the exercise of the powers of natural objects. But if, as seems more likely, he creates a probabilistic system, he intends only that there is a certain probability that specific goods will exist. This may vary from near certainty to an equal chance of existence or non-existence; and God's intention is the complex one of intending that either a or b . . . n should exist, with probabilities assigned to those alternatives in various ways. In this sense, God does not strictly intend all specific goods; but he certainly intends that there shall be goods of this sort. He has, one might say, a generic intention, and he desires and approves of the specific goods which ensue. When a specific good comes to exist in a probabilistic universe, it is less plausible to say that its coming to be is an act of God. God's act, specified by his intention, is the existence of the system and the existence of some goods which include this one as a disjunct possibility. Since he does not intend this specific good, its coming to be is less easily thought of as an act of God, but rather as a desired consequence of his acts. Accordingly, when we thank God for creating this good, we properly thank him for creating the system which makes such goods possible and for including this good as one of the possible goods of the system. It may well be that in our world, the occurrence of some goods is virtually certain, whereas others will be very improbable. The former are more easily thought of as acts of God than the latter, even though we may not be able to tell which class many specific goods belong to. It is quite natural, therefore, that we should be very cautious about speaking of the coming to be of natural states as acts of God, in this non-basic sense of action.

It is even more difficult to ascribe such things as earthquakes and cancer to Divine activity, even though they too originate by natural causality from the system of nature which God sustains in being. That is because, quite intelligibly, it may be said that God does not desire or intend such states. What God antecedently intends is the system of nature, and he intends it for the sake of the goods which it alone can realize. From that system arise evils of many sorts, and though God foresees that and indeed sustains them in being, as a condition of maintaining the system which is necessary to so many goods, he neither desires nor intends them. For this reason, one may feel reluctant to speak of such things as acts of God, even in a non-basic sense. One could call them unintentional acts of God, except for the connotation that God did them by mistake, which would not be the case. They are unintended but necessary consequences of a system which produces great goods, for those who suffer as well as for others. There is a reason for their occurrence, and in that sense they are intentional. But the reason needs to include the event in a wider description of the total created system, within which the evil event is neither an end nor a means to an end. Thus it would be a wholly inadequate answer to the question, "What is God doing in this event?" to say, "He is causing cancer". One would need to say, "He is sustaining in being a total natural system and its laws, which alone allows the sufferer and many others a distinctive set of goods, but which necessarily results in great suffering at this time".

One traditional way of putting this is to distinguish what God intends and approves from what God permits. As Stewart Sutherland points out, the word "permit" rather underplays the extent to which God must be an active causal factor in whatever exists (Sutherland 1984:65). "The *sangfroid* implicit in such a conception of God is morally grotesque", he claims, remarking that many a war criminal has been found guilty for less. But war criminals intend to oppress and torture others; they do not care about the dignity of the human person. Their torturing is not necessary; it results from a hatred of goodness; and it has no possible good outcome for the victims. God *ex hypothesi* intends eternal happiness for those creatures which are capable of it. He cares so much about human dignity that he has assumed a human nature in Christ. The suffering he causes is necessary to a world in which such goods are possible; he shares in it himself, and he calls creatures to eliminate it wherever possible. Such a God is not fairly called cold-blooded, though he is bound by necessities which are ineliminable even from the existence of the most perfect possible source of all being.

Thus far basic, specific and generic non-basic acts and the non-intentional exercise of causal powers, have been distinguished in God. Further, and more important, distinctions arise when one considers the creation of rational agents. The main reason for sustaining a universe of causal regularities, with all its inevitable defects, is that it is the condition of the emergence of a certain sort of rational agent. If God, by a basic act, sustains such a rational agent in being, it will possess powers which may be freely and responsibly exercised, and this opens up further complications in the relationship of God to creatures. Suppose God commands a rational agent, A, to do x, and A does x. Then, in a sense, x is God's act, since God is a primary cause in its coming about, though he is not the only or sufficient cause. This is even clearer in the case where God gives A paranormal powers to do y, and A does y. Then God's agency becomes particularly apparent, though it is still true that God is a co-operative agent and that A possesses a real agency which must be distinguished from that of God. "That we can come to know God and love him ... are matters of grace, marks of divine favour, for which we owe no thanks to ourselves at all, but to God only: but the final decision, the final right of refusal, he has vested in us, and we, not God, are answerable for the answer we return" (Lucas 1976:15). These events, of obedient response to God, may be called mediated acts of God, acts mediated through the response of obedient creaturely wills. It is important to note how different they are from particular basic acts which God can and may perform, which bring states about, not by means of prior causally efficacious acts. Thus raising a man from death would be a basic Divine act. In a probabilistic universe, the determination by God of one alternative which would otherwise have been left to chance would be a basic action. So would be the exercise of any power of a creature which was identical with God. But a life of complete obedience to God, lived by a human creature, would be a mediated Divine act, or set of such acts. This distinction will turn out to be important when thinking of what incarnation might mean.

We can clearly distinguish God's acts from the acts of creatures, as they respond to God and freely exercise the powers he gives them. So we have possibility that a creature may disobey God and do what God forbids. Now the act of the creature is not an act of God at all – though of course its continuing existence is due to the basic act of creation. As acts of creaturely disobedience multiply, they will affect the structure of the created order itself, so that more and more of that order fails to reflect the Divine intentions. In the case of cancer one must add to what has been already said that many instances of such sufferings are not acts of God even in a non-basic or unintentional sense; they are the results of evil or careless creaturely acts, not the results of physical forces alone, but of free choices wrongly made, stretching over generations. God still sustains the order of freedom, but what happens is not only what he does not intend, it is what he forbids, but allows for the sake of freedom.

It should be clear that it does not follow from a doctrine of creation *ex nihilo* that everything in the universe is an act of God, even though a basic act of God is involved in everything that exists. I have distinguished the universal basic activity of creation, possible particular basic acts within the created order, particular non-basic acts (intended events brought about by the natural powers of objects), generic non-basic acts (events of an intended class, brought about by natural powers), mediated acts, the exercise of non-intentional causal Divine powers, and occurrences which are opposed to God's intentions. Of all these, the clearest and most unequivocal sense of "act of God" is that which refers to particular basic actions, and that is the sense that will be generally used in subsequent discussion. If this sense is clearly defined and distinguished from the other senses outlined, it should be quite possible in principle to know what sort of thing an act of God is, and to distinguish various sorts of such action both from the exercise of the powers of natural objects and from free creaturely acts. I am therefore not convinced by Professor Sutherland's searching argument which ends in the conclusion that "acts of God ... are incredibly difficult to individuate" (Sutherland 1984:65), so difficult that one must give up the concept. He is supposing that as creator God must somehow be active always and everywhere, so that one can never distinguish what is not a Divine act from what God is doing. But one does not have to think of God as engaged in a "frenzy" of activity which leaves no room for other beings to act at all. On the contrary, even though God is in one sense involved in all events, it is quite possible to distinguish particular basic acts of God from other sorts of acts, events and processes. It is another question, to which much of my argument will be addressed, whether there are any such particular basic acts. Whether or not there are, one can certainly say that many things can happen in a created order, wholly dependent for its existence upon God, which God does not intend, desire or approve of. Yet the order itself may be the necessary condition of an overwhelmingly great good.

It is right for me to thank God for creating the world-system within which alone I can exist. Of course, I will not thank him for the suffering I endure, taken on its own. But I may believe that such suffering is an inevitable consequence of the sort of world in which I exist, and that it can be used by God to bring about an overwhelming good. My gratitude will be for my existence, taken overall and in view of my supernatural destiny, when I see that it is part of a world-structure which must contain suffering of the sort that I endure. If I see that to be so, it is even possible for me voluntarily to accept suffering, if thereby someone else may suffer less or be helped in some positive way. One must be careful, however, never to turn this into an argument for increased suffering, as a means to greater good. It is simply a statement that suffering can be used for good, by a heroic commitment that no one has a right to demand of anyone else. Suffering can in this way be turned into a prayer of intercession for the good of the world – even though it would have been better for that suffering, considered in isolation, not to exist. It is that mystery of freely accepted suffering that is expressed in the Christian symbol of Christ on the cross. In acceptance of that mystery there lies the possibility of a practical and of a theoretical resolution of the classical problem of evil, even though the details of such a resolution must be as far beyond human comprehension as is the necessary nature of God himself.

4

The Integral Web

It is an important thesis of theism that the existence of this world is desirable by a perfectly rational being. Is this plausible? Many have thought not. Even Plotinus thought it would have been better for the world not to be, though it necessarily is ("It unfolds itself desirous of becoming all things, although it would have been better for it not to have desired this", Plotinus 1966:111,8,8). Obviously, there are many parts of the world one would prefer not to exist. But, I have suggested, if these can be seen to be necessary as part of the system, one may still will them as part of one's primary willing of the system. In such a manner, I will prefer not to be seriously ill, but I may still say that I desire to exist, that my existence is desirable. There are many who may not agree, who may take their own lives, so full of misery do they seem. But it is possible to suggest that they have not seen the full context of their lives, the meaning that their sufferings may weave into them, the overwhelming good that lies in store for them. We may be overcome by misery for a while. But if there is an endless beatitude awaiting us, that may make all our sufferings worthwhile.

The classical statement of a powerful objection to this view is put by Dostoevsky into the mouth of Ivan Karamazov, in his novel, *The Brothers Karamazov*. Ivan protests that if it is inevitable to torture a baby so that its unavenged tears are the foundation of final human happiness, such a world is not worth creating. Even an endless ecstasy for all people is not worth the torture of an innocent baby. The protest makes its point strongly, and Alyosha, Ivan's brother, has no reply. But it is built upon the supposition that there is an alternative to the existence of this world, or one like it in relevant moral respects, and that the torture is a means to the happiness of others. Suppose, however, that there is no alternative, that universal happiness, for the baby as well as for the torturer, is only possible in a world where that torture may occur, and where, given many evil choices by finite wills, it does occur. Suppose that the torture is not a *means* to happiness, but a foreseeable though forbidden consequence of the existence of such a world. The torture is not chosen that through it happiness may come about, but it is accepted as a possible consequence of the only sort of world in which happiness is possible for free finite creatures. And suppose that the baby itself can only have supreme happiness if it is born into a world where it is so tortured. Perhaps the proper question to ask then is: would that baby, after its terrible death, finding itself as a rational and mature agent in a world offering endless bliss, still say: "I would rather never have existed"? In the perspective of endless bliss, that torture will soon diminish to the merest speck, an atom of misery lost in an eternity of bliss. Why should any rational agent hesitate then to accept the universe as good, and affirm existence with all the misery it entails?

A suspicion perhaps remains that we are here replacing reality with a dream. The horror of innocent and terrible suffering is real; the hope of endless bliss may be a dream. We cannot see why our suffering should exist. We cannot see what good will come of it. Our faith in endless bliss is born of real despair. So, when we hear Sonia, in the concluding speech of Chekhov's *Uncle Vanya*, say "I have faith", we cannot help thinking that this is a pitiful delusion born of an insufferable life. Does it not trivialize our real present suffering to say that all will be well hereafter?

One must never confuse the pastoral with the doctrinal. Of course it would be absurd to say to someone suffering agony, "Do not worry; you will soon be very happy". What one can offer, often all one can offer, is shared experience, silent companionship and preparedness to listen and care. Grief, desolation and sorrow are real, and not to be denied. The doctrinal question, however, is always silently present. Does this desolation and pain have a meaningful place in one's life? Can it possibly be seen as an integral part of a desirable existence, an existence willed by a loving God?

If one thinks only of one's own life, so short in duration

and so bounded by chance and accident, pain may have no meaningful place in it. It will be an absurdity, a destruction, an opposition to all meaning. One must begin the theoretical exercise by thinking of the universe as a whole. Human beings are integral parts of a huge cosmic structure, and modern physics helps to spell out how much the various parts are bound together into a quasi-organic whole. The physicist David Bohm has called the universe an "implicate order", in which each part affects every other, even at surprisingly large distances in space and time (Bohm, D. 1980). And we can see, in part, how apparently unrelated facts in the universe may be necessarily related to produce the sort of world we now have. For instance, the universe is approximately 15 billion light years in diameter. That may seem very wasteful, if it in the end only produced human beings on this small planet. Why so long before conscious life appeared? The surprising answer is that conscious life originates from carbon-based molecules, which are born out of the ashes of dying stars. It takes just about 15 billion years for stars to be born and die, and during that time the universe has been expanding from a first "Big Bang". So it turns out that the size of the universe is directly related to the existence of rational life on earth. In short, we need a universe that big to produce conscious life of the sort we have! Two apparently unrelated facts, the size of the cosmos and the existence of human beings, turn out to be related in what seems to be a necessary way.

There are very many instances of what physicists call "fine tuning" in the universe – the ratio of hydrogen to carbon atoms, the exact value of Planck's constant, the rate of expansion of the universe, and many more – which all need to be correlated to a very fine degree of accuracy before human life could appear. It is not possible to change one of these and leave the others intact. So, if a world anything like this is to exist, we cannot take one chunk out of it and leave the rest the same. To put it briefly, if I am to exist, it has to be in this universe as a whole, or in one extremely similar. One cannot just take me and put me in a different, apparently more comfortable world. I would not belong there. I could not exist there. I have to be where I am or not at all. And so it is for all of us.

There may seem to be a tension between this stress on the interconnectedness of everything in the universe and the alleged facts of freedom and indeterminacy. If I cannot take out one part of the universe without changing the whole structure, how can there be real alternative courses of action? The tension is, however, only apparent. It is true that a change in one part of the universe will have effects over a much wider range. But the principles in accordance with which such changes occur are themselves exactly specified within the system. It is not that everything in the universe has to be exactly the way it is, without there being any alternatives. At every stage of the universe's existence, alternative possibilities for the future exist. The point is that these alternatives are specified by the nature of the universe itself, and that the taking of one alternative in one part of the structure will have effects on all other parts of the structure, in some way. Everything in the physical universe is interconnected, but the web of connections is a constantly changing one, as specific options are actualized out of the range of possibilities which exists at any particular moment of time. The important fact is that any change in one part of the universe has implications for the total structure, and thus the sorts of changes that are possible at any time will depend upon changes at all other points in the structure. That is what is meant by saying that the universe is an implicate order.

There may seem to be an uncomfortable consequence of this view. If almost any degree of earthly suffering will be rendered worthwhile by the enduring possibility of endless bliss, am I not compelled to have as many offspring as I possibly can, however miserable they may be? The creation of new human souls will always be worthwhile, however terrible their disabilities and however much suffering they endure. What is uncomfortable in this thought is that I may seem obliged to procreate lives of enormous and certain suffering, because of some disputable theory about God and immortality. Even the convinced theist may pause at this consequence. Fortunately, the consequence does not in fact follow from the theory. What is true, if the theory is true, is that every human life is worthwhile and must be regarded as such. But the fact that it is good for x to exist does not mean that there is an obligation on anyone (even God, much less me) to bring x into existence. There is no obligation to do every good thing. Indeed, there could not be, since many goods are incompatible. There is an obligation on humans to do much good in their lives. But few people have a particular obligation to procreate new human souls, though it may be good, in particular circumstances, if they do. So there is no obligation to have children even at great cost. There is, indeed, an obligation to bear children responsibly and with as great a concern for their earthly welfare as possible. It is an important consequence of theism, nonetheless, that the procreation of children is good, and that every human life is of enormous and irreplaceable value. I do not regard this as an uncomfortable consequence, but as a profound moral implication of belief in God.

Just at the time when the problem of evil has come to seem insuperable to many theologians, physicists have constructed a picture of the universe which promises a theoretical solution to it. Our theological picture of the goodness of God will need to clear itself of sentimental attributions of a cosmically indulgent sugar-daddy, who would like to eliminate all suffering, but for some reason fails to do so. The classical theologians provide the means to do that. For them, the goodness of God lies in his supreme perfection and desirability ("God is called good as being the first source of every perfection things desire", Aquinas 1964:1a,6,2). We might add to that the Divine promise of endless bliss and the religious affirmation of a presently offered loving presence and empowering creative spirit. It remains true that from this God issues a universe containing suffering and ills of countless kinds. Nevertheless, it is not an evil universe, nor does God will (antecedently) that anyone should suffer ill. In the universe he has made, ills must necessarily come upon us, but when they do, God wills that they should be opposed and overcome wherever and whenever possible. Evil does not come from any source other than God. But though evil derives by necessity from him, his actuality is without evil. Nor is God evil because evil originates from him, any more than a lion is evil because it kills and eats it prey. What derives from God by necessity is not a matter of personal responsibility, and he wills or accepts evil only because and in so far as it is necessary to the great finite goods which he does intend. God is good in the ways that are proper to the unique creator of all. He is the supreme instance of perfection; his creation is, as a whole, good; and all evil in it can and will either be eliminated or be transformed ultimately into good, and so redeemed.

These are points that the great theologians of the classical Christian tradition have made. But many of the conclusions of modern physics delineate a picture of the universe which even more clearly helps one to understand how suffering and destruction are necessary features of a universe in which alone beings like us can exist. The universe of modern physics is not a collection of arbitrarily associated events, which a God could alter just as he chose, while leaving everything else as it was. The universe is a total integrated whole of the most elegant sort. The laws of its being are mathematically beautiful, and it may well be termed a perfect masterpiece of rational beauty and imagination. This perfect beauty may seem to accord ill with the evolutionary picture of "nature, red in tooth and claw". But evolution is just an outworking of the same elegant principles at the base of the physical structure of things. A few physicists have even proposed that there is only one really possible universe. For there is only one consistent set of equations from which the basic laws of the universe can be derived (cf. Atkins, P.W. 1981:ch.6). This is almost certainly an exaggeration, for there could surely have been different basic laws, though we can hardly imagine what they could be. Nevertheless, the point made is an intriguing one. It suggests that necessity is built into the structure of things in a very strong way. It suggests that the universe is mathematically ordered and its parts interconnected in a web of quantifiable relationships which is real, but may be quite unknown to us in detail.

This is a world which proceeds, not in accordance with arbitrary and *ad hoc* decisions, but in accordance with all-embracing rational principles. It is also a world which shows emergent order. That is, from very simple and basic principles successive hierarchies of order emerge – from primal matter the atoms emerge; then the level of biologically replicating life; then sentient beings; and finally, so far as we know, rational wills. Each level adds new properties and principles of organization; the most obvious, but not the only, jump being from matter to consciousness, at the level of complex nervous-system structures. Each new level is built on the previous one, and generated from it by a leap from increasing complexity in one sort of property to the existence of new sorts of property. The biologist Dr Arthur Peacocke stresses the emergent nature of the physical world, and the way in which it is not possible to reduce higher levels of explanation to lower. The basic laws of physics remain operative; yet "the laws of the higher-level process are not fully determined by the laws of processes (of a different kind) at the lower level" (Peacocke 1979:117).

In such an emergent universe, the future cannot be predicted wholly from the physical past. No inspection of the first state of a purely physical universe could enable one to deduce the nature of conscious intention in human beings. Physical unpredictability enters into the structure of things, not only via the well-known indeterminacy principle of Heisenberg, but also in the ontological gap between one sort of property and its emergent successors. This may suggest a picture of things, which quantum physics would support, in which the future is truly open, not completely determined by the past (though of course it is limited and prompted by the past, which remains as a basic structure underlying newly emergent properties). In such a universe, randomness, risk and an element of "trial and error" would feature. The analogy of the game of dice would not be wholly inappropriate because it seems that an element of indeterminate emergence is built into the physical structure of things.

Einstein, in a much-quoted phrase which he used in a remembered conversation with Bohr at the Solvay Congress of 1927, could not believe that God played dice with the universe. But Einstein seems to have been wrong in his life-long opposition to physical indeterminacy and quantum theory. The root of his opposition lies in the deep desire that physicists and philosophers have that there should be a sufficient reason for everything. This desire for an absolute explanation is rooted as much in a religious sense that existence should have ultimate meaning as in the rational requirement that everything should have an explanation. But the provision of sufficient reasons entails determinism; and if contingent freedom, in God or creatures, is to exist, there must be a place in the universe for true contingency, that is, for reasons which are explanatory, but not sufficient. Quantum theory suggests that such reasons may exist as a basic feature of the physical universe, if it is stochastic, that is, probabilistic in structure.

Probability is not absolute chaos; it works within defined parameters. As David Bartholomew says, "Chaos and order are complementary; the presence of one seems to imply the other" (Bartholomew 1984:95). There may well be a sufficient reason why those parameters are as they are – a reason founded on the elegance, simplicity, coherence and fecundity of the basic structure. But within those parameters, there is room for creative originality. Think of the artist arranging materials to form new creative patterns for their beauty and novelty. Whitehead's re-interpretation of Leibnizian monad-ology postulates that each monadic unit reflects every other in the universe from its own point of view, and then makes a creative advance into novelty by a re-organization of these materials and a forward leap into originality. The sense of unreality that afflicts most of us as we consider this prospect arises from its breathtaking pan-psychism. It speaks as though each monad – each "actual occasion", in Whitehead's term – is a little creative genius, prehending all and adding its little spark of creativity to reality in the very moment of its passing away. Even David Pailin, who has been a foremost defender of Process Theology, admits that "on analysis, the psychical description of reality as a whole seems to be either meaning-less, misleading, or deeply obscure" (Pailin 1989:148).

Perhaps we can accept that the importance of indeterminacy lies in the room it leaves for the exercise of creative imagina-tion. But we need not give all the creativity to the atomic units of being, leaving God little or nothing to do. We may, with classical theism, regard God as the prime creator, but, revising classical theism, regard him as a genuinely creative imagination. Then we could understand why reality might have a stochastic character. For we would not have a Newtonian universe which runs in predetermined grooves, with God interfering, as Newton thought, on rare occasions to keep the balance right (to keep the planets in their orbits, he supposed). Instead, we would have a probabilistic physical system, open to the creative shaping of the Divine imagination at very many points. A stochastic and emergent universe allows and invites the continual activity of God, normally hidden in the complex interweaving of law and probability which constitutes the energy field of physical being.

The work of contemporary physicists allows us (though it hardly compels us) to construct a picture of the physical universe as a process whereby primal matter is structured and developed to become capable of expressing and consciously relating to the primal Spirit which is its origin, foundation and goal. God is one, perfect, pure spirit and creativity. The material universe, considered just as such, is many, limited, unconscious and containing many possibilities of conflict and destruction. It is of the nature of the energy of which it is constituted to destroy as well as to create, to renew itself precisely by destruction, and so generate the new by its own continual perishing. It is the nature of the physical universe to live by opposition. Its vast energies continually interact and annihilate one another, yet generate new properties in the process. In such a world-system of many delicately balanced energies, held in an elegant mathematical web of rational principle, capable of generating emergent properties, including all the mental properties involved in the existence of a community of free rational wills, the creative originating Will can act to form and realize the structures of the physical order and bring its diversity into final unity with itself.

This may seem rather an ambitious metaphysical picture, based on what must surely be provisional conclusions of science, and even then generalizing beyond the scope of physics itself. That is so, and I do not suppose that it is a finally adequate picture. Yet what I think it does show is that the universe may be such as to have been created by an omnipotent and perfectly good God, while necessarily containing much evil. It is a provisional picture. But if we are to seek an understanding of how God may originate such a world as this, we need to work with the best provisional hypotheses we can find. There are other scientific views of the world which would also yield an adequate theodicy, at a certain price. If, for instance, determinism turned out to be true, one would have a very strong appeal to the necessity of things being as they are, though the stress on contingent freedom would have to be given up. So I am not suggesting that theism depends on the truth of an indeterministic world picture. But that picture does seem to be the leading one in modern science. And it is strongly compatible with the sort of emphasis on Divine and human freedom that I think a positive understanding of Divine creativity requires. So, though we understand little of the ultimate nature of things, modern physics does open up a positive way of understanding how individual suffering may find an intelligible place in a Divinely created world. Humans are parts of a universe which must be considered as an integrated totality; which offers a unique and distinctive set of goods; which necessarily contains many actual instances of conflict and suffering, and many more possibilities of such suffering; but which also offers the prospect of an overwhelming good and happiness obtainable in no other way. Suffering is a conditionally necessary consequence of having such a world-system at all. God cannot play this game and change the rules.

But should the game by played? My suggestion has been that some such game must be played. God is, by necessity, a creator God. Would it have been better never to exist, because of the virtual inevitability of suffering that our existence involves? It seems to me that if one could be convinced that one's suffering was either just or inevitable, and that endless happiness was always genuinely possible, then it is entirely rational to think that existence is desirable and good. God is good in that he wills our happiness and makes it possible. He is the ultimate good, in that the supreme desirability of his own being is what brings us endless bliss. He is omnipotent, in being the source of all that is, and in being more powerful than any other possible being. Thus, I submit, the problem of evil, in its precise intellectual sense, is capable of adequate resolution; no contradiction can be shown between a good and powerful God and the existence of innocent suffering; and one can even see, at least in principle, how such suffering could co-exist with such a God. None of this removes the real agony of suffering, nor is it meant to do so. It does not pretend that suffering is good. But it supposes that out of suffering, God can bring good if we join our wills to his in seeking to oppose and remove its causes.

The defence I have offered is a variety of the "free-will defence", which naturally had only subsidiary appeal for Augustine, with his much stronger doctrine of Divine necessity, but which has figured prominently in recent discussions, as greater emphasis has been given to both Divine and human freedom. I think this defence, very ably expounded by Alvin Plantinga and others, works, but it leaves two major questions: how can one account for the great deal of naturally caused suffering in the world? and is free-will a great enough good to justify the suffering whose possibility it entails? Plantinga's suggestion that Satan causes natural evil seems to me most implausible (Plantinga 1977:58) for suffering is involved in the whole course of the evolution of life, from the preying of one fish on another to the development of cancer cells in the body. Though some prophets have thought that lions might lie down with lambs, that would involve a great change in their digestive systems. And I cannot think that fallen angels changed the digestive systems of dinosaurs long before the first human being existed. Nor is it quite convincing to be told that one is free to choose between good and evil; for what is the point of such a choice, and why is it so important as to justify a world of immense suffering? Perhaps one would rather not be free under those conditions.

In view of these problems, I have sought to put a great deal of emphasis on the necessities inherent in the Divine nature. We are often presented with a picture of a God who might not have created morally free creatures, but determined and happy ones. Thus J.L. Mackie argues thus: God can create any possible universe. There is a possible universe in which every person chooses good. Therefore God can create that universe. God could, and should, create a universe in which all free agents always make good choices (Mackie 1982:165f.). But it does not work. For the fuller description of the universe in question is that, in it, P *freely* (i.e. not determined by God) chooses x. That is a possible universe, but it is not a possible universe that God can wholly determine of himself. Then we would have the contradiction that God determines wholly a universe in which some things are not determined by God, i.e. there is some event which God both does and does not determine. So there are many apparently possible universes that God cannot create, since creating them would be self-contradictory. He cannot wholly determine any universe in which some events are free (i.e. not wholly determined). He can, of course, create any universe in which there are free agents, but he cannot know, before they choose, which of the alternatives he places before them they will choose. He can thus only foreknow such a universe as about to be actual if it will actually exist. And that cannot be wholly within his power of choice.

So God cannot create a universe in which free creatures always choose the good. Nor can he make the laws of nature, which bring about much natural suffering, quite other than they are, while still creating us, since we can only exist in this universe, with these laws. Brian Hebblethwaite says, "The evils men experience from their physical structure and environment are not just by-products of a created order which is the necessary condition for particular goods which they experience; they are by-products of a process which is the necessary condition for their being created finite persons at all" (Hebblethwaite 1976:75). That is an extremely broad claim, and I am not sure that all possible finite persons must exist in a process very like ours. Perhaps we can be content with the more restricted claim that any finite persons who arise by the sorts of emergent physical processes that we do, who have the same general nature that we do, must be parts of a world of processes very similar to those of our own world. That is still a substantive claim, which the insights of modern physics about the integral nature of this universe render plausible. It is therefore useless to complain that God should have avoided the suffering that exists in this universe, while yet creating free human beings, or indeed any sentient and rational creatures like them. It may even be pointless to complain that God should not have created any rational creatures at all. Tickets for existence may be non-returnable, and moral indignation may be an inappropriate response, even if we hate the journey, despite all assurances that all shall be well. For, just as God is necessary in some respects (in his existence and perfection, for instance), so it may be necessarily part of his nature to create some autonomous, nomological, stochastic, emergent, dialectical and integral world-system, in which many other dependent but truly creative wills can come to be.

Such a universe will be autonomous, in not being wholly determined by God in every respect. Thus it, and only it, allows for beings other than God. A real other must be at least partly self-determining. It can be shaped and sustained, but not determined, by God. And perhaps God necessarily creates others, in order to realize part of his nature in relationship to them, and to unite beings quite different from himself to his own being by the free persuasion of love. He does not do so out of any lack in himself, but out of the fullness of his unlimited reality, which must include all possible worlds. The history of the universe is the unfolding of these possibilities in one of the many ways in which they could be actualized, and in some one of which they must be actualized.

The universe will be nomological, or ruled by general laws. For only thus can it provide a rational, predictable and dependable basis for action and existence. Only thus can creatures be freed from dependence on God's arbitrary willing, and exist in a world with its own proper structure and comprehensible form. It was this perception of the created order which helped to make possible the rise of the natural sciences in the seventeenth century – a thesis argued at length and forcefully by Stanley Jaki (Jaki 1978).

The universe will be stochastic, or probabilistic. For elements of indeterminacy are necessary to permit the exercise of free creative action. We do not have a universe with absolute laws, and a few gaps where God might act. We have a universe with probabilistic laws, where alternatives frequently exist, and can be chosen. This God is not a "God of the gaps", interfering on rare occasions to correct errors or omissions in the system of physical laws. He is a God who constantly and continually sustains and guides the universe by purposive choices among its alternative pathways. He is the constant presence of purpose in the universe, not an external interference with an otherwise perfectly running machine. How this purposive influence is to be conceived is a matter of intense and unresolved debate. David Pailin, renouncing the Process idea of a God who lures every actual occasion towards its best possible future, advocates that "divine activity ... is to be understood in terms of an overall influence ... a restlessness that agitates ... a desire for greater flourishing" (Pailin 1989:172). This cosmic urge to greater value sounds suspiciously like Bergson's *élan vital* returning.

Or can this urge be dropped, and the nisus towards value be seen as implicit in the physical structure itself, so that, as Arthur Peacocke puts it, the creator unfolds "the potentialities of the universe ... by a process in which the creative possibilities, inherent, by his own creative intention, within the fundamental entities of that universe and their interrelations, become actualized within a temporal development shaped and determined by those self-same inherent potentialities" (Peacocke 1979:106)? Once one begins to speak of generalized urges, spread over the whole creation, is it not simpler just to speak of an unfolding of possibilities inherent in the structure itself, and revert to a clear-sighted deism? Dr Peacocke, aware of this danger, has recently written of the possibility of "top-down causation", by which total complex structures can exercise causal constraints upon the physical behaviour of lower-level entities.

T. F. Torrance, whose works on science and theology have broken new ground in twentieth century theological thought, also writes, "As a unitary intelligible whole the universe must be thought of as ultimately integrated from above through the creative bearing upon it of the Trinitarian relations in God himself" (Torrance 1980:38). Perhaps this notion of "integration from above" will help to show how God can exercise a purposive influence upon all things, without being just an extra element within the physical structure itself. If God is conceived as the total spiritual environment of the physical universe, his nature may exercise a sort of purposive constraint upon the system, which is in one sense causal, though it will not be detectable as a specific "shuffling around" of physical particles, or as the causality of one lower-level agent or cause among others of the same kind.

Fundamental problems remain about how the causality of

such a holistic and purposive set of constraints is to be best conceived. But it seems well-established that the universe has a looser structure than Newtonian mechanics envisaged, and that the probabilistic character of many physical processes permits an idea of purpose and of creative freedom both in particular parts of the universe (in human beings) and in the universe as a whole. Freedom no longer has to be pushed out of the physical universe to a strange noumenal realm beyond, as in Kant. The complex structure of physical laws permits and encourages it, and is thus well suited to the production of beings which can freely respond to their creator's purpose, for good or ill.

The universe will be emergent, bringing forth new levels of structure and new properties through time. This is a condition of true creativity, the origination of the new. It brings creatures into being who evolve from simpler physical elements, and who carry the potentiality for transforming their past natures in new and surprising ways. With this, comes the possibility of real risk, adventure and unique forms of creativity; the possibility of life as a self-shaped journey towards truth, beauty and goodness. It is not just that one is faced with a blunt choice of good or evil, which seems absurd in the abstract. Each finite will which comes to maturity is faced with a multitude of choices. In each one, there is a possible move forward in a positive and creative way, a possible retreat or refusal to act creatively, and a possible path to destruction, to the exploration of darker avenues, having an attraction which is both fascinating and frightening. It is these choices and their consequences, in bewildering multiplicity, which determine human history. The wheel of suffering is chosen because we desire what it promises, even though we fear what it gives. So emergence is both for good and ill; though because God is present always in the process, there is always the positive good to be actualized. And, in the end, on the Christian view of things, when all our choices have played themselves out and we have done all that our perverse wills have desired to do, God will eliminate evil from this creation, and receive to himself all those who will return to him. In the Christian gospel, the parable of the Prodigal Son portrays this thought most poignantly (Luke 15:11–32);

in it we see, in a readily understandable way, both the attraction of evil and its ultimate emptiness. An emergent universe opens up to us the pathways by which we work out this destiny.

The universe will be dialectical, in that temporal change results from an interplay of opposites. A world of many wills is one of a possible conflict of purposes, of disintegration as well as harmony. This dialectic is present in the primal act of creation, in which the one pure Spirit generates from nothing, by his power alone, a world of many physical forms. From that logically first moment ("logically" because there may be no absolute first moment of time), being is played out as a dialectical succession of opposites, death passing into life and life falling into decay. Such a world of oppositions is necessary to the existence of beings which, by their very finiteness, exclude others. To understand this is to understand why there cannot be joy without at least the possibility of sorrow. In a perfected world, such oppositions may be checked, the negative possibilities of destruction held at bay by free submission to a harmonious purpose. But the possibilities must be there, and they will be realized by wills which choose their own desires in preference to the surrender of self.

The universe will be integral, in that it will be a unity of wills bound together in one organic whole. Each affects the others, for good and ill. And the final purpose of the whole is that completed integration in which all who freely assent will freely conform to God's purpose and creatively co-operate with his design. There must be such a final purpose, if this universe has its origin in a being who is the exemplar of all perfections and who desires to create the world for the sake of the overwhelming good it alone can realize. Belief in immortality, in some sense, is a necessary implicate of belief in a loving creator. Without it, no theodicy is possible. But if we can accept it, then we can see how Augustine and Aquinas could say that evil is a privation of being. They were not denying its reality, but seeing it as a lack of perfection or as a disorder necessarily possible in a world capable of being distinct from the source of all perfection. That necessity is what the classical Christian theologians discerned. Contemporary physics helps us to a clearer view of its nature and limits. And when the "free will defence" is placed within that context, it can be seen to provide the foundation of a comprehensible theodicy.

Having placed such a stress on necessity, it may be asked how this account differs from Plato's account, in the *Timaeus*, of God doing the best he can with a world of eternally existing and partly recalcitrant matter. One difference is that matter remains an inexplicable uncreated surd for Plato; whereas this view sees it as necessarily arising from God, and so as having an intelligible reason for existence. But the more important difference is that, for Plato, the world of eternal Forms is the truly real world. Matter is essentially the tomb of souls, and it will never become wholly transparent to the Divine will. So he says that "such as have duly purified themselves with philosophy live henceforth altogether without the body" (Plato 1982:391). Matter has no final or enduring place in the Divine plan. For the theistic view I have outlined, the material world is intended to be a sacrament and expression of Divine reality, with its own proper reality, and its destiny is to be transformed into a fully adequate vehicle of spirit. The recalcitrance of the material is partly a condition of creating free and autonomous finite wills, and partly a consequence of the refusal of those wills to be vehicles of the spirit. The doctrine of atonement and redemption is the story of how such refusal is being overcome, and the world returned to its true and intended unity with the Divine. In such a story, God acts in a more physical and particular way than a Platonic Demiurge or a Deistic first cause could do. The outlines of that story are yet to be drawn, but the provisional narrative so far sketched is intended to show that Christian theism can in principle provide an account of how necessity and freedom, eternity and time, perfection and evil, can be held together in one coherent view.

5

The Death of the Closed Universe

A great deal of stress has been placed on the necessity with which God creates a universe, and on the necessities which govern the structure of any such universe. This stress is entirely consistent with classical Christian theological writing. What is new, with respect to tradition, is the stress I have also placed on Divine freedom to create imaginatively and originally, and on a sort of human freedom which faces genuine and undetermined alternative futures. Thus I have supposed that the universe is open at many points to the influence of Divine and human choices, though all those choices will work within parameters of necessity which are sometimes very strict. Both God and creatures will often act in ways which affect the future, determining it to be in a state which might otherwise have been different.

It is not easy to tell when such an action has taken place. When a change occurs in the physical state of the universe, we normally assume that there is a cause of this change. We may not know what the cause is, and until the seventeenth century even the most intelligent observers were not generally aware of the true causes of most of the physical changes in the universe. That is to say, virtually no one thought that changes occurred in accordance with universal, mathematically quantifiable laws of nature, governing the interaction of fundamental particles. So for most of human history even those who most assiduously sought to discover the true causes of change were mistaken about those causes.

The lesson to be digested is that it is not at all easy to say what causes physical changes, to say what the causes of things are. Even now we cannot be sure of the most fundamental physical causes. We accept, for very good reasons, that there are fundamental equations governing the interaction of sub-atomic particles. But we do not know whether there is room for genuine indeterminacy in such interactions or whether there are "hidden variables" which remove indeterminacy at an even more fundamental level; whether all the fundamental forces (types of interaction) can be reduced to one or not; whether these fundamental forces give a complete account of complex phenomena – in the human brain, for instance, or whether there are sorts of causality we have not yet discovered. In modern physics, there is a host of disputed and undecided questions. Hypotheses abound; some seem much better attested than others; but a startling new discovery which upsets our present way of looking at things is always possible.

It is therefore not to be expected that there will be a generally accepted answer to the question: where and how, precisely, does God act to cause physical changes in the universe? To answer that question, even in part, we would have to have a very clear idea of just what the boundaries of natural physical causality are, and of how forms of purposive causality could coherently relate to them. And that requires an answer to all the disputed questions just briefly mentioned, which we are very far from having. It is most unlikely, therefore, that we could be empirically certain of where God acts in the world, even if he does so constantly. This is not an objection to the possibility of Divine action, as Maurice Wiles seems to suggest (Wiles 1986:4). It is a natural consequence of our general lack of knowledge of the complete causal bases of physical change.

The picture of causality just presented may be thought to imply a discredited "God of the gaps" hypothesis. Surely it cannot be true that God can only act in the gaps left between existing causal laws? Suppose we try this argument in the case of human acts. We assume that we perform actions which bring about changes in our bodies and in our environment, that we can act freely and for reasons. We also assume that we are physical objects among others in the world, and that we are accordingly subject to the same forces of physical causality as objects in general. But there is little inclination to say that our free actions must take place in the gaps left by a framework of physical laws. We are subject to physical laws; and we do act freely. However difficult it may be to give an adequate theoretical account of these facts, it seems that if human action can be integrated with natural causality, there is little reason why Divine action should not also be so integrated. And since most of us believe that humans act freely without having any idea of what an adequate philosophical account of such action in relation to natural causality would be like, it is hardly a serious objection to Divine action that we do not possess an adequate philosophical explanation of how God's acts integrate with the realm of natural causality.

We can say rather more than that, however. Richard Taylor has argued persuasively that a "purposeful explanation" can be, and should be, given of much human behaviour, which is not reducible to a causal explanation. "A purposeful explanation of an event or series of events is some statement that represents the events in question as the *means* to some end or goal" (Taylor 1966:213). Further, he suggests that "only the actions of agents can be purposeful"; in which case certain processes are properly explained only in terms of the purposes or intentions which an agent has in bringing them about. On such an account, explanations of human actions in terms solely of the laws of physics will be incomplete, in that they will omit quite proper forms of explanation which are needed to account for such actions. But does that imply that as agents we are somehow outside the nexus of physical forces, and have the power to bring about physical processes different from those material causes would have produced on their own (cf. Swindburne 1986)? Or is the non-reducibility of purposeful to causal explanation compatible with an ontological identity of the agent with some set of purely physical processes (say, brain-states) (cf. Armstrong 1968)?

I do not need to investigate these questions further – fortunately, since they are subject to radical philosophical dispute, not to say confusion. Although cases of human action are clear and indisputable, it is very contentious whether or to what extent some non-physical or mental entity or state plays a real causal role in human behaviour. If there is no agreement over these questions in cases of human action, one can hardly expect that the question of whether God makes a causal difference to the world will be easy to answer or clearly decidable. There is, nevertheless, one major difference between human and Divine action. While it is possible that human mental states may be identical with brain-states, it is clear that God is not identical with any physical state of the universe, much less with some intergalactic brain. Whatever we say about human causality, Divine causality cannot be reduced to or identified with some set of causal physical processes. If God, a purely spiritual or immaterial being, by a basic action produces some change in the world, then no set of physical causes can provide a sufficient explanation of that change. For a sufficient explanation is one that gives a cause or set of causes which, together with some causal law, entails the existence of a state of affairs. Now if God, an immaterial being, has the power, as a basic action, to bring about a state of affairs or not, that state cannot be entailed by states other than God. A state whose existence is entailed by previous states is not one that any being can have the power to prevent, while leaving those previous states the same. So, if God has the power either to bring about or to prevent a certain state, that state cannot be entailed by prior states; it cannot, therefore, be sufficiently caused by anything, much less by purely physical causes. So to say that God, or any non-material intellect, brought something about on purpose entails that, on that occasion, no purely physical set of causes provides a sufficient explanation of its coming about. Perhaps some set of physical causes *could have* brought the same state about; which means that we can never be sure whether God's choice is the real cause. But if physical causes did bring it about, then, necessarily, God was not the efficacious cause.

This argument does not show the God acts in the world. It shows that, if God acts (brings changes about intentionally) there are states of the physical universe which are not sufficiently explained by the operation of physical causes alone. To put it in the words of the crude formulation, there must be gaps in physical causality, if God is ever to do anything. It also shows, as if by the way, that it may be in principle impossible for an observer to be sure whether or not God has acted on a particular occasion. To know that, she would need a complete knowledge of all physical causes operating at a given time. Such a thing is well beyond present human capacity; and is in principle barred to anyone who thinks that there may be as yet unknown physical causes in operation at any time. It is always open to anyone to say that there *are* sufficient physical causes operating, though we cannot observe them. Whether it is more probable that there are such "hidden variables" or that there is a non-material intentional cause at work, will depend upon a more general assessment of such things as the nature of mind–body causality, the existence of God, the limits of physical causality and so forth. Since such assessments are extremely hard to make, it is highly unlikely that a definitive answer will be forthcoming in the foreseeable future. But it breaks no canons of scientific thought or procedure to suppose that non-physical causes may be in operation. Such causes will simply be beyond the purview of physical science – by such science's own self-definition.

In his acute and stimulating discussion of this problem, Dr Peacocke valiantly, but in my view unsuccessfully, attempts to preserve a real sense of Divine causality while denying the existence of any causal "gaps" in nature. He starts from the position that "the mental events which are the experience of being an 'I', an agent, are identical, under another description, with neurophysiological events in the brain" (Peacocke 1979: 131). "Thus", he says, "in my mental experience I am a transcendent causal agent"; but my behaviour can also be truly described in purely physical terms. He then suggests that we might conceive God's transcendence and causality in a similar way, so that we might see talk of Divine action as talk about "the meaning of the nexus of physical events". The laws of nature remain in place; but the very same physical events, spoken of in terms of their meaning and purpose, can be seen as Divine actions. Such an account would require no gaps in natural laws, which God might utilize. The account promises a certain theoretical simplicity and elegance; but is it coherent?

The most obvious problem is that, whereas human minds are emergent and supervenient upon physical processes, God can hardly be conceived both as the creator of the universe and as an emergent and supervenient being, generated by the physical universe. For the identity theorist, the real causal basis of change is physical; for the theist, the real causal basis of change must be a transcendent and subsistent immaterial being, God. Moreover, human mental events are aspects of an immensely complex and particular physical structure, the brain. Yet the universe as a whole does not have such a structure, and it is vastly implausible to see it as the brain of God. There just does not seem to be the requisite complexity of structure in the physical universe for it to be correctly described as the external aspect of the mind of God.

Peacocke himself emphasizes that the universe "is a system of much more change and open potentiality than was envisaged in the heyday of Newtonian science" (ibid.:135); but he is reluctant to think of God as utilizing this openness by determining particular events in ways which otherwise might have been left undetermined. However, if the openness is really present, and is part of the structure of scientific law, then God would not be "violating" the laws of nature if he did determine particular events within the limits allowed by the structure; nor would such action be detectable by scientific methods. So why should he dislike the idea? He wishes to think of Divine purpose as existing before and therefore apart from the physical universe. He wishes to think of it as setting the limits of physical change. So why should it not continue to operate within those limits to exercise a continuing, creative and responsive constraint upon physical processes? This would mean that physical laws alone would not provide a sufficient or complete explanation of what happens in the universe, though they would remain in force at their proper level. But that is just to say that the universe is open to the purposive guidance of God, which makes a material difference to the way things go. If God's intentions plus the physical laws do give a sufficient explanation of what happens in the world, whereas the physical laws alone do not, it is clear that the existence of God contributes substantially to an explanation of what happens in the world. This contribution will not impugn scientific explanations, which will remain content with non-sufficient causal explanations, but its possibility entails that in some sense scientific causal explanations will be incomplete.

I conclude that the "God of the gaps" objection is not a serious one. Its apparent force derives from the thought that there must be things science cannot explain, while God must enter into scientific explanations at some point to make them work; and from the fear that, as science explains more and more things, God will have less and less room for manoeuvre, until he is driven from the universe entirely. God and scientific laws are attempted explanations of the same sort, so the more the sciences explain, the less there is for God to explain. Sometimes God *has* been used as part of a scientific explanation. The classic example is Newton's suggestion that God is needed to adjust the planetary orbits from time to time (Newton 1952: query 22, p.352). Laplace, by a refinement of the calculus, famously showed that "we have no need of that hypothesis". It is now fairly clear that God does not occur as an hypothesis within physics. But that is because theistic explanations of why things happen are not of the same sort as the explanations used in the natural sciences. They do not compete or exclude one another.

To understand how this is so, one needs to explore the nature of scientific explanation. I shall use the example of physics, since it is the science which has often been regarded as the fundamental explanatory scheme, to which all others can be reduced, in principle. And I shall seek to show how perfectly adequate explanations in physics do not exclude Divine activity, though they do not mention it either. What is needed for the account to succeed is that a physical explanation should provide all that is required of it, but that it should not explain, or even mention, many real and important features which exist in the real world, and that it should not need to provide a sufficient, or determining, explanation of all changes that occur in the world. If this is so, then Divine activity can be a real feature of the world not mentioned by physics – or by any other experimental science – and it can be a causal factor in the temporal process of the universe which is not, or perhaps which cannot be, included in the conceptual scheme of physics, or of the experimental sciences in general.

It is important to note the fundamental features of the experimental method which revolutionized human understanding of the world in the sixteenth and seventeenth centuries. It is not just a matter of looking at the world very hard – this had been tried for centuries, without much effect. The revolutionary insight was to devise measurable and repeatable sets of observable conditions, to construct theoretical models from which consequences could be deductively derived by a formulatable set of general laws, and to devise ways of showing how observable facts confirm or disconfirm the model. Plato theorized; Aristotle observed; but the world waited until Galileo and Newton for observation and theory to be brought together by the notion of a repeatable, mathematically formulatable set of observations in carefully controlled and quantitatively described situations.

Far from being commonsensical or obvious, this approach to the study of the natural world was brilliantly daring. The proposal that a set of observable properties can be isolated and precisely measured; that a set of completely universal laws could be framed mathematically; that from one initial measured state a second, different, measurable state would inevitably ensue, whoever the experimenter may be, and wherever in the universe he carried out his experiment – this is a breathtaking idea. It has worked with astonishing accuracy, and seems to confirm that human reason does not, as Plato thought, tell us about some supra-natural realm beyond sense experience. On the contrary, it tells us about the world of sense-experience itself, when and in so far as it is subject to carefully controlled interaction and dispassionate and accurate observation.

These qualifications already suggest that Divine action may be outside the scope of the experimental method. It is very hard to see how anyone could carefully control the ways in which God might act or interact with the universe. To set up an experimental situation in which God's action could be tested is impossible without undertaking to manipulate and control God. If God cannot be controlled and measured, we shall not be able to set up a control situation within which his actions could be included. Thus one can easily see that it is no defect that natural science fails to mention God and his actions in setting up its theoretically explanatory models.

God, as the one who is beyond all manipulation and control, cannot be subjected to experimental testing.

Moreover, there is good reason to think that humans cannot observe God dispassionately or measure his actions precisely on any quantitative scale. Our relations to God, like our relations to other persons, cannot be wholly neutral. Our emotions, attitudes and whole personalities are involved in such relations. In the case of God, the appropriate human relationship is one of worship, awe and gratitude, involving submission and a re-orientation of self. To compare this with the calmly analytic attitude of the scientist in a laboratory is crass. In short, if we see what sort of being God is, we shall immediately see that the experimental method is wholly inappropriate for discerning his being and activity. That is why God cannot occur in any properly scientific account of the world, and why explanations of what happens in terms of Divine action must be different in kind from the explanations of natural science.

One of the methodological presuppositions of the rise of the experimental method was the de-sacralization of nature. That is, physical nature had to be seen as a neutral ground which could be controlled, manipulated and experimented upon, rather than as a part of the Divine being or the abode of spirits who might resent such human activities. Further, all formal and final causes had to be banished from physics, which would deal henceforth only with efficient and material causes. The revolutionary nature of this change of attitude is attested in Sir Francis Bacon's *Of the Proficience and Advancement of Learning* (1605), which helped to prepare the ground for the new scientific age which was just coming to birth. Only when the physical world was seen as quite distinct from God, and therefore as potentially subject to human control, could modern science begin. On the other hand, as Newton testified, belief in God remained psychologically important for the new scientists, as the guarantor that nature was a rational and intelligible order, which human reason, created in the image of the Creator, could hope to understand and control (cf. the General Scholium of *Principia Mathematica*, Newton 1962).

Newton and his immediate successors, however, created a

problem which to some seemed impossible to resolve. Once the physical universe had been sharply distinguished from God, how could the two be coherently related? The problem was made more severe by a philosophical presupposition which was widely accepted, and given canonical expression by the German philosopher Immanuel Kant. The presupposition was that all changes in the physical universe were governed by the principle of sufficient or determining reason. That is, physical causes sufficiently determine their effects – if the cause exists, a specific effect must necessarily exist, and no alternative is possible – "All that is required for a complete and necessary determination must be found in a possible experience" (Kant 1952: A.540). If you add to this axiom the admittedly complex hypothesis that there is a finite number of completely describable physical causes, which exhaust the set of possible causes of physical change, then one arrives at the immensely influential Laplacean model of the physical universe.

In its most general form, this model supposes that the whole universe consists of nothing but a large number of elementary particles, all of whose properties can be precisely measured, plus a finite and completely exhaustive set of discoverable and universal laws of physics. Then, Laplace famously declared, from the first state of the universe and a knowledge of all the laws of physics, everything that ever happened thereafter in the course of the universe's history could be infallibly predicted (Laplace 1951:4). There are at least seven highly dubious assumptions involved in this hypothesis. Is there nothing that really exists except elementary particles? Are all properties even of the physical universe subject to precise quantitative measurement? Can one ever exhaustively describe every feature of the universe, much less know that one has done so? Is there a finite and closed set of physical laws? Are these laws completely universal in their application, so that nothing lies outside their scope? Is every event in the physical universe completely predictable, even in principle? And do causes necessarily determine their effects, in such a way that nothing could happen except what does happen? Despite the immense difficulty of answering these questions, Laplace's model has had an almost hypnotic effect on the human imagination. Perhaps it owes something to the half-forgotten thought that God has determined everything to happen just as it will. But in Laplace's universe there is nothing left for God to do. Perhaps God is needed to construct the clockwork machine of the universe in the first place. But it is difficult to see why God should need a machine like this. And is it really necessary that the machine should have a maker at all?

With a sort of inner inevitability the idea of God, the great designer, soon drops out of the picture, and the material universe is left as a free-standing, deterministic entity. It exists purely by chance; and the fact that it is intelligible is an accident. Out of the infinite array of possible universes, there must be one which is intelligible. The chance of any one of such an infinite array of possibilities existing is infinitely small, but no smaller in any particular case than in any other case. Thus it is quite consistent to say that the existence of this beautifully rational universe is infinitely improbable, and that it exists as a random accident. The existence of any other universe, or of no universe at all, would be equally improbable. And that is that.

Is this an assured result of the scientific revolution? If it is, it causes peculiar problems for anyone who reflects seriously about human thought and life. One problem was formulated very clearly by Descartes. If all that exists, according to science, is an array of physical particles with a number of measurable properties, governed by a set of absolutely universal and unchanging laws, where can human thought, experience and freedom of action fit into the picture? When I formulate the thought, "There is no highest prime number", it does not seem that my specific thought could possibly be predicted from Laplace's complete knowledge of the first state of the universe. For in any valid deduction, there cannot be more in the conclusion than there was in the premisses. One logically cannot predict such a thought from initial premisses which do not in some way contain it already. But thoughts are not parts of the Laplacean initial state. So this thought, and thousands like it, does not seem to consist of physical particles, or to be predictable from any set of statements about physical particles alone. Does that not entail that the Laplacean model of reality is incomplete?

Descartes' resolution of this difficulty was to place thoughts in a kind of substance quite different from material substance, not amenable to scientific analysis – the mind. But this did not resolve the problem very well. For there is a very close relation between the mind and its brain, between mind and a physical body whose mind it is. As Descartes himself saw, "I am not just lodged in my body like a pilot in his ship, but ... I am intimately united with it, and so confused and intermingled with it that I and my body compose, as it were, a single whole" (Descartes 1960:161). Now if all physical particles in the brain are predictable on Laplacean lines, and if my thoughts are not physical in nature, it seems to follow that my thoughts are incapable of having any effect on my brain, or more generally on my body. Descartes supposed there was an interaction between mind and body; but the scientific account seems to preclude the intrusion of such extraneous factors into the causal network of the material world. So Malebranche suggested that the physical motions of my brain and the sequence of my thoughts must run in parallel, without real causal interaction. Yet that is contrary to what seems to be the obvious fact that physical stimulation of the body can cause me to have certain thoughts (like, "Ouch, that hurts!"). For the parallelist view, it must be a coincidence that I have a thought that something hurts, when the pin pierces my flesh. And that is too much for most people to stomach.

The Cartesians got into such problems because the Laplacean model forced them there. The idea of the completely determined physical universe left nowhere for the mind to be. Recent attempts to replace Cartesian dualism by a theory of central state materialism are simply resurrections of the same type of theory under another name. On such theories, thoughts are said to be identical with certain brain-states. But what is meant by "identity" is precisely that they run in parallel with physically determined states, without exerting any causal influence of their own. On such a theory, brain-states do not *cause* thoughts since obviously if a brain-state is identical with a thought, it cannot cause it. Things do not cause themselves. The new identity thesis is old parallelism writ large. It inherits all its disadvantages with the added obscurity of having a *sui generis* notion of identity which no one can coherently explain.

What needs examination is the Laplacean model itself, for it is not wholly extinct. Even though particle physics works with a strongly indeterministic theory, Bohr's "correspondence principle" is well-established, that quantum considerations cancel out at the macrocosmic level, at least for the most part. We could ignore them for all practical purposes, and accept Laplace as a complete theory for most of the macrocosmic domain.

However, one large concession must certainly be made. It can no longer be said that Newton's laws, or anything like them, will account for all phenomena, everywhere in the universe. Those laws simply do not apply at the sub-atomic level – if they did, electrons would collapse into the nuclei of atoms. A new set of laws obtains both at the sub-atomic level and at very high velocities or over vast interstellar distances. Even at the observable level, such entities as neutron stars and superconductors require the application of quantum principles. Newton's laws, then, are not complete, in the sense that they apply throughout even the observable universe, without exception.

There are much more severe restrictions on their efficacy, however, which can be brought out by considering more closely the experimental method, from which they generalize. It is essential to the experimental method that one regards phenomena as occurring repeatably, observably, and in some precisely quantifiable relationship. Now it is not at all obvious that phenomena will be like that – either that any will be, or that all will be.

First, in classical physics, when one regards an experiment as repeatable, one means that the same initial conditions will always produce an identical result. But the world does not have to be like that; and at the particle level, it is not like that. Fortunately, even at the particle level, one can at least produce statistical results of experiment – one can state the half-life of a class of atoms, without knowing exactly when any one of them will decay.

But it is not necessary that repetitive patterns should be as tight as they are assumed to be in classical physics. In the case of human actions, for example, there are detectable patterns of behaviour, the range of options open to human beings is not unlimited, and very many human acts can be predicted. Yet surprising and new creative acts do take place. To take a specific example, humans can only hear a rather small range of sounds, out of all possible wave frequencies that exist. The possibilities for arranging these is rather limited, again by the human ability to discriminate differences of timbre and pitch. One might predict, then, that if someone sits down to compose a piece of music, she will use only certain timbres and pitches, and will follow certain rules of melodic and harmonic structure. With more detailed knowledge of the sorts of music which already exist, one can predict in more detail what is likely to result – a symphony for orchestra or tune for pipe. Yet we cannot predict what Beethoven will write, and a great composer will extend the constraints of convention in surprising ways. The new and creative is not something *wholly* unforeseeable. It is constrained by physical factors which set general human abilities. It is constrained by cultural factors, which set standards of what is acceptable. But the actual work seems to be quite unpredictable in detail; and it may extend the standards of cultural acceptability bit by bit.

The correlation of predictability and creativity is worth examining further, as it is of the first importance for understanding the nature of the material world. For creativity to operate, there must be some wholly predictable events. I cannot write music if I cannot predict with complete reliability that the written notes will remain constant on the page and will produce the desired sounds when played. It is not enough to know that something rather like what I want, but unpredictable in detail, will result from my composition. In other words, there must be a wholly predictable, regular process, before I can use it to write new tunes. Creativity requires predictability of the processes it utilizes.

The simplest analogy is the game of snooker. If I could not predict that a ball of a given mass moving with a certain velocity in a specific direction would have predictable effects on the balls it hits, I could never play the game, since I would not know where the balls would go next. Once I set a ball moving, its movements are wholly predictable. Snooker is a game, however, because it requires skill to move balls just as I wish. I must impart a certain momentum and direction to the ball; and that is very difficult to do. The difficulty of snooker lies, not in lack of predictability, but in deciding what momentum to impart (where I want the balls to end up) and in being able to impart exactly that momentum. The laws of classical mechanics apply perfectly to snooker tables. They state exactly what will happen when balls interact by collision. If one could imagine a friction and gravity free snooker table, floating in space, with no outside influences at all, one could have an endless motion of snooker balls, all perfectly predictable in their movements for ever. That is the perfect Laplacean universe – and very boring and pointless it would be. Snooker becomes a game when a goal is assigned to such movements – to get all the balls into pockets, and prevent an opponent doing so, by giving him shots too difficult for him. The goal is arbitrary, in that any goal would do – it might be to get all the balls into a perfect triangle, for instance. In fact, the point lies, not in the goal as such, but in the exercise of skill and competition.

The skill is precisely to alter the conditions of the snooker table from what they would have been, left to themselves, as a "closed" system, free of other influencing factors. It is thus an axiom of snooker that *I can alter the conditions of an otherwise closed system*, with difficulty. Of course, in most games, luck plays a large part, too. But luck enters into snooker only in so far as my causal alteration is so unskilful that I am unable to control it exactly. I make a difference I cannot wholly control; and in that sense "leave the outcome to chance". Luck does not require any objective indeterminacy in things; it requires lack of control in my causal interactions with things, whether deliberate or not.

Experimental science is surprisingly similar. It is a competitive enterprise, the goal of which is to arrive at the simplest, most comprehensive theory to explain certain sorts of physical phenomena. Creative scientists show great skill in devising experimental procedures and in inventing complex and elegant theories. The very notion of an experiment supposes that I can alter the conditions of the physical world, with some difficulty, to achieve a desired goal – the demonstration of my theory. For instance I will need to control temperature, speed and mass of the objects I am interested in, and then discover their behaviour when they are isolated from all other known influencing factors. How very ironic it is that a method which is based on the idea that I *can* alter the conditions of an otherwise closed system, has given rise to the conflicting notion that everything is so pre-determined that no unpredictable, creative actions can ever take place.

There are very important invariances at work in nature, most obviously the various conservation laws. It has been said that in particle physics, there are no laws which state exactly what has to happen; but there are laws which state what cannot happen. In all interactions, for instance, it cannot happen that energy is not conserved; that is a limit on the sorts of interactions which can take place. Even then, it must be noted that such properties as linear momentum are only conserved as long as no external forces act on the system. For example, momentum is not conserved in a system if an external force of gravity acts on it, causing momentum to be increased continuously.

Experimental science deals with systems which are closed with respect to all known interacting forces, including the action of the observer. Heisenberg's Uncertainty Principle shows the limits of this procedure dramatically, in pointing out that the act of observation, since it releases photons, necessarily interferes with observed particles, collapsing wave-mechanical phenomena into particles, and thereby changing the system under observation. The idea of a wholly closed system is thus only relatively available; it is an idealized model, which breaks down in certain very basic instances.

The strength of the experimental method lies in the fact that it devises techniques for measuring those forces which act in closed systems of interaction, which can then be used more skilfully for accomplishing human goals. But is there anything in the method itself which suggests that the whole universe is such a closed system, without goals or creative action? Surely not, since the very method is a prime instance of creative action taken in furtherance of a goal. Yet it is characteristic of the human mind that it is captivated by its own metaphors. So it presses the idea of *a closed system of quantifiable forces* to its extreme limit, and proposes that it is all-embracing – the Laplacean picture.

That is a bold and imaginative hypothesis but it must be open to refutation by counter-examples. What would constitute a counter-example? One clear example would be unpredictability in principle. There are logical limits on what can be predicted. One can only predict precisely if one has a universal (or at least widely applicable) law, together with an exact specification of the conditions under which the law applies. If the law may not apply in a given case, one cannot predict with certainty what will happen. And if the conditions cannot be completely and precisely specified, one cannot predict exactly what conditions will ensue from application of the law.

I have argued that it is a condition of creativity and knowledge that there are such universal laws; laws stating what happens in a closed system of specifiable properties. But it by no means follows that all phenomena are bound by such laws; it is enough if a large class of phenomena are so bound. Nor does it follow that even such phenomena as are bound by such laws are subject to no other influences than those laws. All we need is that certain phenomena are bound by laws, other things being equal, or under carefully controlled conditions. Then prediction will be possible in controlled experimental conditions; or in normal conditions, most of the time; but not necessarily in every real case in the world.

The problem is, if events are not bound by laws, why do they occur? Could anything account for them? One simple answer is given by reference to the snooker case. One ball hits another because John wanted it to. The notes in the symphony were written thus because Beethoven invented a new tune, never heard before. In the case of a Beethoven symphony, here is something which has never existed before in the whole history of the cosmos. Sounds were put in this order by a conscious effort to bring about a new tune. The symphony consists of a set of sounds, arranged in complex order. As such, it is a phenomenon not bound by laws of physics. That is, no law of physics states what must happen next in a symphony. There are, one might say, some laws – discords must be resolved in certain ways. These are not laws of physics, but of composition. Beethoven worked within those laws, which leave a vast range of options open, for creative activity which aims to produce dramatic or beautiful or expressive sound-patterns. A piece of music is a phenomenon in which sounds follow each other in an orderly and planning way, but not in accordance with any universal laws, at least for most of the piece. Is this a counter-example to the theory that all phenomena are connected by universal laws of physics?

What the determined Laplacean will say is that sounds are "in fact" wave-frequencies of a certain sort, and the occurrence of such frequencies is determined by purely physical factors. Beethoven may think he is trying to write a good tune; what is *really* going on is that millions of physical particles in his brain cause certain wave-frequencies to occur, with precisely specifiable inevitability. No one claims this has ever been shown; it is like a bet that it could be shown. Consequently, those who reject the bet do not have to produce a proof that such a reduction is impossible – to show impossibilities is usually impossible. All one has to do is to bet differently; to bet that it can't be done.

Still, this may seem like going on the defensive; such bets have been lost so often before in the history of science. It was said that humans could never fly, never go to the moon, never see at a distance – but all those things now happen. How can we place limits on science? But if we look at all those claims that something was impossible, we find that they all placed physical limitations on what could be done. Physical laws were adduced which ruled out space-flight – rather like the Einstein theory which says that one cannot travel faster than light. These laws turned out to be mistaken; but they were properly physical theories. What we are considering now is not a physical theory. It is the question of *whether one sort of explanation* – which all admit to be necessary in certain areas – *extends without limit to all actual and possible phenomena*. The sort of explanation in question is an explanation in terms of universal, non-purposive, quantifiable laws. It is not like asking if certain physical actions will be technologically possible. It is asking whether one sort of approach can cover every possible aspect of reality. It is asking whether the scientific approach, as such, has limits. And that is asking what the scientific approach is; and then, whether there is anything it could not, precisely because of what it is, apply to. We are asking, not about physical limitations, but about logical limitations, limitations which may be imposed by definition, once we are clear about just what scientific method is.

It is immediately clear that, as a matter of logic, scientific method – as the provision of completely universal quantifiable laws for a closed system of forces – could not cover every possible sort of reality. That should not be seen as a limitation on science, any more than the inability of music to produce good paintings or to solve Schrodinger equations, should be thought of as a defect. It is just a consequence of the simple fact that, if we assert that science can only do operations of type x, it is necessarily true that it cannot do, and *would not wish to do, operations of type not-x*. At first it might seem that anyone who points to something science cannot do is placing an arbitrary *a priori* limitation on the progress of science, which may be empirically refuted in time. But it is not like that at all. It is rather that, once one becomes clear about what science is and what its methods are, one also becomes clear about what it is not and what sorts of things its methods could not logically deal with. To point out that the methods of science, as at present conceived, cannot deal with x, is, if one has got it right, something not capable of empirical refutation. Of course, if one holds that the methods of science might change out of recognition, it is surely fair to respond that this will not be science as we know it, at all; so one can have an open mind about that.

What can experimental science not deal with? By definition, it cannot deal with any phenomena which cannot in principle be quantified, which are unique, in not following any universal law or which do not form part of any closed system of physical forces. But are such phenomena logically possible? The answer to this question is not wholly clear, but one can think of an event occurring only once, for no apparent reason, and never being repeated in identical circumstances. Miracles are events which are claimed to occur and not to fall under any scientific law. But one can also think simply of wholly anomalous events, like a pencil floating in the air for five seconds, doing so for no traceable reason or because of no assignable physical cause and never doing it again. Whether or not such events happen, they are clearly possible; we can imagine them without any trace of self-contradiction. Here, then, is one sort of event science could not in principle deal with – the unique, anomalous event.

To revert to miracles for a moment – and again prescinding from whether they actually occur – a miracle is said to occur because a spiritual being caused it to do so. Some being, whether God, angel or demon, forms an intention to make the sun stand still; and it does so. Let us suppose that a very powerful God is possible and can bring things about simply by intending to do so. It may not be clear whether this is possible, but there is no proof that it is impossible. So we may assume it without absurdity, as a theory innocent until it is found guilty. Now if God decides to stop the sun, this seems to contradict Newton's laws, or any set of physical laws of nature. For Divine intentions are simply outside the otherwise closed system of physical forces. Of course, such Divine action would not in fact contradict physical laws, since it would introduce a new force into the system, and so change its parameters. But the point about this "new force" is that it could not be brought under some wider physical laws. There is no physical law which can say what God will intend, or which can correlate the strength of his intentions with their effects in the material world. Divine intention is not a quantifiable force; it cannot be measured for intensity; so no equation between cause and effect can be set up. It is clear, therefore, that if there is a God, and if God can act in the world, science is incompetent to explain those acts for they will be unique; they will not form part of a system of physical forces, and the causing intentions cannot be measured and correlated with physical forces.

So much the worse for God, it may be said. But if we recall the course of this argument, it began with the bet that science could explain everything. That is because everything is reducible to physical factors in a large but closed system. The opponent who wants to bet that there are things science can never explain is then seen as a mealy-mouthed pessimist, who is anti-scientific and wants to place arbitrary limits on progress. What I have tried to bring out is that the opponent has more on his side than that. For if there is a God, there is at least one thing not reducible to physical factors in a closed system. And that thing can have effects on anything within the system. Belief in God, then, provides a very strong reason for saying that there are many things science can never explain – and among them are the actions of God in the world. The weaker belief that there could possibly be, or have been, a God, still shows that there are *possible* things that science cannot logically explain. And even if one is not sure about that, at least the hypothesis that all realities are purely physical, measurable and repeatable is as bold, as risky and as indemonstrable as the hypothesis that there is, or could be, a God. At the worst, the bets are pretty evenly balanced.

If the complete explanatory power of science cannot be pushed through as an *a priori* hypothesis, it may nevertheless be urged as an empirical one. It is anyway a matter of fact, it may be said – whatever the merely logical possibilities – that scientific laws will explain all phenomena satisfactorily. We can explain everything perfectly well without recourse to God, to purpose or objective value. Much now depends on what is meant by "explaining all phenomena satisfactorily". It is absolutely false that we can at present explain all phenomena even to our own satisfaction. Hundreds of facts remain puzzling and unexplained. We do not know how the embryo develops; we do not know how to resolve many of the dilemmas raised by quantum theory; we do not know if one unified explanation of nature can be achieved. Once again we are in the area of taking bets on the future. Now the fact is that we *can* say what sort of view of reality would make it impossible for science to explain everything satisfactorily. We have seen that the existence of God would, for a start.

However, God is not needed to make the point. If there really is creative, new and original activity in the universe, prediction, and thus general-law explanation which makes exact prediction possible, cannot apply to it. For the radically original does not fall under any general law, by definition.

Thus the Laplacean model is deeply inconsistent with any truly evolutionary view of the material universe. For such a view, new properties come into existence, properties which have never before existed. Thus at some stage in the history of the universe, consciousness existed for the first time. Shortly after that, no doubt, the whole range of phenomenal properties – sights, sound and so on – came into existence for the first time. These properties are wholly and in principle unpredictable on a Laplacean model, which can never have more in the universe than the physical properties that were there at the beginning, in various mixtures and combinations.

Thus there is a huge number of things the Laplacean model cannot explain – including all those phenomenal properties which are of most interest to us in life. Another obvious problem which is beyond the range of scientific explanation is that of why things should be related by the precise laws which do regulate their behaviour. One might suppose that the laws of nature are the simplest, most elegant, set of laws which can generate the complex forms of conscious life we have in this universe. The so-called anthropic principle, in a weak form, states that certain sets of finely tuned conditions – the ratio of protons to neutrons, the exact strength of the weak nuclear force and so on – are necessary conditions of the existence of observers such as ourselves (Barrow and Tipler 1986:15–23). This principle does not show that everything is designed to produce us. But it does show that there is a relationship between the basic structure of physical laws and the existence of human sentient beings which is more than simply co-incidental. So one might explain the fundamental laws of physics in terms of aesthetic and purposive criteria – namely, that they are the most beautiful laws which can realize the purpose of bringing about sentient observers in a physical universe in the most economical way. Such an explanation would not, given the present understanding of physics, be absurd; it might even be useful in suggesting the sorts of laws scientists should look for (elegant, simple, integrating laws), and in suggesting certain functional relationships between them (laws can be seen as functionally directed to the origination and sustenance of sentient life). One might then say that, either there is no explanation for why physical laws are as they are; or, if there is an explanation, it must be in terms of purpose. Such purposive explanation does not fall within the province of experimental science, as we now understand it. But it is interesting that the progress of science, which began with the firm rejection of purposes in nature in the seventeenth century, may be interpreted as pointing towards a form of purposive explanation in the twentieth century. The major difference is that this purpose is concerned with the general structure of the universe, not with particular occurrences within it. But the appeal to purpose still points to a dimension of explanation – a personal, purposive explanation – which is significantly different from that of the experimental sciences.

Once one has the notion of the universe as purposively ordered towards a goal, it is a very small step to seeing some particular processes within the universe as intentionally brought out in furtherance of that goal, or intermediate steps towards it. And if one has accepted that many emergent features of the universe cannot be completely explained in terms of antecedent physical laws and states of affairs, the way is open to consider the possibility of Divine actions within the physical structure which are not completely explicable in purely physical terms, though they operate within the normal parameters of physical laws.

The Laplacean view that physical laws alone completely account for all changes in the physical world leaves no place for Divine action. The God who acts, if at all, in the gaps left by physical theory, therefore seemed to have been effectively exorcized by the mathematical incantations of the seventeenth century physicists. I have tried to show that the philosophical theses underlying this view are not in fact entailed by the methodological practice of the sciences or by the specific conclusions of particular sciences. They are generalizations to a world-view of cosmic proportions, and are deeply problematic; even those who accept them must admit, if they are honest, that the theses are far from obvious and indeed are as mysterious and contentious as most of the hypotheses involved in a theistic world-view. It is important to remember that belief in Divine action does not derive from physics, but from religious and historical experience. The question is not whether modern science compels us to admit specific Divine acts – which it certainly does not – but whether it permits us reasonably to speak of them. My minimal suggestion is that contemporary science does not rule out such theistic beliefs, since a Laplacean model is no longer essential to it. As John Polkinghorne bluntly puts it, "The clockwork universe is dead" (Polkinghorne 1989:33); "even at those macroscopic levels where classical physics gives an adequate account, there is an openness to the future which relaxes the unrelenting grip of mechanical determinism" (ibid.:30). More positively, I have argued that at least some of the philosophical theses underlying a Laplacean model of the world are mistaken, and that they conflict with well-grounded beliefs about human freedom, creativity and rational action.

Anyone who rejects the epiphenomenalist or identity theory of mind, and who thinks people really do act, in the sense of bringing about changes in the world in accordance with intentions and purposes, is bound to believe that many purposive processes – which might include both human and Divine acts – are not sufficiently explained by physics alone. One is not claiming that physical laws need supplementation from elsewhere to remedy their deficiencies as explanations. It is rather a question of what a physical explanation is trying to do. The physicist Ian Barbour, in his magisterial study of scientific and theological methodology, says, "The critic may object that *any* mention of God's influence, whether large or small, sudden or gradual, runs counter to the modern assumption of the sufficiency of scientific explanations in terms of natural causes. The reply to this objection would recall that scientific laws are always selective and abstractive and often statistical" (Barbour 1966:463). No working scientist ever tries to come up with a formula which will explain everything. There are many natural sciences, but if one takes particle physics as an example, then the first thing a physicist has to do is to isolate certain aspects of physical phenomena so that they can be described in mathematical terms and placed within an overall theory. The theory will describe the interactions between component parts of the system, in accordance with general principles described by mathematical equations. A physical theory is essentially an abstract model of how things would go, if they consisted only of particles having only precisely described properties and if no other factors ever interfered with the system.

It turns out that there are good reasons, arising from physical theory itself, for doubting whether any such model could apply exactly to the real physical world. First, we are now clearer about the status of scientific models, about the ways in which they abstract and isolate aspects of physical phenomena. There is no reason to expect that the world will fit any such precisely constructed model exactly. It is a great bonus that things fit as well as they do; but few would now claim that our models picture true states of affairs exactly. As Einstein said, "As far as the laws of mathematics refer to reality, they are not certain; and as far as they are certain, they do not refer to reality" (quoted in Capra 1976:49). This means, of course, that there may be all sorts of causal influences in nature not covered by present models; but we may only become aware of them if we look in the right way, or take the right approach to them. In the case of God, the right approach may involve the attempt to achieve a personal relationship and an acceptance of a Divine self-disclosure – things which physics, as such, cannot require. So it may be that physics will only ever reveal the mechanics of the universe. It will not disclose the underlying meaning and purpose, which may be – and, the theist, believes, is – just as real.

Second, there are difficulties in the claim to have achieved a complete description of any physical state, let alone a vastly complex one like the universe. The "complete explanation" model requires us to say, "These are all the physical forces there are; and there are no others". Such a claim is enormously difficult to substantiate. Godel's theorem claims to show that it is impossible, in principle, to prove both consistency and completeness in any rich mathematical system (Nagel:1959). The implication is that one can never be sure of having achieved a complete system, so long as one is concerned to ensure the consistency of the descriptive system.

Third, there are fundamental doubts whether one can precisely specify every physical state. Heisenberg's principle of indeterminacy suggests that one cannot. But a wider doubt is raised by the quantum view of sub-atomic phenomena as consisting of probability-waves rather than of precisely valued particles at precise positions. Perhaps the basic structure of the universe is loose and fuzzy; perhaps it is, as Professor Polkinghorne puts it, "fitful and probabilistic at its constituent roots" (ibid.:2). If so, our elegant mathematical models may never completely describe it.

Fourth, there are basic doubts about whether any describable physical system can be regarded as completely closed, so that no new influences can ever operate upon it, either by the emergence of new sorts of property or by influences operating from beyond the system as described. The emergence of new properties, such as consciousness, in the physical universe, necessitates new models to describe what is going on. No model is ever complete, once and for all; new models will always be necessary to enable us to understand a constantly changing and developing world. One could confirm that there was a truly closed system only if it could be completely specified and predicted accurately in all circumstances, in principle. But this has been ruled out as impossible in principle both by the Uncertainty Principle, which rules out a complete specification of all physical forces at the same moment, and by studies of the dynamics of complex systems far from equilibrium, which show that we would need an infinite amount of information to make such predictions (cf. page 125). The "closed system" view cannot be confirmed. Indeed, if anything, it is not established by science, but rendered unconfirmable by it. It cannot therefore by regarded as so strongly established as to overthrow a theistic view which begs leave to doubt it.

Fifth, the postulate of sufficient causality, with the deterministic view it entails, seems to be undermined by quantum theory; and it is clearly unprovable that nothing could happen except what does happen. The idea of sufficient causality is an ideal for regulating scientific investigation; but it needs to be balanced by the ideals of creativity and personal responsibility, which enable us to regard persons as making new and imaginative contributions to the way things go in the world. Both sets of ideals can live together, as long as neither claims authority over every possible realm of experience. And such complementarity is strongly suggested by much work in twentieth century physics, as the quantum physicist Neils Bohr suggested (Bohr 1958).

All these tendencies in modern physics suggest a view of the universe very far removed from the clockwork model associated with classical Newtonian mechanics. The universe remains a supremely elegant rational set of systems. But there is every reason to think that no one consistent model that humans can devise will ever provide a complete account even of its physical structure, let alone of all the causal forces which impel it into the future. It is not that there is a complete model, which just happens to have a few gaps in it, where God might operate. There is no consistent and complete model at all; so gaps do not become apparent in the model. It is the models themselves which operate more or less well for specific human and scientific purposes. In view of this, the theist might reasonably suggest that the models of physics work very well for their own purposes; there are no gaps in them which God might fill, as far as the physics is concerned. But a huge ontological gap does exist. It exists between any and all models and the complex, fuzzy, dynamic and opaque real world. In such a situation, we will always need a plurality of models, related to each other in highly problematic ways, continually subject to re-interpretation and revision. The theistic model need not, in all its versions, conflict with a particular physical model. It will simply offer a different way of describing reality. The theistic model and the physical will be complementary – but this entails that neither of them provides a complete account of why things happen in the world as they do. The principle of complementarity turns out to have philosophical implications of deep significance.

God and his purposes will not occur within the models of physics, any more than human thoughts or emotions will. In that sense, he is *not* a God of the gaps. But such models will provide a necessarily incomplete and partial account of the real world; what they omit may be just as real, but capturable only by means of a different model. Physical principles alone do not give a complete description of everything that happens in the universe. That seems a plausible enough claim. It certainly does not mean that there is some inescapable defect in physics which prevents it completing its proper tasks. And, as has been noted, it does not mean that one will be able to tell when God has to come into the story, to fill in an obvious gap. The gaps, far from being obvious, may be indiscernible, since they lie outside a particular model. God never *has* to be appealed to in giving an account of why things are as they are, since one can, if nothing else, claim that one's model is complete in principle, though not yet completed in fact; or appeal to physical causes as yet unspecified.

One implication of this "complementary models" view is that events will occur in the world which one model does not wholly explain. So, if the model is taken as completely predictive – as predicting everything exactly – it will fail. Exact prediction will work only in so far as the modelled system functions without the influence of outside forces – as in controlled laboratory situations. Heisenberg has built unpredictability into physical systems in a fundamental way, so this should come as no great surprise. It simply emphasizes that we must give up the clockwork-prediction view of physical science; and replace it with a multiple model view, wherein each model works efficiently for specified purposes, yet is an abstraction from the concrete complexity of the temporal universe. Each model is a product of human imagination, attempting to understand why things are as they are. One may fail to perceive some aspect of reality, however basic it is, because one has not devised a suitable model for understanding it. Knowing what the world is like is not just a matter of staring very hard at it. One needs to develop the appropriate conceptual models, which can be a slow and arduous process.

The theist supposes that a truly adequate account of how the world progresses into the future will require reference to the purposes and acts of God, its underlying creative source. But that does not mean that there will be just one all-embracing model of causality, one complete and unified language for understanding all forms of causal change. Physics will continue to deal with the principles governing physical interactions, which are built into the universe as part of its structure. But this structure, for the theist, allows of Divine action to direct events towards desired goals. The wise physicist does not claim to tell the whole truth about absolutely everything. Neither does the wise theologian. Both may have important truths to tell; each must listen carefully to the other, if claims to unlawful monopolies of truth are to be avoided, and a more comprehensive account of the mystery of human existence in the world is to be achieved.

6

The Enfolding Spirit

I have suggested that God may be continually active in the world, even though his actions – the particular causal processes which realize, and are intended by him to realize, a specific purpose – remain undetected by creatures. But am I really saying that God's acts can never by discerned? That they are doomed to be for ever invisible? Surely, one may think, if God acts at all there must be some occasions we can point to – as we can in the case of human beings – and say, "There is a *prima facie* case of God acting". Otherwise, why should we talk about acts of God at all?

It may be said that the idea of purpose belongs to the social context of human life; and it cannot properly be taken outside that context. We can identify human behaviour which is purposive without inferential guesswork to some set of hidden intentions. Identifying a purpose primarily depends upon identifying some purposive behaviour. But God has no body. There is no observable behaviour on the part of God which we can identify, so the idea of God's intentions can gain no purchase on reality. God's acts cannot be discerned for the basic reason that the idea of an action which we cannot identify by means of a particular body which performs it is incoherent.

This objection seems to me wholly misplaced. We are not confined to human beings, when we talk of purpose. We can attribute purpose to animals, to chimpanzees and porpoises. We can ascribe it, in principle, to any extra-terrestrials we may happen to meet. Of course we normally ascribe it on the basis of familiar and recognizable behaviour. But we are not confined to what is normal. Once we have the idea of changing a physical state to bring about a desired result we can apply it to many hypothetical situations. It can easily be seen that cases may arise when we do not know whether it properly applies or not. In fact, such cases do arise in the animal world. Are we really sure whether cats act for a purpose? Or, if we are sure of cats, what about ants and bees? There are many cases where we are not sure whether beings think, or imagine or are intelligent or not. When it comes to frogs, I would say that I am genuinely not sure whether they act intentionally or not. If they do, it is in a way very different from any that I can readily imagine.

But, even if we disagree about how to analyse it, at least we know what we *mean* by purposive action in the case of humans and animals. We can point to their behaviour and say, "We may not know how to interpret it; but that is the behaviour which is ambiguous and puzzling to us". What is the analogy in the case of God?

God, by hypothesis, is one agent who is the ultimate cause of everything that exists, other than himself. He cannot be an item among the things that exist; so he cannot be picked out as one finite agent among others. Nevertheless, since he is the cause of everything, one can frame the question: "Are there any changes of physical states in the universe which are intended to bring about some desired result, when that is not the desire or intention of any finite agent?" We might have got the idea of such purposive causality from observable human cases. But there is no reason why we should not extend it to the maximal case, the case of a purposive agent causing the whole universe. The behavioural analogy for God is simply the nature of the whole universe and its processes. We observe the behaviour of the universe, and ask whether it is purposive at all, in part or as a whole.

It is no use objecting, as David Hume did (Hume 1935:Pt.2) that we cannot see the universe as a whole. We do observe much of its behaviour; and scientists do not hesitate to generalize to the character of the universe as a whole from what we observe. It therefore seems to be a perfectly meaningful question to ask whether some processes exist in order to bring about a purpose or purposes. Whereas Aristotle thought that purposiveness was built into everything, most modern science assumes that the basic laws of the universe are not purposive, that there is no need to appeal to purpose to explain what they are and why things happen. It is widely thought that there are no objective purposes in nature. This would rule out the occurrence of particular Divine actions; and it is one main reason why the idea of God acting in history has become less plausible to many people. But one can at least see the class of phenomena which are in dispute. The *prima facie* case of Divine action is the nature of the universe as a whole, and the general causal principles which are needed to explain it. It is entirely meaningful to ask: Is there anything in the structure of the universe or of particular processes within it which looks as if it could be purposive?

When the question is framed in this way, it becomes clearer that the "invisibility" of God's action expresses a dispute about the fundamental causal basis of the physical universe. His acts are "invisible" in the same way that the laws of quantum mechanics are invisible. They may be one of the most fundamental features of everything, and yet never be discerned because nobody has the insight to discern them. In the case of quantum mechanics, we are speaking of physical principles which can be discerned by observation, when the right theoretical framework has been developed. But in the case of Divine purposes, it is hard to see what observations could give us insight into these, since the mind of God is not open to observation. If we really could see the whole of the universe, from beginning to end and in its whole extent, we might make a good guess at his purposes. But at this point in history, any such guess might be rather hazardous and primitive.

Nevertheless, it is not hard to see what is *prima facie* purposive about the universe. Contemporary scientists are well aware of the large number of apparently improbable coincidences which need to be matched for the universe to have evolved rational, moral and sensitive beings like us. They are well set out in many recent scientific works, a good example of which is *The Anthropic Cosmological Principle* (Barrow and Tipler 1986). After the first minutes of the "Big Bang" with which the universe originated, hydrogen had to form, if water, the basis of life, was to be possible. Carbon and iron had to be formed by nuclear reactions in the interiors of exploding stars. So the ratio of weak nuclear force to the other basic forces of nature had to be precisely matched to make such formations possible. Even a slight difference in that ratio would have made any subsequent development of sentient life impossible. Consideration of a very large number of facts such as these, each highly improbable taken alone, can make it look as though the universe is directed towards the evolution of rational sentient beings, and to a further evolution which we can hardly imagine. Even humanistic atheists like Julian Huxley think of evolution as a process of developing greater complexity and intensity of consciousness, in a quasi-purposive way. Without belief in God, there is a compulsion to explain such a process simply in terms of chance, or some outworking of a blind shuffling of physical particles. One cannot disprove that hypothesis; but it may seem simpler – and it is certainly possible – to posit a purpose urging the process towards its destined goal. Despite Darwin and the general refusal to appeal to purpose in modern physics, there is a strong inclination to see the point of the physical universe as lying in the evolution of a community of rational agents of complex sensitivity who can come to know the nature of the universe and perhaps direct its future course. I am not proposing this as a "proof" of God, but as a pointer to those aspects of the universe which look, even if ambiguously and disputably, intentional. If such is the overall purpose of the universe, more local and particular purposes can be seen as those which are conducive to that general aim. That is where, revelation apart, we must look to decide whether and how God may be active in the world.

Those who believe in God will think that there is at least one process directed to the realization of an intention; namely, the universe itself, in its general structure. Atheists may see how that structure could look purposive, but coherently deny any purpose, accounting for its nature in terms of unconscious causality and chance alone, as Jacques Monod has done (Monod 1972). This dispute is difficult to decide, and different people will decide it in different ways. Yet the universe either is purposive or it is not; so one disputant must be mistaken. Will the dispute ever be finally resolvable? Theists usually think that the ultimate purpose lies in a fully conscious union of rational creatures with the creator, in the fruition of perfect knowledge and love of God. The religious life is aimed at the furtherance of such union. If this purpose is achieved, dispute about it will be resolved by the experience of unity with God, the supreme consciousness which is the origin and goal of the world. As John Hick says, there is a conceivable state of affairs in which "the prediction that the universe is leading to a limitlessly good end-state in communion with God would have been fulfilled" (Hick 1989:179). Indeed, it is easier, in principle, to confirm the hypothesis of purpose than to disconfirm it, since we can never be sure that further experiences will not come which will show there was a purpose after all. Nevertheless, there is something most unsatisfactory about having to wait for some long-delayed cosmic confirmation in order to resolve the issue.

This suggests that the debate is not solely about what will turn out to be the case in some far future, or about the best interpretation of purely physical processes. It is about whether those processes relate us to an origin beyond them and underlying them at all times, which they can mediate. If they do, then while the world may be autonomous in its structures, it will not be wholly self-contained. It will essentially point beyond itself to a transcendent source. "Acts of God" will not only be processes conducive to realizing ultimate objective purposes. They will be processes which tend at many times to realize a consciously experienced unity with "the Self of all", or to inhibit and perhaps destroy processes which undermine such unity. Any such processes in the world, or at least processes which can be plausibly interpreted in this way, are *prima facie* acts of God.

Gordon Kaufman helpfully distinguishes God's "master-act" of creating the world as a whole, from his "sub-acts", which are particular parts of the process which contribute to realizing the overall purpose. The analogy is with the master-act of a King who may be said to build a temple, though in fact many particular acts performed by other people are necessary to the completion of the building. So God creates the world in all its complexity; but this necessitates many particular acts which contribute to the realization of his master-purpose. "Only those natural and historical events which directly advance God's ultimate purposes – those which are essential constituent phases or steps of God's master act – may properly be regarded as (subordinate) acts of God within nature and history" (Kaufman 1972:145).

There is a tension in Kaufman's account, however, which puts this analogy in doubt. For he insists that there must be an "unbroken web" of causality in nature, so it is questionable "whether it is even possible to conceive clearly the idea of a finite event without adequate finite causes" (ibid.:130). It is questionable, that is, whether it is intelligible to think of God as acting directly and immediately in nature. But then can the sub-acts be properly regarded as acts of God at all? If the King builds a temple, it does not follow that he places the bricks one on top of another. His act properly consists in ordering others to do things; and, since they are obeying orders, he takes responsibility, at least in part, for what they do. It is always possible to identify specific things which the King does, even if it is only handing over authority to his Vizier. One can identify specific things which others do, in carrying out his orders. And one can see that the specific things builders do are not done by the King, even though he may take ultimate responsibility for them. In other words, the only proper sub-acts of the King – or of God – are those he does himself, not those done by others at his command.

It is not enough to say that events which advance God's purposes are acts of God, even if they are acts he commands to be done. One needs to add that God performs them himself – and then one faces the possibility that not all his specific acts may, or need to, be essential to or directly related to his ultimate purposes. God may have specific, non-ultimate but local and important purposes, too. Kaufman holds that "this whole complicated and intricate teleological movement of all nature and history should be regarded as a single all-encompassing act of God" (ibid.:137). But is it really plausible to think that the whole cosmos realizes just one Divine act, with one Divine purpose? Of course, one can always speak of the cosmos as realizing a single Divine intention, in the sense that it is intended to bring into being communities of loving agents. But that is rather like saying that an author intends to write a novel – that purpose needs to be filled out with many subordinate acts, specifying the characters and plot. Only in a Pickwickian sense is writing a novel "one act". It is rather a continuous process, consisting of many particular acts, all contributing in some way to the rather abstract intention of writing something. In other words, the intention of creating a cosmos requires many particular acts of God, if it is to be realized. The goal does not lie at the end of the process, but in the many acts which constitute the process itself. It seems that Kaufman's account remains ambiguous between God playing a causal, purposive role in the world – he speaks of God as "governing", "guiding", "ordering", "redeeming" and "enabling" – and his setting up a system within which he plays no further part, since his acts are already built into the "one purpose" which creates the whole system.

It is clearer to say that, for natural or historical processes to be acts of God, they will have to be intended by God and efficaciously caused by God's basic action, in combination of course with many requisite physical conditions. But it will be virtually impossible for anyone, by observation, to tell whether some process naturally tends of itself to a state of (for example) "believing I am experiencing God"; or whether that process is efficaciously caused by a particular contingent act of God causing one to be in such a state. The difficulty is compounded by the fact that God is the primary cause of everything; and the world-system as such is caused by God's intention that it should be as it is. So it is not wholly clear whether God wills a process as a necessary part of willing the world as a whole; or whether God wills this particular purpose, though he has not done so simply in willing the world as such.

If one adopts the account offered in the previous chapters, God brings the universe into existence for the sake of the good of conscious unity between creatures and himself. His creation is not one timeless act or one act at the beginning of time; it is a series of acts which continually bring into being new states of the universe by his positive or permissive willing. In so willing, he leaves many alternatives open to free choice; and many others open, at a sub-rational level, so as to permit that open-ness of structure which will subsequently allow free choice to operate – an argument convincingly expounded by Brian Hebblethwaite (Hebblethwaite

1976:ch.25). God cannot both leave these open and determine them. Many events must occur which God does not (consequently) will. It is possible that God may simply create the parameters of finite freedom, setting the system up so that in the end cosmic unity results, but leaving many details and whole stretches of the intermediate story to finite choice. One could then speak of the universe as a whole as God's primary act; and deny that there are any additional and contingent Divine acts within the history of the universe. This is the view Maurice Wiles takes, in his Bampton Lectures (Wiles 1986). It is in some ways surprisingly close to the classical theological account, for which Divine action, being timeless, must be completely unitary and without any addition which might be a response to how things subsequently happen in the world. Thus, for example, God must will prayers to be made and answers to be given to them in one and the same eternal act. There can be no contingent additions to his primary and immutable decrees.

If there are finitely free acts, however, in the strong sense I have defended, then God must be changed by the world at least in his knowledge of which contingent futures become actual. He must order the world in response to this growing knowledge, since he cannot determine what precise future states will be actualized before he knows what the free actions of creatures will pick out as the new initial conditions. So many of his creative acts will be in response to contingent choices. They will therefore themselves be contingent. On such an account, one must find a place for contingent and responsive Divine activity, as well as for a primary originative act of creation.

If the Divine purpose is to bring creatures into growing relationship with himself, a further reason for contingent Divine action lies in the consideration that he may wish to make himself known to creatures, to inspire them to do his will, and to respond to their prayers in a personal way. Personal relationship is essentially an interactive mode of being, in which each partner initiates and responds in a complex interweaving pattern. If it is an appropriate model of the relationship between God and rational creatures, we will have to envisage a great many contingent Divine acts, growing in complexity as rational creatures develop. Moreover, as God wills to bring all evil into a pattern of goodness or to eliminate it, the particular ways in which he does this must be contingent upon the sorts and degrees of evil which are actualized by creatures. Given radical creaturely freedom, it is thus natural to postulate a great many contingent Divine actions – purposive processes conducive to particular knowledge and love of God – within the universal process. Finally, it may be, as I have suggested, that God is himself a supremely imaginative creator. If this is so, he will generate new and previously unpredictable states at many points of the world's development, even before rational or conscious creatures exist.

There are at least five distinct types of Divine action here, though they shade into one another in practice. First, there is the originative act of bringing a universe of this general nature to be. Wiles and Kaufman have little difficulty with this notion; and it does enable one to think of the universe as having a generally purposive structure. Second, there are particular acts of imaginative development, which shape this universe in particular contingent ways. Peacocke's notion of "top-down causation" and Pailin's concept of a cosmic "urge to novelty" allow such a shaping constraint to operate, without sudden and arbitrary interferences with the natural order. Third, there are acts in response to the "chance" permutations of natural forces and to the free choices of rational creatures. Fourth, there are acts by which God relates in a distinctively personal way to created persons, revealing himself to them, inspiring or impeding their actions, in so far as they are in obedience to or in rebellion against his declared will, and responding to their prayers. And fifth, there are acts of the redemptive shaping of good out of evil, or of the destruction of evil, to achieve the final consummation of this created universe. The Christian theist will seek to discern acts of all five types in the general structure of the universe and in the particular ways in which history develops.

However, there is a theoretical difficulty with the notion of such particular Divine acts. If God acts freely and contingently within the universe, he will be limited by his own antecedent choices; by the general law-like structure he wills for the world, by the indeterminacies he has built into that structure, and by the free choices of rational creatures, when they have evolved within the structure. These constraints may seem so severe as to exclude the possibility of particular Divine action altogether. In the terms of an analogy suggested previously, he cannot both set up a particular game and then step in to alter the rules whenever he feels like it! Once God creates an autonomous universe, is there any room for him to shape events within it in previously undetermined ways?

Two extreme positions which are ruled out by the general account I have given are: first, the view that God can do absolutely anything at any time; and second, the view that he cannot act contingently within the universe at all. The first position is ruled out by considerations of Divine necessity and his antecedent intention to create an autonomous world of emergent rational creatures. He wills to create a world-system in which the laws are a simple, elegant compossible set able of themselves to produce emergent sentience. Random events occur to a degree which is necessary to permit the emergence of freedom in due course. And free creaturely acts enable individuals to have responsibility for shaping a communal life. Having willed this structure, God cannot alter or contradict it without contradicting his antecedent will. There are a great many things in this universe that God cannot (consequently) do.

But the second position, that God cannot act in the universe at all, depends either upon a view of unrestricted creaturely autonomy or upon a theory of complete determinism with regard to the physical structures of the universe. Creaturely autonomy is not, however, unrestricted; for rational creatures achieve their proper fulfilment only in relation to, and by obedient response to, a personal God. They can only be truly personal, in this view, if God does act to disclose himself as one who can be loved and obeyed. As for determinism, the existence of a degree of randomness and of creaturely free choices throw doubt on such a theory. We can see the universe as law-like without supposing that it is wholly determined, as if it were a totally closed physical system. The game of dice will again provide some sort of analogy. The throws, we may suppose, are governed by the laws of mechanics. Yet the dice have to be thrown; and there are many points of interaction between the system and what is quite external to it, the acts of throwing which initiate new physical sequences. It might be possible for someone to alter the state of a die in mid-throw. But if he did, the game would be destroyed. Alterations of state can occur; and they must occur if the game is to continue. But they can only occur at points laid down by the initial rules – points at which the dice have come to rest, and another throw is needed to continue.

So we might see the universe as consisting of sequences of law-determined events, which terminate in points where new initiating acts are needed to begin a new sequence. Both the structure of the sequences and the occurrence of the initiating points are laid down by the primary act of creation. Further, each initiating point will not provide an unrestricted possibility for action. It will present a point of choice between alternative sequences, the limits of which are laid down when creating the system as a whole. We can see human choices as made possible by the complex structure of neuronal discharges in the brain, which create the possibility of alternative pathways of electro-chemical discharge, and so of human action. So, in the general structure of the universe, there may be many specific "junctions" at which branching pathways open up, a choice between which will engender, in the end, radically different states of being.

It is sensible to look for some rational principle in accordance with which God acts in the world. It is not satisfactory to say that he so acts whenever he wants to – for then it seems impossible to understand why he does not want to more often, why there is so much suffering and frustration in human existence. A commitment to the intelligibility of the universe and to the wisdom of God requires us to provide a reason for the hiddenness and apparently limited nature of Divine action. Such a reason can be given if we can discover specific points within physical processes which permit creative choice, while limiting it to conformity with the general principles of physical law. Contemporary physics suggests that such points may occur within basic physical processes, when small probabilistic changes occurring at critical stages within wider physical systems open up the possibility of major changes of state of the system as a whole. "Points of instability are circumstances in which it is not possible satisfactorily to treat the system as isolated from the effects of its surroundings", as Polkinghorne puts it (Polkinghorne 1988:43); and at such points systems are susceptible to major changes of state, triggered by seemingly trivial causal inputs. An example would be that of a metal ball balanced precariously at the top of an elliptically curved wire. The tiniest force exerted upon the ball in one direction will bring about a major change, when it rolls to the bottom and perhaps breaks a diaphram, releasing poison gas. The tiniest force exerted in another direction would cause it to roll another way and leave the gas sealed up and safe. This simplified analogy shows how critical junctions can exist in the physical world, which can bring about large changes by small determinations of otherwise random probabilistic changes. Such junctions will only exist at certain points of the physical world, and this may be one constraint on Divine action within the parameters of normal physics. Such determining action will be in principle undetectable, since it always could have happened by chance.

It is important to stress here that I am not trying to lay down *a priori* from theology what physics must say about the world. The problem is primarily an internal theological one: it seems that God does not directly choose every outcome of physical processes, since many are deleterious. So, if he acts in particular ways at all, he must determine some but not all outcomes. One then needs a rationale for explaining, at least in general, how many outcomes God may determine, and which ones he will be likely to determine. Otherwise, his acts will be irrational, arbitrary and implausible. To do this, one needs a structure which will permit Divine determination on some, but not all, occasions, and which will cause some occasions to be more conducive to Divine determination than others. Michael Langford argues that "it must be the case that God's action can make a difference to the world". If this action is not to be an arbitrary interference in nature, "the action must be such that, after the event, a natural explanation is possible". So it follows, he argues, that "it must be the case that there be several possibilities within the natural order at any one time ... God's action is the steering along one of these possible routes" (Langford 1981:87). Modern physics, tentative and reformulable as it may be, does suggest such a physical structure. At the very least, it releases us from Newtonian determinism, and it suggests one account – though not necessarily the final one, by any means – which gives the theist just what is needed. It needs a step of faith to believe that, however much the scientific account will be modified in years to come, its present insight that nature is open to emergent ordering will not be refuted. But such a step of faith is not especially "religious"; it is of the same order as the Laplacean faith that nature is as a whole mechanistic. And it has the enormous advantage that it does not create a yawning gulf between the experience of human freedom and creativity and the objective and impersonal processes of the physical order. In uniting the introspective experience of human being with the observations of the natural world in one unitary pattern, this view of the world had the virtues of coherence and elegance. We may well suppose and believe that it is a decisive advance in the understanding of the world, however embryonic it may yet be.

Theists are not leaping on to a bandwagon of obscure and ephemeral physical theory. They are seeking to integrate their faith with the best scientific knowledge available, and finding that they need no longer hold religious faith and scientific knowledge in two quite separate compartments, awaiting the day when they could be adequately united in one unitary understanding of a theistic world. That day seems to have dawned. God can determine just so many outcomes as leave the general probability laws of nature intact; and he is likely to determine those which have a focal structuring position within an integral structure – a key position in an unstable dynamical system far from equilibrium – which will maximize novel patterns or consequences for good within the system as a whole. This is only one possible model suggesting a rationale for particular Divine action, but it is one which is consistent with recent work by Prigogene on the dynamics of complex physical systems (Prigogene and Stengers 1984), and which offers a plausible account of the creator's continuing and particular action in the world.

In this way a certain sort of account of physical law provides a reason for the hiddenness and limitedness of normal Divine action, while it renders the idea of the objective reality and importance of such Divine action intelligible. We may thus suppose that God will be able to act creatively upon inorganic nature, as he makes imaginative choices at critical points in the universal process. Examples might be: the generation of specific types of sub-atomic particles from more primitive energy-states; the selection of specific constants of physical relation, and the evolution of DNA based forms of life. It is true that some physicists claim that these factors are necessary to the universe being what it is. But, while accepting the general argument to much necessity in nature, it is not widely accepted that these factors could not possibly have been otherwise. They give some indication of a purposive tendency to issue in forms of rational life. There might have been other forms of rational life, for all we know. So it seems possible to say that God can play a creative role within the universe, which is an implicate and emergent order, leading it to produce new states without contradicting its basic principles.

God can play a providential role in the natural order. He can bring into being a physical universe containing many creative possibilities, which permit the possibility of his acting "in a way that is analogous to the use of opportunities by the human artist" (Langford 1981:90). This analogy of God as creative artist is widely used by scientists interested in the continuous and emergent complexity of the natural world. One can find it in Capek (1961) and Peacocke (1986) as well as in many other authors. As I have pointed out, however, such accounts often remain ambiguous about the extent to which creative agency really plays a part in the developing process. Dr Peacocke says, "Thus might the creator be imagined to unfold the potentialities of the universe which he himself has given it, selecting and shaping by his redemptive and providential action those that are to come to fruition" (ibid.:97). But does the creator in any real sense "select" and "shape", as a composer might select which notes come next in his sonata? Or is it, as Dr Peacocke also says, that "we see a world in process that is continuously capable, through its own inherent properties and natural character, of producing new living forms – matter is now seen to be self-organising" (ibid.:54)? To put the issue sharply, is it matter which does the shaping, or is it God?

Bishop Montefiore objects that this is still "the God of the deists, remote, unmoved, unloving" (Montefiore 1985:98). He proposes that "the Holy Spirit is infused into the very elements of matter itself, enduing them with this tendency which is consonant with the Divine plan" (ibid.:138). But that seems to be exactly what Dr Peacocke wants; and Peacocke rebuts the charge of deism by holding that "the being of God includes and penetrates the whole universe, so that every part of it exists in Him" (Peacocke 1986:99). For Peacocke, matter *is* God, or at least part of God, so that when one says matter does the shaping, that is equivalent to saying God does it.

Is this an acceptable view? One can see the view to which it is opposed. The material universe is not a non-purposive machine, which God would have to adjust discontinuously to give it any purpose. So the "interference" model of Divine action is rejected. The universe is a continuous, emergent and open system, or set of systems, with an inherent drive to realize certain goals. But the crucial question for theism is that of the primacy of the causal impetus. The theist cannot see the emergence of mind and purpose as a later emergent phenomenon of an initially blind physical process. If the universe is part of God, it is God who has the substantial and causal primacy; he generates the universe in all its detail; he is not its product. Just as music does not compose itself, so the universe does not drive itself forward into a goal-directed future. One needs fully conscious mental direction of the processes of nature at every stage. If this is so, one must see God as a causally directing power, in addition to the powers of natural objects themselves. God's action is not merely an unfolding of the inherent powers of material objects. But it need not be conceived as an alien manipulation of such objects. It can be seen as an efficacious causal shaping of those objects, in accordance with and in fulfilment of their natural powers. The structure of the universe is essentially open to such shaping; it calls for it but cannot of itself provide it. That is given by the self-existent spiritual reality which surrounds and enfolds the physical universe, giving it inherent powers and drawing those powers to new realizations by its environing teleogy. The theist may then say, not that matter is wholly self-organizing, but that it has an inherent capacity for realizing organization, and is essentially open to teleological shaping by the spiritual reality which is its source and goal. Nature is not a machine, but nor is it a wholly self-contained organism. It is, for the theist, an inherently emergent system, existentially dependent upon and open to the creative influence of the self-existent supreme value which is God. Supreme Spirit enfolds the physical, gives it the potential for continuous creative emergence, and draws out that potential by its own perfect actuality.

Naturally, the mechanics of this unique form of purposive causality are hidden from human knowledge. But work in contemporary science enables one to unite the vision of an emergent and holistic physical universe with the ancient religious vision of the world as a contingent expression of an infinite being of supreme value. The acts of God in nature will be those hidden but all-pervasive causal influences which shape the emergent processes of physical reality towards goals which take specific form only in the process itself, but the general character of which are laid down as archetypes in the being of God. Those goals will involve conscious knowledge and love of the God towards whom the whole process is directed. But God may be seen everywhere as the artist of nature, shaping it to forms of beauty which are original and inexhaustible. Divine action can be discerned in the world; but perhaps only by those who are themselves open to that creative and transforming influence which gives purpose and value to nature.

7

The Constraints of Creation

Many theists have a strong sense that God acts providentially – that he leads one to a particular job or opportunity, or puts one in the right place at the right time. Yet I have admitted, or indeed stressed, that we can rarely, if ever, know when God is acting, specifically. And it is clear that misfortunes and disasters happen to people. Is it possible to present a coherent account of providential action in a universe where God's acts are so undetectable and where so many counter-providential things seem to happen?

To set the scene, we must bear in mind that God creates the universe with the structure it has for a purpose – because that structure will have the best chance of achieving the particular set of unique goods he has in mind. As the omnipotent creator, he can change the structure; but if he wills it to exist for a purpose, and he does not wish fundamentally to modify that purpose, he will be limited by his own prior decision to changing the structure very occasionally, and then only for very good reason. Normally he will act in ways which leave the structure intact. So the first constraint on Divine action is that it must normally operate within the possibilities inherent in the structure God has created.

What one thinks such possibilities are will depend on the sort of structure one believes there to be. If we have a tight mechanistic structure, as in Newtonian science, there will be no possibilities of Divine action. All special Divine acts will be strictly miraculous, violations of the natural order. However, if one sees the models of the sciences as mapping ideal possibilities, so that there is always an ontological gap between any model or set of models and the real processes of nature, then this much looser, more open structure leaves many opportunities of modification by an intentional causality operating from beyond the system as modelled by our scientific

119

laws. Such purposive action does not "violate" the laws; it introduces a new modifying factor, which would be needed in any complete account of how the world is. The particular sciences, however, do not need or attempt such a "complete" account. All we require, therefore, is good reason to think that the sciences leave open the theoretical possibility of such an account – which could probably only be given by the omniscient being itself.

Quantum physics presents a picture of the universe which is sympathetic to this looser view. Any recent account of physics makes this clear, but a particularly helpful overview is given in John Polkinghorne's *The Particle Play* (1979). Subatomic physics pictures a world in which at every moment the future is partly indeterminate. It is not that anything can happen. Possible futures are quite strictly limited by probability laws. Some possible pathways have a much higher probability of occurring than others, and some have a null probability. This means that the highly probable will happen most of the time, and the highly improbable will happen only rarely. Nevertheless, the improbable can happen at times unpredictable in detail; and there may often be a number of possibilities which are of virtually equal probability, so that any of them may occur. In such a universe, while there are precisely formulatable probabilistic laws, there are many cases in which the future is neither specifically determined nor exactly predictable.

God may work within the probabilistic structure of physical laws to select a set of paths which would not necessarily have eventuated by physical laws alone, though the possibility of such a path exists in the natural world. Thus God could act within the natural world, intentionally bringing about a particular future. If God exercised this selectivity at all times, the laws of probability would change. So, if the laws of probability are to remain the same, God cannot so choose as to make physically less probable states happen continually, or even very often. From this it immediately follows that, if God is to leave the structure of physical law intact, he cannot cause the unlikely to happen very often (though he could do so sometimes).

It is clearly not enough for God simply to determine one

or two otherwise indeterminate electron-probability states. Even if he selects a very improbable state, it will normally be cancelled out in the vast number of random or freely willed fluctuations which are occurring elsewhere. One selection will usually be irrelevant to a macrocosmic outcome. To effect a significant change, God will have to select a great many sub-atomic states, which will mesh in a coherent way to produce an overall state-change. Or he will have to determine behaviour at one of those critical points within a complex dynamical system at which a very small change can produce an overall change of state, what is sometimes called a phase change. In such circumstances, a small and relatively improbable change, leaving the laws of nature intact because the overall sum of probabilities is not affected, catalytically produces a significant change of overall state.

One might expect God's actions to be normally located at these critical points. For then, the rationale of nature can be preserved, while contingent Divine actions can use the physical structure to effect particular purposive sequences of events. This causality cannot operate in any way at any time. There are law-like constraints on the system. Those constraints allow only certain sorts and degrees of purposive change. We might model the situation in a very much oversimplified way as follows: think of one elementary particle, with a specific amount of energy. That energy can be used in various ways – it can be converted into motion, mass or magnetic charge. Such changes are governed by a probability-rule, which makes some changes more likely than others; yet a great many changes are possible. This is a one-unit stochastic system. How could God, a purposing agent external to the system, "act within" or modify the system? Clearly, he could cause one possibility to be realized rather than others. Any such particular action would be undetectable from within the system, since the realized possibility might have happened in any case.

What God can do is limited by the range of available actions; there is a finite and quite determinate number of possibilities, one of which he may choose. He cannot do just anything. But there is a further constraint. He is limited in the number of changes he can bring about. Crudely, he can bring about more probable changes quite often, and less probable changes very rarely. If the stochastic structure is to remain intact – and that is the hypothesis – then probabilities can be assigned to actions with some precision. Suppose one spins a two-sided coin. Over a long run, it should come down an equal number of times on each side. It may come down heads twenty times in a row; though improbable, this is quite possible. But things will balance out later. That means God cannot make it come down heads every time; and if he makes it come down heads many times, he may have to balance things up by making it come down tails on many other occasions. He can cause it to come down heads a few times, without the laws of probability being noticeably infringed. Generally speaking, the more improbable an event is, the less often God can make it happen. The more likely it is, the more often he can make it happen.

It seems, then, that God can act on such a system; he can do one of a limited range of things on any occasion; and he can act on a number of occasions which is directly proportional to the probability of the event's occurring in any case. This would still be a significant mode of action. For instance, God could make a coin fall the way he chose (but only either heads or tails!) on a large number of occasions, as long as he balanced out the overall odds in the long run. This action would be undetectable, though God might make it obvious by predicting in advance what he was going to do, for instance. But it would be a real purposive change, all the same.

What God can do, in this very simple system, on any one occasion is governed by the range of possibilities set by the system, and by the overall probability-pattern which he must conserve. It would be false to say that he could do nothing, to say that he could do absolutely anything, or to say that we could ever know exactly what he can do (for we are not in a position to know how he intends to adjust the system elsewhere to make the probabilities come out right; or how his past acts may now require him to balance the system). It would also be false to say that there is only one thing God can do, on any occasion, that he is either metaphysically or evaluatively constrained to only one course of action.

He is not metaphysically constrained, because he can choose any option that the probability-pattern allows; and he can adjust individual events in many different ways while conserving the pattern. His choices may often be very limited, if his past acts impose a strong probability of a specific balancing event. But even then, he *could* choose another option, at the cost of further balancing elsewhere. Clearly, however, his acts will be much more limited at some times than at others, depending on how much leeway he has left himself by other actions, performed or intended. We will never be in a position to know the extent of such limitations.

Even at this very simple level, God is not generally evaluatively constrained to only one action. Suppose he chooses to actualize a particular pattern because it exhibits the value of elegance, then there is not just one most elegant set of events. Some sets are more elegant than others; some are very inelegant, showing little discernible pattern. But almost any event can be worked into an elegant pattern, given time. Perhaps on some occasions a consideration of pattern would constrain an action, if the pattern needed just one element to be completed. But normally the patterns can be continued in various ways. It may be most satisfactory to say that concern for pattern will impose constraints on Divine action on many particular occasions. Yet which pattern is chosen; and how it is developed in many particulars, allows many open possibilities. However, we have uncovered another sort of constraint on Divine action, the constraint imposed both by the general values God wishes to implement and by the particular creative ways in which those values are implemented. In each respect, there is much room for alternative choices, with no one "best" being obvious. Once again, we could have only the most general idea about what those values might be; and only the vaguest guesses about how, in detail, they might be implemented.

Even on the simplest one-unit stochastic model, one can make an intelligible case for Divine action, given only the assumption that there are some outcomes God desires more than others. And one can identify four sorts of constraints upon Divine action – a range of possible acts must be specified; a probability-pattern must be conserved; a general set of

E

values must be selected from a wider possible range; and the particular pattern of their implementation must be intelligibly developed. These constraints will sometimes be quite tight, and leave few options open to God. But at other times, they will be very loose, and leave him with possibilities of decisively different actions. Even then, however, the actions he chooses to perform will have effects on the rest of the system. Divine acts cannot be considered in isolation, for they will alter the rigidity of the constraints upon other parts of the system, and that will be a relevant feature for God to take into account when deciding whether to perform them.

If this account seems fairly complicated, that complication increases exponentially as we come to consider anything like the actual physical universe in which we exist. For now we have a system of millions of stochastic units, interacting to give rise to emergent properties which introduce factors apparently irreducible to the properties of their constituent parts. The way in which hierarchies of emergent properties is generated is set out in Arthur Peacocke's *Creation and the World of Science* (1979: esp. ch.4). The most obvious new feature of the situation is that God will have to consider the character of the whole, in addition to the individual units which go to make it up. For it is the structure of the combined units, integrating them in functional relationship to one another within a self-sustaining total system, which makes organic life possible; and the units then need to be considered in relation to their function and placing within the whole, not just as isolated units.

Such units combine to form wholes with new properties, and they act as total systems in relation to other similar systems. The properties of individual units then become modified by their placing within a wider structure; and this will affect the primary allocation of probability-states to each unit. Such systems will be "holistic" – the properties of the parts will at least partly be governed by the nature of the structural whole of which they are parts. Moreover, changes in a small but critical part of such a structure may cause wholesale changes throughout the whole structure.

It has been pointed out in a previous chapter that the work of Prigogene and others in the relatively new subject of chaotic dynamics shows that sometimes a very small fluctuation, occurring at a critical point, may cause a total change in a much larger physical system. This need not be a case of the improbable happening. It is rather that indeterministic changes of a seemingly trivial nature can, if the situation is right, bring about wholesale changes in a macrocosmic situation. A very simple and familiar example of a phase change in nature is the way in which liquid turns into a solid at a specific critical temperature. The continuous operation of physical laws produces a radical change of state. This case does not involve indeterministic change; but it illustrates the way in which a small continuous but critical change in one variable – temperature – may in the right circumstances bring about a total change of physical state.

Such critical changes often occur quite unpredictably; and Prigogene's studies of the behaviour of complex dynamical systems far from equilibrium emphasize the enormous degree of such unpredictability. As John Polkinghorne points out, even the precise position of molecules in a gas can be affected by a variation in gravitational field caused by the genesis of one electron on the other side of the universe, fifteen billion light years away (Polkinghorne 1989:28). This point is picturesquely described as "the butterfly effect", since it shows the possibility that a storm over New York could be caused, ultimately, by one flap of a butterfly's wing in Beijing, setting off a chain of critical disturbances in the planetary atmosphere.

Recent studies in dynamics certainly stress the presence of important phase-changes in nature, the enormous subtlety and unpredictability of any particular dynamical system, and the way in which such systems are open to forms of influence which the tightly closed world of Newtonian dynamics could not take into account. They do not establish conclusively the presence of indeterminacy in such processes. Even at the quantum level where the Copenhagen interpretation insists on radical indeterminacy, it is possible, as Einstein famously held in conversation with Bohr at the Solvay Congress of 1927 (*"ob der liebe Gott wurfelt"*), that hidden variables exist which will impose a tight causal grid upon sub-atomic particles. And Polkinghorne himself speaks disparagingly of those who pin their hopes of freedom on sub-atomic indeterminacies, as believing in a "hole-in-the-corner" God (Polkinghorne 1988:58).

One must therefore speak rather carefully about contemporary physics. But this at least can be said, that a deterministic system of universal physical laws rules out both human and Divine freedom to develop the future in genuinely novel and unpredictable ways. Such a deterministic system has not been established by contemporary physics. Further, it is clear that it could not be established by any foreseeable physical techniques, since the "infinitesimally balanced sensitivity to circumstance" of dynamical systems in our universe results in "an almost infinitely multiplying variety of possible behaviours ... not open to prior prediction" (Polkinghorne 1989:28). Minimally, then, physics does not rule out human or Divine creativity.

But more can be said than that; for since the development of quantum theory in this century it has become most plausible to see the physical world as a set of emergent, flexible and open systems, and Newtonian mechanics as "no more than an approximation to a more supple reality". In this sense, the material world is open to a purposive shaping of the flexible cosmos of becoming – it is open, as Prigogene and Stengers put it, to "the reenchantment of nature" (Prigogene and Stengers 1984). When the universe is most naturally seen as an open and emergent system, a much more positive space has been cleared for a creative dimension either to emerge within this reality, or, as the theist would believe, to direct its processes at their root.

Polkinghorne's objections to a reliance on quantum indeterminacy alone are due to his feeling that such microcosmic indeterminacies cancel out too much on the everyday level, so that they do not seem suited to provide the fairly large degree of free action that appears to characterize human life. In a system of many probabilistic units, strong probabilities will tend to be reinforcing, and make some outcomes virtually certain. Weak probabilities will correspondingly become virtually impossible. Other probabilities will balance out, leaving some set of outcomes equiprobable. This gives rise to the familiar fact, enshrined in Bohr's correspondence principle, that microcosmic probabilities at the sub-atomic level give rise to apparently certain law-like processes at the level of ordinary perceptible objects. Polkinghorne does not deny that quantum effects can sometimes be amplified to have macroscopic consequences, but he dislikes the idea of God scrabbling around in the basement of sub-atomic particles, furtively adjusting quarks when no one is looking.

My inclination at this point is to admit to ignorance as to the precise nature and location of the flexibility and openness which characterize the causal processes of the physical world. What a theologically sensitive account requires is the existence of law-like regularities which Divine faithfulness will not (or will hardly ever) impugn; and the existence of such a degree of openness in the causal sub-structure as enables and encourages free and creative action, both human and Divine. Both quantum theory and chaotic dynamics give strong support to the general philosophical hypothesis of an emergently open but law-governed universe. They help us to see how it is quite beyond our powers to identify the precise points of Divine determination in nature; how Divine action must be understood within a broadly probabilistic framework, which enables laws to be preserved while not exhibiting deterministic necessity; and how such changes within a stochastic system, or set of systems, will have consequences which reverberate through a total interlocking network of physical forces (as the Einstein–Podolsky–Rosen experiment makes clear). This reinforces the point that changes caused by Divine actions cannot be considered in isolation. Each one may cause major changes in remote parts of the physical system. It will be a major constraint on Divine action that such consequences, unknowable by us, will have to be taken into account by God in considering what to do.

Particular Divine acts will not occur at random, or arbitrarily. Their occurrence will be subject to rational principle; there will always be a good reason why a particular act occurs when and where it does. This reason is unlikely to be discovered by simply looking at the event in isolation very hard. A rather limited analogy might be to think of a giant balloon made of plastic material which will tear under pressure. Gradually it is filled with air, until at last a tear appears in one part of the surface, and the balloon collapses. Suppose further that you are standing on the surface of this balloon. As it deflates, you suddenly find the surface collapsing around you as you begin to accelerate rapidly through space. Now you ask why this should happen to you, just when it does. There is, of course, a reason, but you are not likely to discover it by imagining that some malignant demon specially decided to cause a balloon-quake to teach you a lesson. In fact, the collapse has nothing specifically to do with you though it certainly makes a very big difference to you.

The events involving you occur because they are part of a much wider pattern of interconnected events. The total structure of this web of interconnections has been changed dramatically by one far away rupture in the balloon skin. The rupture occurred where it did because that part of the skin weakened first; and that in turn happened because the total surface was subjected to immense pressures which caused adjustments throughout the whole area. The point of rupture may look arbitrary. It could have happened almost anywhere else. Yet there is a reason why it occurred where it did – because of the developing strains and relationships within the total structure, when subjected to air-pressure.

So what happens to you is the result of one far-away event, of which you may not even be aware. That in turn is the result of a whole complex of interconnected strains produced by air-pressure applied over a whole surface. The relevance of the analogy to Divine action is this: a Divine act may be just one extraordinary event; but it occurs within a web of interconnections which extend over a vast physical area; and it may well produce dramatic changes in the total structure, even at points far away in space and time and in ways unknown to those who will experience them. Moreover, the occurrence of the act at just that place and time may look arbitrary. But it was enabled to happen, it was made fitting, because of developing strains, opportunities and relationships within the total complex of history, subjected to the constant pressure of the Divine purpose.

In the case of the balloon, the application of air pressure is not a purposive thing. Whereas when God seeks to realize his purpose in the universe, he forms particular intentions in accordance with his knowledge of various situations. So a Divine act is not really like a puncture produced by blind application of air pressure. It is more like an intentional act which is made appropriate or fitting because of its place within the interconnected web of events which make up human history. And it is only actualized in view of all the foreseeable future consequences in the system as a whole that its occurrence will have. The point is that God does not decide to perform an action at one point just because of the intrinsic characteristics of that point. What is in question is the place of that point within a total structure, its appropriateness for expressing or revealing Divine presence and purpose, and the consequences its occurrence would have elsewhere in the system.

In addition to considerations of synchronic structural formation, we have to take into account the obvious fact of diachronic structural development – the fact that increasingly complex structures give rise to new emergent properties with structures of their own. Thus self-replicating organisms give rise to brains, which give rise to consciousness. New sorts of properties come into being, and their relationships to the already existent properties of physical systems is as yet extremely obscure. It looks as if the universe is organized as a hierarchy of levels of structure of increasing complexity and that the physical constraints at each level cannot be wholly reduced to the constraints of the lower levels which form their sub-structure.

In the present state of scientific knowledge, it is not possible to provide details of these processes. But, in considering how God might act in such a world, it should be apparent that possibilities of purposively initiated change from outside the system could exist, subject to varying degrees of constraint, at various structural levels and stages of development. The constraints would be those of preserving the general diachronic and synchronic structural patterns of development, while giving purposive direction to events that occur within those patterns. How exactly this Divine causality is exercised, rather unsurprisingly, remains unknown.

Austin Farrer has argued that "the doctrine of analogy ... shews us that we are bound to break down over the joint between infinite and finite action, unable as we are to do better than talk about infinite action as a sort of finite action" (Farrer 1967:85). Certainly, we cannot conceive of God as one cause among others of the same sort, as merely a finite agent within the created order. Yet we do have to say that God gives a purpose to the events of nature, that he orders them to a goal or series of goals. At this level, conceiving of such ordering as a determining of otherwise open structures in the physical world, or as a "top-down" form of holistic causation, or as a "nisus" or "urge" towards value, are perhaps not wholly contradictory notions. All of them suppose some sort of purposive causal input which makes a difference to how things go in the world. Once one admits such an influence, there is no reason to confine it to a sort of generalized pressure, insensitive to the particularity of events, or perhaps differentiated only by the receptivity of events to its uniform force. That would be to press the analogy of "impersonal pressure" too far, and to neglect the important element of personal responsiveness in the character of Divine action.

The fact is that any of these analogies suppose that the being of God in some way causes events to take a certain course which a set of laws of nature alone would not necessitate. They suppose a form of interaction between God and the world, which is not just that of having set it up in the first place. Even Maurice Wiles, who comes closer than most to giving the created world total autonomy, draws back from the full implications of his view, and says, "God's purpose is fixed and unchanging only in the most general sense. God is affected by our actions in such a way that the particular form of that purpose is changed to take account of them" (Wiles 1986:51). But if the particular form of God's purpose changes in response to human acts, and if it is really a purpose – an intention to bring some state about – and not just a desire; then his changed intention must change the causal process of the world.

This is the heart of the theistic contention: that God changes his particular purposes in response to what happens in the world, and therefore that there are Divine causal influences not already set up in the act of creation, which govern how the world goes. God's purpose is not one and unchanging in all respects, whatever happens. It is constantly redefined in response to events in the world, so it is particular and responsive, not wholly general and unchanged by whatever happens. Any doctrine of providence must render intelligible such particular and responsive action of the Creator. The account I have offered is not meant to reveal the mechanics of "the causal joint" between God and nature. It is intended to suggest how there can be such responsive Divine actions, which are enacted within the structures of nature, and not by some sort of interference with them.

The hypothesis of Divine agency is not one that would enter into any scientific account, for it would not explain anything in ways which are amenable to scientific study (we could never experimentally predict God's purposes on particular occasions). But it does postulate that not everything that happens is wholly accountable for in terms of any natural science. A complete account of what happens in the world would thus need to mention God's purposes. In this sense, there are "gaps" in the scientific account, since that account does not wholly explain everything that happens. However, we could never know for sure that this is so, for the simple reason that it is always possible to suppose that no such complete account is necessary or possible for human beings. We can always ascribe to change or undetected and possibly undetectable law anything that happens in a physical system. It is not, after all, that we have clear cases which science is unable to explain. The question is rather whether an explanation in terms of probability and chance is a sufficiently good explanation, without bringing in purpose. There are no obvious gaps in a scientific account which does not refer to purpose, for such accounts deal only with the physical relations between event. Yet God can cause specific options to be realized, thereby introducing a new causal factor into the system, which would have to be included in any full description of the nature of the universe, even though it would not be part of any model used by the experimental sciences, and might not even be detectable by us.

This picture of Divine action in a partly probabilistic and partly law-governed physical universe is complex enough to bring human understanding to a standstill, when it tries to puzzle out the exact relation of causal necessity and purpose in any specific case. But we have yet to mention the most important complicating factor of all – human freedom of choice. Thus far, I have suggested that God might determine various options within a physical system, subject to a set of highly complicated constraints of which we can give only the most general and tentative account. But the system we have been considering is wholly passive in relation to God. He can manipulate it as he wishes, within the limits he has set down. What now if conscious beings exist as part of the system, which are supposed to co-operate with the Divine actions and purpose for the world, before it can be effectively realized? It might be God's purpose that rational creatures should freely bring about certain states of affairs, finding their own greatest fulfilment by co-operation with the Divine will and by a self-transcending loving awareness of the Divine being. It is plain that such creatures could refuse to co-operate or to take the path of self-transcendence which love of God requires. If they turn to selfish desire and self-will, the most general purpose of God will be frustrated. If his design is that most of his purposes will be effected by the co-operation of creatures, it may happen that many of his purposes will then be frustrated by their lack of co-operation.

God could still manipulate creatures to make them do what he wants. But that would contradict any purpose he has that they should co-operatively and freely act in specific ways. Manipulation would contradict God's purpose (one might note, however, that God might manipulate sometimes without this destroying his purpose; but such manipulation would have to have a very good reason). So God's actions will be constrained immensely by his antecedent decision to leave relevant human freedoms intact, and to permit these millions of creaturely decisions to play a large part in determining what happens in the world. If God must take human responses into account, this will modify his purposes considerably and it will give both human virtue and human vice a positive part to play in shaping course of history.

Now we are in a position to see how it is that God might lead me providentially on many occasions, while he yet may allow disaster to befall those I love or me in future. The structure of the world is such that God has many possibilities of acting within it. He will be able to determine one of a number of alternative options, to bring about some purpose, on many occasions. But what God is able to do on any particular occasion will be subject to many constraints. Much will depend on the ways in which general probability-patterns must be conserved, on past and projected future actions within such patterns, and on the ways in which free creatures respond to what happens to them. It follows that the scope for Divine action is quite wide on some occasions, and narrows to virtually nothing on others. Very often, a process will not be capable of being prevented without quite drastic manipulations of the system – which would constrict actions elsewhere. So even when it comes to points at which a small determination can produce a marked effect, although God will usually be able to effect such changes, on many occasions his action may be constrained by what has been done elsewhere. God does act providentially; but each action requires a corresponding balancing of the total system of probabilities. So he cannot act providentially on all occasions when it may seem to us that he should. In such a situation, it is no doubt better that God should act providentially sometimes than that he should not act at all. But many events will occur which God does not desire, yet cannot eliminate without destroying the structure he antecedently wills to exist. Thus a clear account exists of why God should usually act in ways which are undetectable by creatures, and of why he will not always act to do what I think best, though he may always be active for good in the universe that he creates and sustains at every moment of its existence.

8

The Particularity of Providence

I have suggested that God, having set up a system for encouraging self-developing beings to find their fulfilment by eventual union with him, could not act providentially all the time, as such action would destroy the system. If he saved everyone from harm every time, no harm would ever come to anyone, and the world would be a very different place. But he can act providentially on many occasions; and it is better that he acts sometimes than not at all. So the question is: does God have any reason for acting when he does, and not at other times? If he has no reason, then his acts seem arbitrary, which does not befit a wholly wise God. But it is not easy to see the sort of reasons he could have.

One reason which may suggest itself is that God would save good people from disaster, but leave the wicked to their doom. That is an answer which tempted the Biblical writers from time to time ("I was young and now I am old, yet I have never seen the righteous forsaken", Psalm 37:25). But it seems to be definitively rejected in the Book of Job ("I am innocent, but God denies me justice", Job 34:5). It would mean that we could all immediately pick out the good from the bad – the good would never come to harm, and anyone who suffered would deserve it. Good people would not need to take out insurance policies or worry about accidents. Medicine could be abandoned in favour of moral rehabilitation centres. Sympathy would never be in order, since people would get what they deserved; and goodness would become a matter of simple prudence. God would have to intervene on a massive scale, to prevent the innocent being harmed by accident or by the malice of the wicked. In such a moralistic world, it would be senseless to suppose that God himself suffers, as he does on the Christian view, for suffering would only come upon the guilty. Any sense of human solidarity would be undermined, as the good and the bad would be separated into two distinct groups, which could hardly interact even in the most elementary ways. The idea seems vastly over-simple.

There may nevertheless be a connection between virtue and happiness, even in this life, such that the truly virtuous tend to be happy, and the wicked tend to be dissatisfied and self-destructive. The connection will have to be a rather general one, if humans are really to live together in community, with responsibility for one another and for future generations. So it may be one reason for Divine help that a person is virtuous, so long as it is not a reason that can be guaranteed to operate on all occasions, and so long as it does not invidiously enable us to pick out the virtuous and spiritually advanced by the amount of apparent good luck they have.

We may assume at first that God's providential action would aim simply at making everyone as happy as possible. But that supposition does not fit the observed nature of the world at all well. It does not seem as though the primary Divine purpose in creation is just to make beings happy. God will be concerned with happiness, but not with happiness of any sort, achieved in any way. One might expect it to be happiness resulting from the fulfilling of one's potentialities, or, as Kant put it, happiness in accordance with virtue (Kant 1956:117). As Michael Langford says, "The immediate plan by which the human order is providentially governed has more to do with the development of the person as a person than with happiness" (Langford 1981:119). However, a fully theistic account will probably wish to modify the Kantian notion of a self-won happiness and of virtue as an end in itself, by suggesting that true human happiness lies in conscious relation to God, in loving him for himself alone, and in being the vehicle of his creative will. If that is so, God's purpose will not be simply to give people happiness, on any terms. It will rather be to bring people into obedient, loving relation with him, and to find their fulfilment in that relationship. Such a relationship cannot be compelled. Nor can it be simply quantified, as happiness might possibly be.

If happiness was the aim, one might say that God should be the ideal cosmic utilitarian, aiming at the greatest amount of happiness for the greatest number of creatures. The best act to perform will be the one that makes most creatures happiest; and that is what God should be doing. That great English moralist, Bishop Butler, once suggested that God might be a Utilitarian, even if human beings would not dare to be (Butler 1906:272). But for once Butler overlooked the significant fact that God must be more concerned with virtue, with personal perfection and with loving relationship than with simple happiness.

On a Utilitarian account, on any occasion, there will be one best act, the one that maximizes happiness, and God should do it. But if God's aim is the more complex one of bringing people to love him freely, the nearest one could get to the felicific calculus would be to say that, on any occasion, God should do whatever brings most people to love him most effectively. There is, however, no such possible action as "doing whatever will bring most people freely to love me". I could give people lots of good things, and they will like me – because of what I give them. But will they love me freely for myself? Will they love me unselfishly? Hardly; in fact such a course of action may be self-defeating. I cannot make people unselfish by giving them lots of things they want, and so encouraging their selfish tendencies!

If I want to encourage others to be loving, the best thing may be to act in self-giving ways to others, and hope that they will imitate me. Or I may try to get them to think of others instead of themselves by putting them in situations where their sympathy may be aroused, where their selfishness may come to seem indefensible, or where their affections may be engaged. There will be no guarantee of their response. I will probably have to deal in a different way with each individual. Can I perhaps do "what has most chance of getting people to love me?" The implausibility is to think that there will, on each occasion, be just one thing which will have the most chance of evoking love. People are rarely predictable in quite so determinate a way, and the best I can do is probably "what is an appropriate way of influencing people to become more loving?" There may be quite a lot of possible acts in that category. Many possibilities of creative action may remain open. Just as there is no best possible world, since many goods are incommensurable; so there is no best possible act for God in every situation, since there are many incommensurable ways of evoking love and of restraining or defusing hatred.

The emergence of rational creatures creates a radically new situation in the universe, and enables God to relate in distinctive ways to parts of the universe. With a purely physical force, all he can do is select possible futures within the limits of causal laws and without wholly eliminating the elements of randomness which are the necessary basis of subsequent creaturely freedom, thus directing the universe in a purposive direction. In this respect, one might conceive of God as "the nisus of the universe pressing onwards to levels as yet unattained" (Lloyd Morgan 1926:34). The theist will not conceive this "nisus" as some sort of blind upward groping, but as a conscious directive agency, acting as a directional constraint upon the physical processes of the universe. These processes issue in the highly complex physical structures which are human persons, which have the capacity to implement conscious purposes of their own. God can then relate to persons in a different way, by revelation, persuasion and co-operation. At this point the work of Whitehead is very helpful, though his account extends the personal analogy rather unhelpfully to physical particles as well as to human beings. He is surely correct to say, however, that the most appropriate sort of relation God can have to conscious beings will be one of love, of personal disclosure, moral demand and promises for the future, "with tender patience leading (the world) by his vision of truth, beauty and goodness" (Whitehead 1929:490).

The Christian God is above all a God of love, and as such he is bound to act to realize specific purposes for particular human persons. A love which is purely general, and exactly the same for everyone, is not real love, since it neglects precisely that uniqueness and particularity of the person which it is the place of love to celebrate. As Vernon White says, "If God's purposive activity for the world is uniform and undifferentiated (except through particular creaturely response) then it is liable to be impersonal, amoral, and relatively impotent" (White 1985:69). Real love is always active, responsive and particular. A person shows love by helping others to grow to their full potential, to realize their positive qualities and overcome their disabilities. It would not be loving either to give people too much of what they want too easily, or to do nothing at all and tell them you sympathize with them. Love requires co-operation; it requires letting people be themselves, while giving help and companionship when it is wanted. If God's relation to us is one of love, he cannot determine what we think and do. Nor can he leave us alone to get on with it. He will make himself available to help us realize our potential, in knowledge, creativity and happiness, as we turn to him for help. He will reveal himself fully enough to evoke prayer from us; and he may respond to that prayer by giving us new capacities and resources of strength. But he will not take away our responsibility, or free us from those bonds of chance and necessity which are part of the necessary structure of that world within which alone we can exist.

If the fulfilment of God's purpose is the establishing of a conscious communal relation to him, we might expect him to reveal himself and his purposes, showing the destructiveness of selfish desire, the true purpose of eternal bliss and the way of self-transcendence which can lead to that goal. He will arouse a sense of his personal presence, a presence which is inherently attractive, evoking love in one who apprehends it truly, offering forgiveness of the past to all who turn to him and promising a fuller awareness of his glory to all who live in him. This is his revelatory mode of action.

He will empower those who respond to him, giving new abilities, insights and the gifts of inner peace and joy. He will unite finite selves to himself by creating a relationship of intimate knowledge and love, in which duality seems overcome in a unity of mind and will. He will infuse the virtues and excellences of hope, loyalty and justice into those who assent to his invitation to love. This is his interior mode of action.

Finally, he will respond to the prayers of those who turn to him, creating situations of opportunity for growth and healing; enabling the physical processes of the universe to be drawn into final unity with the fulfilment in himself. This is his responsive mode of action. In each of these modes, God acts directly upon mental states (which entails, of course, that he acts upon those physical states of the brain which are causally related with our mental states), giving a sense of his presence and an increase in the spiritual powers possessed by creatures. Nor can he reasonably be conceived as confining his actions to human brains. For if human persons apprehend him through the events and in the circumstances of their lives, he must be conceived as acting in the physical order, enabling it to mediate a knowledge of his presence and purpose, and to be moulded in co-operation with creaturely responses to his initiating will and purpose.

One may understand why the actions of God may be hidden in general causal processes of nature. But if a personal God may be expected to disclose himself to creatures in all these ways, why should such disclosive actions, too, be so hidden and disputed? One important consideration is that, since love is an interactive relation, much will depend at every point upon human decision and response. What God reveals of himself will depend largely upon what humans have prepared themselves to perceive. Augustine suggested that we become what we see; but we might also say that, in religion, we see what we are prepared to become. Divine love asks for a free response from the soul. It raises our minds and hearts to new inspirations, insights and strengths. It unites our wills to the Divine will in a final perfecting of human life. God's action real and efficacious. It works within the soul and within the physical environment within which souls are embodied. It co-operates with human responses, to achieve its purposes with infinite patience and non-coerciveness. But love must be met with acceptance, before it can work as it wills. So the ways in which it is realized, and in which it is perceived, will depend upon the existence and character of co-operative human response.

As creatures come to awareness of God, we may suppose that he will offer love, healing and power to them, opening up new possibilities and enlarging human capacities and insights. If creatures reject him, however, the world becomes more closed to the Divine presence. God's action will then be experienced as judgment, frustration and impediment. To the person who rejects God, the Divine purpose will either be hidden or it will be fearful and threatening. God will not empower selfish desires; he will bring them to self-destruction. And God will not open up new opportunities, but close off possibilities, trapping sinful creatures in the despair and slavery of their own self-created Hell – what the Bible sometimes refers to as the "hardening of the heart" (Exodus 10:27). These, too, will be works of love, since they will be aimed at turning perverse wills to repentance. But they will not be apprehended as acts of love. They will seem to be acts of destruction and terror, threatening the very existence of wills which are set against their own true purpose. Thus many of the limits of Divine action in the world are set by the nature of creaturely response. The refusal of love closes off possibilities. Its acceptance permits God to modify the world for good, without interfering with its structure or the freedom of creatures. Divine action in relation to rational creatures is most coherently conceived as a form of personal interaction, God making himself known to them and giving them the power to love and obey him, or destroying their hope and joy and entrapping them in their own self-deceits.

If these are the forms of Divine action in the world, and if we ourselves are at least partly enmeshed in the structures of evil and sin, it is hardly surprising that God's acts should seem puzzling and ambiguous to us. When we come to identify specific cases of Divine action in the world, we cannot wholly avoid supposing that they are to be found in processes which support our own values and purposes. Since human beings are notoriously partial in their conceptions of justice, it is not surprising that there will be deep and irresolvable disagreements about what God is doing. However, just as we should not let the fact that we disagree fundamentally about moral values undermine our belief in moral truth, so we should not let our disagreements about what values God supports undermine our belief that he does support some set of values. One of Maurice Wiles' difficult cases (Wiles 1986:1) is that of thanksgiving for the end of a war, and he asks whether God really takes sides in war. I think it is obvious that God is on the side of justice and right. Our hesitation here is because we see how easy it is for people to assume they are in the right, when in fact they are partial and prejudiced. The fact of such partiality provides an additional reason for a certain agnosticism in claiming that God is on our side. But that he is on the side of justice is not at all in doubt. There may be no theoretical way of resolving such disputes, because we do not know enough about the objective moral truth, about our own self-deceptions and partialities, and about the limits of physical causality to understand the full causal substructure of historical processes. But that in no way suggests that God is not really acting for good in the world.

Maurice Wiles takes it to be a great difficulty for Christian belief that "the initial identification of what might constitute instances of divine action, as well as their more specific location, is increasingly problematic" (ibid.:7). I suggest that this is not at all a great difficulty, but a useful and necessary insight into what the nature of Divine action is. Once we see what it is, we see why it must be difficult, uncertain and often downright impossible for us to locate and identify specific cases where God is acting in the world. A commitment to Divine action is compatible with, and, when carefully reflected upon, requires, a measure of agnostic diffidence about what precisely God is doing, especially when it seems to support our own plans and desires. "My thoughts are not your thoughts, neither are your ways my ways, says the Lord" (Isaiah 55:8). Religious faith perhaps requires a much greater degree of reverent agnosticism about the ways and specific purposes of God than it sometimes displays.

Thus far, it may seem that God's purpose may not simply be to make people happy, but to persuade them to become truly loving, and in the end to respond to his love above all things. Yet, even if God cannot save *everyone* from harm, we may still feel inclined to ask: will his purpose be best served by saving some individuals from harm? This is an extremely difficult question to answer. Of course, we would all *like* to be saved from harm, we pray to be delivered from evil. But suppose I put the question to myself: would it make me more loving if I was delivered from some harm which threatens me? The answer is not always or obviously "yes". Indeed, I may give up selfish desires and seek for God only if I come up against a grievous harm which shocks me out of my complacency.

Perhaps one might suggest, then, that God should save from harm only those whom it will positively help to find God. That, I think, may be near the mark. Only God has a good idea of what harm may do to me, and of how I may react to it. And his concern might be to bring me closer to him, through whatever happens to me. God must consider how others will be affected, too, by what he does. So one reason for God acting on some occasions might be that such action is well designed to bring many individuals nearer to knowledge and love of God; and that the consequences of his action elsewhere in the system, which perhaps prevent him from saving other persons from harm at some time, will not adversely affect individuals' relations to God to an avoidable and unacceptable degree. Sometimes, however, allowing harm to fall upon individuals is more likely to turn their hearts to God; and in such cases suffering can be a testing of patience and a training in self-abnegation which can serve a positive moral purpose.

Moral revulsion is often felt at the thought that God wishes to train souls in the art of loving by subjecting them to intense pain and sorrow. Some philosophers react angrily to the idea of the world as a "vale of soul-making", on the grounds that character-training may require some hardship, but it hardly justifies debilitating illness, torture or fatal accidents. To see the tragedies of human life as tests set by God to shape our characters is to see God as a particularly callous and insensitive Commanding Officer in a particularly brutal army camp. But that is not what is being suggested at all. It is rather that, in a "fallen" world of many ills, it may not be right, even if one had the power, always to exempt the virtuous from the harm that evil brings upon the world, or which is implicit in the structure of this universe. A life of perfected love in a world alienated by selfish desire from God, may not be a life which would choose as much freedom from harm as possible. The pattern may rather be that of the life of Christ, who gave himself for the sake of others and freely chose to share in sorrow and pain. God will not deprive the soul of such a choice, and so will not always choose to maximize the happiness of creatures. Of course, he wills them to be happy. But, in the redemptive pattern of this world's making, he may decree that happiness is finally achieved in ways that seem dark and strange to us.

I am not suggesting that God causes disasters in order to bring people nearer to God. On the contrary, my suggestion is that disasters happen by nature, that God cannot eliminate all, or even most, of them. But he can save some from disaster, and when he does, one main reason is that such action is designed to bring as many people as possible, now and in the future, nearer to God. It is not that God will use me as a means to the future happiness of others, but that, in considering which of a class of individuals to help, when he can save any but not all of them, God must take into account all the ways in which such an action will affect the implementation of his general purpose of the ultimate redemption of all humanity. God's providential action does not have human happiness, whatever its character, as its aim. His purpose to increase true knowledge and love of the Divine nature, without undermining human freedom. We are in no position to say when the optimum conditions for such action occur.

For this way of looking at the world, many things happen to people accidentally, or without there being any specific intended purpose in their happening. They happen by chance, or in accordance with laws of nature which are oblivious to their effects on people or because of the thoughtless or evil acts of others which scatter harm indiscriminately around them. Without interfering with this structure, God can save some people from harm, and he can decide not to save others, whom he could save, when their suffering can possibly bring about a greater human good. He can also bring suffering upon particular individuals, in circumstances in which this may have a punitive or reformative effect. But it is not possible, in this structure, for God to allocate reward and punishment with strict fairness. And it is not true that God consequently and directly wills everything that happens to people.

Vernon White, in a perceptive account of Divine action, argues that "such an account can only be offered either at the expense of God's sovereignty (i.e. God *cannot* bring about intended ends in relation to every individual, in every particular event, but only in relation to some generalized sub-acts within the master act), or at the expense of his goodness (for how could a good God ever consign individuals to the category of mere means?)" (White 1985:130). He suggests that, if God is really creator of all, "every event is in some sense 'end' and never purely 'means'" (ibid.:128). That is, every event is directly intended by God for a good purpose, and "whatever happens is caught up to serve God's intention" (ibid.:133). "No event is ultimately without some kind of rationale, no evil is pointless" (ibid.:173).

However, White runs together two distinct thoughts to get this conclusion, one of which is true and the other false. The true thought is that "God's universal activity is able to take the specific occurrence of evil and weave some good end out of it for all involved" (ibid.:183). No evil is utterly unredeemable, and all suffering can be used by God to contribute to some future good, which would otherwise not have existed in precisely that form. But the false thought is that every event is willed by God, even such things as earthquakes, so that it is possible "to take every event of the earthquake and find some good end within it" (ibid.:135).

This thought seems morally dubious in the extreme – as if God wants me to suffer, and directly causes me to suffer in precisely the way I do, in an earthquake. But it is also impossible to reconcile with genuine human freedom; for if I freely choose to disobey God, and harm another person, it can hardly be said that the harm they suffer is directly willed by God. Dr White tries to reconcile freedom and Divine sovereignty by supposing that there is "a God beyond time, 'already' acting to arrange all contingent events into a pattern of meaning, weaving free decisions and the contingencies of the world into an already prepared context" (ibid.:163). But that only compounds the incoherence; for it supposes that God waits for free decisions to be made before he weaves them into a pattern. Yet he weaves the pattern timelessly, and therefore "before" the decisions are made. Even God cannot have it both ways; if he responds to free decisions, and permits them to contravene his will, then many things may happen which contradict his purposes, and it cannot be true that God wills every event to happen just as it does. Finally, it can be said that it is not limitation on Divine sovereignty that he should create a system which is precisely such that not every event in it can be directly willed by him. One might even say that it takes more power to create a system which has in it relative autonomy and creaturely freedom, yet which never passes beyond ultimate Divine control. There is moral and intellectual coherence in the idea of a universe in which accidents occur, but in which God can act sometimes to save creatures from harm or to bring harm upon particular individuals as a form of punishment.

People who are saved from disaster often say that God looked after them. But what about those who were killed? What was God doing there? Was he punishing them, or guilty simply of neglect? Another of Maurice Wiles' hard cases is of the hostage who thanks God for his deliverance, when a companion was killed and thrown out of the plane (Wiles 1986:1). This, he implies, is "both morally and spiritually unacceptable". But is that really so? Is it not better that God helps some people, even when he cannot help all? And might not an omniscient mind have good reasons for particular forms of help, directed to particular persons? If I ask the question: why does God save x and not y?, the answer is not that y is worse than x, or less deserving of saving. It might be given by considering the total situation of x and y. First of all, God cannot save every x and y. X may be in a situation in which deliverance is possible, without causing vast and unacceptable changes elsewhere. But the saving of y may involve vast changes which are virtually impossible, given the other choices which have already been made, or which God intends to make. On the other hand, x and y may be such that they may be saved with equal ease, though *both* of them may not be saved, since that would unbalance the probability-pattern unduly. Then there may be factors about x and those around x which increase the possibility that knowledge and love of God will be actualized more than they would around y. It may not be a matter of there being more spiritual or better people around x. Quite the contrary: they may be sinners, in need of repentance. In general, it is impossible for us to know the factors involved. But we may say that the factors will usually be factors inherent in the total situation, rather than properties of x or y as individuals. What God will consider is the way the historical process may be affected by his action. It is not that he has no wish to save x or y; the question is what reason he may have for saving only one of them; and the answer is then given by the situation they are in as much as by their intrinsic properties. The point of this over-simplified example is only to suggest that there can be morally acceptable reasons for God acting as he does; he need not be thought of as acting arbitrarily. Even though he cannot save everyone, he is actively present in every situation; and at some points that presence may open the possibility of providential deliverance.

Perhaps I have been speaking as if everyone wants to love God as well as to be saved from evil; and God simply has to choose what may lead to the most loving outcome. But, if the Biblical view is right, many creatures reject God and his purpose. In such a world, God's purpose may be not just to lead people to love him, but to liberate and establish a community of love in a world of oppression and evil. That modifies our understanding still further. In the former picture, God was seen as patiently drawing a basically good-hearted people closer to him. But in this picture, God must liberate those who respond to his call from a world of oppression, as Israel was liberated from Egypt. The Biblical God is a liberating and judging God – liberation from evil necessarily carries in its train the overthrowing, and thus the destruction, of the powers of oppression.

We now have a more dramatic view of God's action. It is not that he has to choose which action will increase love more. He has to place his providential actions in the context of a purpose to liberate the faithful from oppression and from the powers of evil which seem to bind them. God's liberation of his people involves the destruction of the oppressing powers of evil. It is perhaps an unduly sentimental and one-sided view of the Divine action which sees it as solely healing and loving. Of course God's ultimate purpose is to bring creatures to know and love him. But is this just a matter of patiently waiting, enduring and gently persuading? Whitehead's God, "the fellow-sufferer who understands", is after all rather unlike the Biblical God, who is a consuming fire, a mighty and terrible god ("He will defend the afflicted among the people and save the children of the needy, he will crush the oppressor", Psalm 72:4).

If we take evil seriously, then God's purposes of love are being actively thwarted; lives are being crushed and maimed; the world itself is threatened with destruction. Is it really appropriate for God merely to endure and persuade when his creatures are being tortured and destroyed? Perhaps the more he seeks to persuade, the more he will be treated with contempt, as a god without power or sanction for his will. Whitehead's view requires a very long perspective, in which creatures may eventually tire of self and, out of a sheer exhaustion of desire, turn back to God. But what of those who suffer oppression now? And what of those who may not tire of evil, who revel in the destruction they cause?

The prophets of Israel call for God's judgment on their enemies, for the ending of oppression and for the destruction of evil. Are those thoughts morally outdated and inappropriate now? The difficult moral question is this: would a being of perfect love ever harm a creature? At first sight, the answer is "no", for love surely hopes and works for the good and flourishing of all. But would a being of perfect love stand by while one creature maimed and destroyed other innocent creatures? If not, then some creatures must after all be harmed, at the very least in the sense that they are frustrated in their desires and restricted in their freedom. Divine actions will not only be the lures of patient love, but also the just judgments of one who wills to lead fallen creatures to repentance.

Repentance can never be guaranteed, if freedom is to remain, but it may sometimes have a fairly high probability of success, depending on how characters have been shaped and have responded up to that time. Again, God cannot, in this autonomous world, only punish those who strictly deserve it. He will need to consider the total context in which the judgment takes place, and the total set of probable consequences. Divine judgments will work under the same sorts of constraint as Divine acts of grace. They must conserve probability-patterns and structural patterns; and they must not wholly undermine human freedom and self-development. Yet it may be a proper part of God's purpose, not only positively to persuade people to be more loving, but also to dissuade them from sin by particular acts of judgment. Is this not unjust of God? That he should perhaps punish x just because it leads y and z to repentance, when he does not punish a, who is even more wicked? The apparent unfairness of God saving x and not y was countered by pointing out that God could not save both; it is good that he should save one; and a distinguishing reason between x and y may lie in their objective placing in the interconnected system of the human world, which puts x in a better position to forward God's purpose of liberating a community of love in a fallen world. In a similar way, God perhaps cannot punish both x and y; and the frustration of x's purposes may be potentially more effective for the liberating purpose God has, which provides a distinguishing reason between x and y. But is the punishment of x good? It is not what x wants, but it may be good in the sense that it is calculated to bring x (and various unspecified others) to repentance and amendment of life. It is not intrinsically, but it is instrumentally good. And, very importantly, it is just, in the sense that it is a due consequence of x's sin (in this sense, of course, it would be just to punish either or both of x and y, and it is only consideration of the structural system of the world which allays such judgment in y's case).

God may seek to bring about a great good, like the liberation of Hebrew slaves from Egypt. But that may involve the frustration of the King's attempt to enslave them for ever. That in turn may involve the destruction of many "innocent" people, who become involved, as the King's loyal subjects, in the process of frustration. God has not directly chosen to inflict pain on those innocent victims. But in acting at all in liberating ways, he affects many parts of the system for good and ill. God foresees the pain. But he cannot avoid it without either destroying the system or refraining from acting in liberation and judgment at all. It is good that the system exists, and that God acts to judge and liberate; so the pain is inevitable. The theist might then add that such pain may come to have a vicarious role to play in the process of history, and that God will be able to use it for the final good even of the agents concerned, in the everlasting life he places before them as a possibility.

The point that has emerged, then, is that, at least for the Biblical view, God is not concerned only with the relief of suffering. In a sinful world, suffering must often be intensified. as the consequence of repeated and expanding sin. God is concerned with the liberation of human lives from a world bound to self-destruction. Divine action is the battle with evil as well as the attraction of love. It thus has a double face, of liberation and of judgment. If God acts to increase knowledge and love of him, it is not obvious that such action will always be the alleviation of pain or discomfort. He may choose possibilities which seem to frustrate many human desires and bring whole peoples to destruction (one may think of Babylon, Rome, Nazi Germany ...). But always and everywhere, he will be working to frustrate evil to help creatures achieve good.

Imagine a world with three inhabitants. A is greedy, and wants to dominate the others; B is self-deceitful, and thinks he is caring for C, while in fact he manipulates him; C is oppressed, weak and spiteful. God desires that they all be brought into loving relation to him. What can he do? He can hope that A will become satiated with his greed, that he will become disillusioned and despairing. His greed will in some way need to be frustrated or to be self-destructive. So God might act to enhance the self-destructiveness of greed or to increase a sense of emptiness in A. Such action will hardly be seen as helpful by A, who might wish God only to keep him from harm or give him more worldly goods. It will be judgmental with respect to A, increasing the unpleasant consequences of greed in an attempt to turn A from it.

The self-deceit of B is such that whatever is done will be interpreted in self-justifying ways. God may act to increase B's self-knowledge; perhaps expose him to ridicule or humiliate him. But B will always be able to interpret such events as signs of ignorant opposition to his own superior wisdom. He may well interpret his own limited views of the world as insights given by God; and take the acts of God which seek to expose his self-deceptions as trials set by the ungodly. However God acts, in regard to B, it is unlikely to take the

form of saving B from all harm. God may well cause unpleas-
antnesses for B, in the hope that it will increase self-knowledge. If it does not, then further judgmental action may be
appropriate. It is important to see, however, that B will mis-
interpret all God's acts, not realizing their true character or
intent.

What of C? Oppression might not be in itself bad, as it
may turn C's mind to God; and in any case C is not so vir-
tuously innocent as to merit exemption from all harm. Yet
oppression is obviously not desirable; and God may act to
liberate C, especially if such liberation will have historical
consequences which may increase knowledge of the Divine
intentions and awareness of his presence, for A, B, C or their
descendants.

But then one must consider the relations between A, B and
C. God may act to prevent A and B oppressing C, at least
in ways which make spiritual fulfilment harder for C. Of
course, he may wish A and B were more loving, but if they
refuse to be, then he may simply have to frustrate their desires
and actions. Whatever God does to one of these persons will
have effects on the others. If C is liberated, A must have
his plans frustrated, and B will suffer what he takes to be
a calamitous collapse of his wise and paternal rule. Further,
such liberation, far from filling C with gratitude, may make
C arrogant and aggressive, wishing to wreak vengeance on
his old oppressors. When all God's acts can be partly frustrated, it may seem more efficacious for him simply to punish
sin, whose occurrence is past and certain, then to aim positively at good, set so uncertainly in the future. It should be
clear that, even in this radically over-simplified case, the possibilities are almost endless. In situations of multiplying evil,
many of God's acts will be judgmental, acts of opposing
human purposes in ways which may well cause pain and frustration, and at least temporarily increase the amount of suffering in the world.

In general, God will act judgmentally in so far as humans
reject or seek to frustrate his will. He will act graciously in
so far as humans respond positively to him, seeking to worship
and obey him. But judgments and favours cannot come to
individuals as a direct result of their particular acts. Human

beings are not solitary individuals, who can be treated in isolation. They are members of communities, bound together for good and ill. So it is that the Hebrew Bible sees God as "punishing the children for the sin of the fathers to the third and fourth generation of those who hate me" (Exodus 20:4). It is not really that God punishes one person for another's sin, but that our sinful acts have consequences even for generations as yet unborn. It is in this sense that we are born into "original sin", into a social structure of selfishness and partiality from which we can hardly ever escape. In such a world, God's providential action will often take the form of frustrating human desire, or of leaving evil acts to take their due consequences. It is accordingly quite unrealistic to ask that God should save everyone from harm, or that he should sharply distinguish between the "innocent" and the "guilty". In so far as human community is a good thing, each of us will be bound to others by complex ties which make any disentangling of God's judgmental and providential acts impossible. All will to some extent suffer because of the evil of others, and all will benefit from the sacrifice and goodness of others, too. Rather surprisingly, it would be a morally less admirable world if everyone received precisely their just deserts; it is morally better that we should share with others in their suffering and in their joy.

Nevertheless, within such social frameworks, different persons have very different roles to play. Some are much more important to the process than others. They may exist at a decisive turning point in history, they may happen to be in a position which will influence many others for good or ill, or they may happen to have qualities which could tip an important balance in social affairs. In this way, some persons are more important to the historical process than others, and often in ways we cannot predict. What happens to some people just is more important than what happens to others; though each one is equally loved by God. This allows for the development of a concept of "vocation", of one person or group having a special role in the working out of Divine purposes. It helps to give sense to the idea of God choosing one covenant people to work out and codify his will for the world.

Of course, that does not mean that God helps the socially

influential and powerful more than others. On the contrary, the Biblical view is that God raises up the poor to confound the rich; that history is not made by the powerful, but, unexpectedly, by the poor and the weak. What constitutes "an important role" is the role a person might play in the coming of God's Kingdom, the unveiling of his nature and purpose; and humans rarely get that right, as the crucifixion of Jesus shows with some force. God's priorities constantly surprise us. But that is not because they are irrational. It is because the Divine purpose is worked out despite, and in the face of, human greed and pride, which constantly distort our perception of what makes for true knowledge and love of God.

Given that God cannot help both x and y, it is a good reason for helping x that in some way x has a more important potential role in the working out of the Divine purpose than y. Even this consideration, however, is complicated by the fact that x, or the people around x, may not respond as God hopes, and so his full purpose in acting may not be realized. One cannot judge God's acts in terms of their actual consequences in a sinful world. God acts in view of certain possibilities which can but which may not be realized in the world. Only he knows fully what these are; and he will act so as to encourage their realization; though he will rarely enforce that realization by completely over-ruling human freedom.

Despite these complexities, we can know what God's purposes are in general. They are to encourage love to grow and lead hatred and greed to self-destruction. We can, as Christians, claim to know even more about the form of Divine action, because we see it expressed in Jesus. Thus we know that God tends to choose the weak, the outcasts and sinners and reject the comfortably religious. We know that he acts to liberate the oppressed and to throw down the rich. We know that he is found in humility and reconciliation, not in pride, self-assertion and aggression. Because we identify Jesus as God's paradigm action, we can identify with a reasonable degree of certainty many acts of God – acts which free people from pride and arrogance; which cause communities of forgiveness and love to grow, and which bring healing and reconciliation to the human community. In these things, we may fairly claim to discern the activity of the Spirit, enlarging human powers of insight and creativity and forwarding God's purposes of love. We have every reason to think that we can point to many activities and say, "Here God is at work to save and reconcile". But this does not enable us to identify all that God is doing, everywhere in the world. Indeed, it would be morally dangerous for us to try to do so, for that would require us to claim infallible moral insight and intellectual clarity, and it would mean that those who disagree with us could be categorized as ignorant of or even as opposed to God. Too much knowledge of God without a great growth in wisdom, humility and understanding would tempt us to put ourselves always in the right, and to regard those who disagree with us as enemies of God. There is a very strong moral reason, then, for a large degree of ignorance of the acts of God in the world.

It is a wholly misleading picture of God which thinks of him as able to heal or help everyone, but as choosing only to help a few people, apparently at random. One can coherently believe that God is constantly working in the world to increase knowledge and love; and that, as one enters into active loving response to God, God can purposively shape the events of life to enable them to conform more closely to his will. While the details of God's actions will be hidden from me, I may believe that he is at work, as a constant causal influence, interacting with me, helping to shape the course of my life, and helping to make it a vehicle of his purposes. This will be especially true, as I enter into the interactive form of personal relationship with God which we call prayer. In providential action, God works to turn all things to final good. In prayer, he shapes causal processes in response to human requests. But such an understanding of prayer seems especially difficult to many people, who cannot see how or why almighty God could possibly perform actions in response to my requests. That is the notion which must now be analysed.

9

Prayer as Participation in Divine Action

God creates persons for the sake of the good they can realize; but he desires that they should imaginatively construct and pursue new goods for themselves, and so find their proper fulfilment in the self-development of knowledge and creativity. However, human fulfilment is not wholly autonomous – that is, found in the development of personal qualities alone. It is essentially responsive – it is found in creative response to the being of God, who thereby enters into a type of personal relation with creatures. That is the heart of the Christian gospel, that human persons find their true fulfilment in relation to the infinite God.

But what sort of personal relation can a finite person on a small peripheral planet have with the infinite God, creator of a billion galaxies? How could such a God relate personally to me? And why should he do so? Of course God is not another person, of the same sort as humans are. Yet the defining characteristics of his being can be properly regarded as personal, in some respect. He is incomprehensible and infinite; there must be much about his being that we cannot understand. Yet it is proper to speak of him as bringing about the universe through knowledge and will. And as the all-perfect One, God must at least possess the most supreme perfections we can think of, even if his reality is much greater than we can conceive (Anselm 1965: ch.3). So he is all-knowing, supreme Intelligence. Since he is wholly aware of himself as the supremely desirable being, he is possessed of supreme bliss and eternal joy. He is the supremely creative and dynamic will. God may be thought of, therefore, as infinite blissful, creative intelligence.

Such a being is like a person, in so far as persons (and

not inanimate or insentient material beings) experience bliss, desire and intend many things, and understand and are aware of many things. When God relates "personally" to creatures, he does not relate as one material object to another, or by means of efficient causality, inevitably bringing about whatever he desires. Rather, he relates by knowledge, feeling and will. He knows what created persons are feeling and doing; he can share in their feelings, by complete empathy; and he desires that they should do certain things rather than others (at the least that they should be creative and imaginative rather than destructive and obstinate). In these ways, God is affected by creatures and responds to their actions, in so far as they are truly contingent, by forming new contingent intentions and desires.

This relation between God and finite persons is already different from that between God and solely material objects. For God leaves finite persons free, respecting their distinctness, not forcing them to act in particular ways, but appreciating the uniqueness of their inner thoughts and feelings. His intentions for them will not be merely that they should act exactly as he wishes; but that they freely fulfil their own potentialities by relating to him, as the supreme reality which underlies all others, and which opens up possibilities for their action. So far, the Whiteheadian concept of God as "the fellow-sufferer who understands" (Whitehead 1929:497), and who presents possibilities for future action to creatures, captures very well one aspect of the personal relation in which God stands to created persons.

But there is a more positive aspect also, which Whitehead himself does not explicitly embrace. God knows us; but we can also become aware of him. We can appreciate the glory and beauty of his being, adore him and obey his will. We come to know him, not as one who passively lies open to our inspection, but as one who actively makes his presence known to us. He discloses his glory, declares his will, and implants in us a sense of his presence. In a personal relationship, he does not do this by forcing us to be aware of him. As other persons do, he shows of himself those aspects of his being which we are prepared and able to respond to and perceive. He can illumine our minds, like an infinitely wise teacher, who instructs us as appropriate for us. If I revere him, he will open my mind and infect me with a sense of his presence. But if I turn from him, he will conceal himself, withdrawing awareness of his presence.

In a relationship of personal knowledge, what I know is a function of what I am able to know, of my own desires, orientations and beliefs. And it is a function of what the other person permits me to know. It is in so far as I become like God that I am able to know God truly or adequately. Now God is not just another person, who must learn from me, who can only know of me what I reveal, and who reveals a particular sort of personality – taciturn, moody, impatient or quirky – as he interacts with me. I can teach God nothing; he knows the deepest secrets of my heart, which even I do not know; and he is changelessly perfect in being. But he can teach me by showing me that of himself which I am ready and able to perceive. Knowing me fully, he knows what it is helpful for me to know of his being and purposes. He is the infinitely wise teacher, whose ultimate teaching is the disclosure of himself, in his infinite reality. So my knowledge of God is quite unlike my knowledge of another finite person, whose foibles and oddities I must slowly become aware of. It is a growing awareness of infinite Mind, and God actively causes our awareness of him to grow, in response to our own growing desire to find him.

Similarly, God can infect me with his eternal joy. He can enable me to share in that infinitely blissful consciousness, in so far as I truly desire to do so and am able to prepare myself to open my life to his practical and compassionate love. We can share the joy of God – but only in so far as we can share his concern for others. Again, this is very unlike sharing in the feelings of another human person, with whom we must learn to sympathize and whom we must learn to respect by overcoming our own self-concern and pride. It is a sharing in the consciousness of supreme bliss. For that to be possible, we must be united in desire for the same things and enjoyment of the same values. God actively responds to our efforts in this direction by infecting us with his joy – rather as a person I love may infect me with their happiness, as we share experiences together.

When I relate to other persons, I act with them to devise joint pursuits, co-operating with them in achieving commonly desired purposes. Now we cannot help God to plan things more wisely or to achieve ends he cannot achieve by himself. But God does have intentions and goals for us; and we can respond creatively to him, in formulating these goals and pursuing them – or we can ignore him, and follow our own way. God will interact personally with us by inspiring us with his dynamic creativity, in so far as we allow him to do so; that is, in so far as we attend to him, in seeking what we should be. The Divine love is his desire for our fulfilment in relation to him, as our selves are consciously related to the Supreme Self, and so are inspired to discover what he prompts us to do, and to draw upon his strength in doing it.

It is appropriate, then, to speak of a personal relation between human persons and the infinite creative blissful Self of all. We must learn to turn from selfish desires to centre our consciousness upon that Divine Self within which we live and move and have our being. As we seek to know and revere him, he can fill us with a sense of his loving presence and joy; he can illumine our minds to teach and encourage us; he can inspire us with his creative strength, as he actively responds to our desire to know him.

The sharing of experiences and activities is the heart of personal relationship. God is wholly sensitive to our experiences, and takes pleasure in the uniqueness of our lives. He actively enables us to share in his wisdom, joy and creative power, as we allow ourselves to become the vehicles of his will. To love God is to adore him; to discern his beauty; to accept his creative, energizing Spirit, his illumining wisdom, the joy of his presence. Our vocation, as finite persons, is to be witnesses to the Eternal Mind and Love. It is, even more deeply, to become sharers in that Mind and Love, vehicles of its action in the world. That, according to the disclosure of God in Jesus Christ, is the purpose of creation. So God will be active in and through us, responding to our conscious seeking to know and love him in and through all things.

But there is another side to this possibility and destiny of personal relationship. As free persons, we can hurt and

manipulate other persons, ignoring their feelings and seeking
to use them or destroy them in pursuit of our own desires.
It is impossible for us to destroy or manipulate God. But
the choice of such a way of life will destroy the possibility
of personal relationship with God. He cannot appreciate or
sympathize with our hatred of others. He cannot co-operate
with our destructive purposes. If we do not desire God, we
cannot share his mind or do his will. We exclude ourselves
from inspiration and illumination. The personal relationship
is broken, and we make God the enemy of our purposes.
In such a case, we find not joy, but despair; not wisdom,
but foolishness; not creativity, but destructiveness of others
and of ourselves.

Furthermore, human persons are not isolated units, directly
related to God without consideration of their cultural environment. We are bound together in solidarity – in itself a good
thing. But when it becomes solidarity in despair and destructiveness – that is, in sin – then the presence and strength of
God is withdrawn from the world. That is why the sense of
the presence of God is so rare and remote; why religion so
often brings fear and not joy; why the Divine action is so
hard to discern in the world. Nevertheless, it is not absent,
and one may hope to find the love of God still present, actively
seeking to lead our minds back to him, to bring us to repentance and trust.

The full and proper form of personal relationship to God
is prayer, the conscious turning of the mind and will to God.
Prayer will involve adoration and gratitude. It will involve
repentance and trust. And it will involve requests that God
should act to enable his purposes to be realized more fully.
Perhaps one can see how the infinitely perfect God would
be able to relate personally to us; how the precise forms of
this relationship will be obscured and blurred in a sinful world;
and how human persons cannot achieve their true fulfilment
without constant and resolute prayer. Yet many people find
particular difficulty with the notion that we may influence
the actions of the creator of all, simply by asking for things,
by petitionary prayer. Would the all-knowing and almighty
God really allow himself to be influenced by human requests?
As Eleonore Stump puts it, restating a thought voiced by

Origen, "If what is requested in a petitionary prayer is or results in a state of affairs the realization of which would make the world worse than it would otherwise be, an omniscient, omnipotent, perfectly good being will not fulfil that request". On the other hand, "if what is requested in a petitionary prayer is or results in a state of affairs the realization of which would make the world better than it would otherwise be, an omniscient, omnipotent, perfectly good being will bring about that state of affairs even if no prayer for its realization has been made" (Stump 1979:16). It looks as though it would be irrational for God to be influenced by human requests. God knows better than any creature what it is best to do. He knows what we want before we ask. Since he will do what is best anyway, our requests could only make things worse; and they are superfluous, since God knows all that is in our hearts.

There are two points here: first, God will do what is best anyway; and second, God does not need our prayers, since he knows what we want. As to the first point, we have already seen that it is not true that God "does what is best". There is no absolute best act; God always has options for action, options limited by many constraints of structure and human response. In such a system, God may well choose one option – indeed, an option may become open to him within the constraints of the system – precisely because a creature who loves God desires it and asks God for it. "Our asking in faith", suggests Peter Baelz, "may make it possible for God to do something which he could not have done without our asking" (Baelz 1968:118). For this is a positive openness to God. In submitting to the Divine will, the creature is also seeking to direct it in a specific way, not by command or manipulation but by request. God would no doubt not answer the request if it would do more harm than good. But if the Divine plan is to a large extent open, he may consent to realize a certain state just because it is requested. The making of the request is a new fact of the total situation to which God will respond. It is an additional factor of which he will take due account. If he does take account of it, this increases the degree to which a fully personal relationship can exist between creatures and God. It brings into being the fullest possible sort of co-operation between the Divine and a creaturely will. Not only do we modify our actions to bring them into line with God's will, but God modifies his plans because of what we desire and decide to ask for. For this to work, the Divine will must face open and creative options, and human acts, in the form of petitions, can modify the range and character of those options to some extent. It should be noted that this way of thinking puts the problem of prayer into a rather different context than the traditional one. For the Augustinian–Thomist tradition, God is wholly immutable, and the main problem of prayer is how a changeless God can be affected by prayer at all. The traditional answer is to say that God creates the prayers and their responses, in his one eternal act of creation. Aquinas writes: "We do not pray in order to change the decree of divine providence, rather we pray in order to acquire by petitionary prayer what God has determined would be obtained by our prayers" (Aquinas 1964:2a.2ae.83–2). In his immutable and timeless act of creation, God decrees our prayers and his answers to them in one and the same act. In a sense, our prayers have real effects, for God has always decreed that they should have. But the suspicion remains that, in such a case, our prayers are not really freely made, and God does not really respond to them in new and creative ways. In the context I have proposed, however, creation is a continuous series of acts, leaving open new possibilities, often in response to free human actions. Thus in principle prayers could affect Divine action. The main problem is therefore a rather different one – namely, is it reasonable to suppose that an omniscient God should have his "mind changed" by very limited and no doubt often silly, even if well-meaning, human requests? That is the problem I am addressing.

As God may justly leave many outcomes to free human choice, and not determine them himself, so he may permit some outcomes that he would otherwise determine himself to be modified or directed by human choices, in the form of requests made to him in the context of worship. Prayer is then seen as an extension of human freedom. We are not only free to perform certain acts, thus bringing about states of affairs by our choice, but we are also free to ask God to bring about some states of affairs, and thus bring them about by our requests. Of course, we cannot guarantee that they will be brought about, since our requests may be harmful or stupid. But it may be within human power to cause some things to happen by asking God to bring them about. God permits this extension of our free power of choice, because it is a form of co-operation with the Divine will. In Baelz's evocative phrase, "It is the penetration of the human creature by the love of God and the extension through him of the formative power of the divine activity" (Baelz 1968:108). It never becomes manipulation of God, for we cannot *cause* him to bring x about. We must ask, and he may not comply, either because it is outside the bounds of the possible in the system, or because it would be harmful.

When one says that God will always do what is best, the assumption is that there is just one best option, which is what it is whatever we do; whether we request anything to happen or not. But it may be for the best that God does some things in response to our requests, since this makes a fully personal relationship with God possible. Vincent Brummer makes this point powerfully when he argues that "no personal relation is possible unless both partners adopt the attitude toward one another which is expressed in petition" (Brummer 1988:98). What he has in mind is that each person in a true personal relationship must acknowledge the personal independence of the other – so we must ask God, and not command. On the other hand, each person must avow their own independent status – so we must not simply submit ourselves docilely to God, but hope that our wishes may influence his actions. Given all the qualifications we must make about calling God a person in a very different sense from human personhood, it seems true that if I am to be related personally to God, I must both acknowledge my dependence on him and also retain a sense of my own relative autonomy, so that he may respond to my freely made requests. Our asking, and thus our acknowledgment of our reliance upon God both in general and for the fulfilment of a specific desire, will change God's assessment of what is the best possible thing to do. What is best if we do not pray might well be different from what is best if we do pray. So it is a feeble argument that, since God will do what is best anyway, we need not bother to pray.

If there is no "best action", anyway, but almost always a range of creative alternatives open to God, then it is even clearer that the Divine action which consists in "doing x because P asked me to" is a distinctive possibility which has its own value. It will show Divine love for creatures if he responds to their requests, just because they make them. It will both allow a proper degree of creaturely autonomy to influence what will happen next, and also strengthen the relation of obedient love to God, by inviting creatures to trust and depend upon God for the fulfilment of at least some of their desires. In allowing himself to be influenced by creaturely requests, God shows himself not to be an all-determining tyrant, but a co-operating power for good. But in requiring that these are requests and not in any sense commands (attempting to cause Divine response with magical efficacy), God ensures that his own distinctness and sovereign power remain unmistakable. So it is precisely in petitionary prayer that the deepest form of personal relationship between rational creatures and God takes form. Far from petition being an irrational attempt to change the mind of an omnipotent God, it is the supreme form of that fully personal relationship with God which is the truest form of human existence.

But do we really need to make our requests in the form of verbally expressed prayers, since God already knows all that we desire? With this consideration in mind, Aquinas wrote that "We must pray, not in order to inform God of our needs and desires, but in order to remind ourselves that in these matters we need divine assistance" (Aquinas 1964:2a.2ae.83. 2). But is petitionary prayer just a matter of reminding ourselves that we need God's help? After all, it is not just a matter of God knowing what we desire. The point is that we should make the request, not simply *wish* that something would happen. A request lies between a desire and an intention. We do not just think it would be good if x came about. Nor do we try to bring it about by our own power. We do something distinctive – we enact a request – with regard to a being who has said that he will hear our requests. God may know what we want, better than we do. But he only knows what we request, if we actually request it. God has never promised that he will give us all we desire; nor would it be good for us if he did so. To request something of God requires that we think of him, that we turn to him to rely upon his power, and that we trust him to be favourable to us. These are all attitudes that could not exist without our actually making requests of God. That is why it is important for us to make requests in expressed prayer, and not just to hope that he might give us what we desire.

Jesus clearly taught that "the Father will give you whatever you ask in my name" (John 15:16). It would be wrong to interpret this to mean that God will give us exactly what we ask for. The requirement that we ask "in the name" of Jesus is a much more stringent one than we might think. Nevertheless, Christians believe that God will hear our requests, and that, if we make them in obedience to him, he will respond to them. How he will respond we cannot say, since we do not know the constraints of the total system. But the making of the request itself, being part of a positive and particular response to God, may shift the constraints in a direction favourable to the bringing about of what we want. In this way, prayer can have a positive part to play in the realization of God's purpose. Indeed, we may say that, if God cares for human freedom, we might expect that he would act in the world in ways partly directed by our free choices in relation to God, including the acts of prayer we are free to perform or not to perform.

Why does God answer some prayers and apparently ignore others? One popular answer says that he says "no" to some of our requests, and this would be a very reasonable thing to do if our requests were silly. But suppose I pray for x to be healed. Will this have any effect? And if it does sometimes, why not at other times? The situation is exactly as in the discussion of God's beneficent action, except that one extra factor has been added – that God has promised to hear our prayers, and we have prayed for this specific thing. Our prayers become causal factors which help to determine God's actions in the world; but they cannot normally overrule the system of nature, any more than God's actions themselves can do so.

If we are to live fully personal lives, we must make our own decisions about the future, as a result of discoveries that we make, searches that we undertake, and difficulties that we face up to. If God knows that it is best for me to decide *freely* whether to do x or y, that is incompatible with God knowing that it is best for me to do, or obtain, x, without my having freely decided it. He may know that in fact it is best for me freely to choose to do x. But he cannot *bring it about* that I do so, without infringing my freedom. Thus God may know that it is best for me to make my own decisions. But he may also know that it would be best for me if I freely came to a particular decision, x; though he cannot bring that about without my choice. Thus there are some things which are good for me, but which God will not bring about independently of my choices. Does this mean that God will refuse to bring about certain undoubted goods for me if I do not make certain choices? Certainly it does; but that is not at all unfair. It is a precondition of my possessing personal existence and creative freedom that certain goods will accrue to me only on condition that I make certain choices.

It is clearly possible, then, that God may bring about certain goods only if I ask him to do so – for that is one of the choices within my power. In such a case, I do not choose directly to bring something about myself – usually because it is beyond my power. But I may choose to ask God to bring it about. Within the Christian faith, prayer is a duty. We are required to pray for others, to ask God for good for them. Just as I am free to help others or not, so I am free to pray for others or not. God will give certain goods to people only if they are asked for, in prayer. Again, this is not unfair, for it is a consequence of our responsibility for one another before God. As Dr Stump puts it, "If men do not always pray for all the good things they might and ought to pray for, then in some cases either God will not bring about some good thing or he will do so but at the expense of the good wrought and preserved by petitionary prayer" (ibid.). The good preserved by prayer is the good of a relationship between God and humans in which creatures must freely acknowledge and rely upon God (not using him as a magical power-source), and in which God leaves humans free to help shape the future (thereby giving them partial responsibility for some of his actions).

Of course, prayer is not only, or even mainly, petition. In prayer, we praise God for his goodness and thank him for the gifts he gives. We ask for forgiveness for ourselves, and we ask him to help, comfort and heal those who are ill or in need. Our asking occurs in a context of conscious relation to God as creator and redeemer, and it arises out of that relation. For we do not regard God as impassive or as unaffected by our relation to him. We regard him as active and as prepared to enter into personal relation with us. "Prayer presupposes a *personal* God who can freely choose to do certain things even though he has the ability to do otherwise" (Brummer 1988:43). That means that, as we seek to obey his will, so he discloses his will to us and acts to help us obey it.

Some theologians think that God will not change the world objectively in answer to prayer, though he might act to empower the one who prays to do his will more effectively, in a physical or moral sense. We ask him for strength for ourselves, probably to help others more effectively; and sometimes he gives it. So it might be said that "the religious person intercedes ... because in and through the sharing of his concern his total sensitivity to the problems facing God and man is increased" (Bertocci 1951:495). This is a widely held view of prayer. It differs from the purely self-exhortatory held by Immanuel Kant by supposing that God can act to increase our sensitivity, as we make ourselves available to him by renewing our commitment to his will. But if we can ask God to help and strengthen us, why should we not ask God to help others, since that is the ultimate focus of our concern in any case? If he can empower us in response to our prayers, so he could help others by modifying the conditions which surround them, in response to our prayers.

There is a temptation to say that, if God could help others, surely he would do so without our prayers. But this neglects the co-operative nature of the Divine action. God cannot heal all suffering, without destroying the structure of this world entirely. But part of that structure is that people can freely help or harm one another. They can increase or decrease suffering by their actions. As they relate to God, they can increase or decrease the possibilities of the Divine governance of things. Sin closes off possibilities of Divine action; whereas obedient love opens up new channels for Divine action. When we show such love by praying for others, we may open up channels of healing that God can use; creatures and creator can co-operate in making the world more transparent to Divine influence.

God creates a world such that all our actions have consequences for good or ill. Our actions usually involve others, so that our good acts help others and our evil acts harm them. It is not sensible to complain that, if I fail to pull my neighbour out of a ditch when I could easily do so, God is responsible for leaving him there. It is no more sensible to complain that, if I fail to pray for my neighbour when I could easily do so, God is responsible for not doing what my prayer might have effected. Prayer is a good act, which arises from the wish to help others, in the context of relating to God in a personal way. When that help is beyond our power, we may ask God to help. Our request may make it possible for him to help them in ways which otherwise would have been constrained by the structures of the natural order.

It is obvious, however, that prayers cannot be guaranteed to produce the effects they request. Otherwise, prayer would become a direct means of changing the world. We could pray that everyone should be healed of all diseases, and the very structure of the world would change. We could constrain God to do whatever we wanted, as he would have to answer our prayers. And we could pick out the good or the spiritually advanced from the bad by seeing whose prayers worked most effectively. Jesus certainly teaches the efficacy of prayer, in dramatic terms: "I tell you that if two of you on earth agree about anything you ask for, it will be done for you by my Father in heaven" (Matthew 18:19). But this is poetic hyperbole, so typical of the teaching of Jesus. It is not possible to take it as a sober statement of fact, as one can readily see by considering what would happen if two disciples agreed to ask for the coming of a new Messiah. Such a thing is contrary to God's purpose; so perhaps it could not be asked for by true disciples. But that shows that our requests must at least be in line with God's will. And that may be much more difficult than at first it seems. As Geach says, "It makes sense to approach God in the style of a petitioner only if one conceives of God as a rational agent who acts by free choice" (Geach 1969:87). It must be neither impossible nor inevitable that God should act to bring about what we request. Since God is rational and has purposes of his own, there will be very definite constraints on what it is possible but not inevitable for God to do.

There are three obvious constraints on prayer. First, prayers must arise in the context of worship, of a relationship of loving obedience to God. It is no use disobeying God in most things, not caring about him or bothering to establish a firm relationship with him, and then complaining that our prayers do not seem to "work". The difference is between asking a stranger to do something and asking a dearly loved friend to do something. Only when we truly love God, or try to love him, will he be able to respond to us as one in a loving relationship would. That is why Christians pray in the name of Jesus, or "through Jesus Christ", thereby naming the object of their ultimate love and loyalty.

Second, prayers must be for the good of others; so they must be validated by loving action wherever that is possible. It is useless to pray for someone when it would be possible to visit them instead, though it would be more trouble. Genuine prayer must be backed by appropriate action. Moreover, it is idle to pray for something that would not be for the good of another, even if we do not realize that. So we must leave God to judge whether what we pray for is truly good, and whether it is genuinely intended by us for good. Very often, both the genuine intention and the wisdom to see what is good will be lacking in our prayers – in which case they ought not to be answered.

Third, prayers must be for what is possible. We cannot be expected to know this; but it can readily be seen that, if two people pray earnestly for opposite effects, it is not possible for both to be heard. Moreover, a prayer that all suffering should end at once is beyond the bounds of possibility. I have suggested that what is possible for God, within the structure he has created, will depend upon factors of probability, system-stability and alternative causal pathways, which cannot in principle be known to us. Terence Penelhum offers too restricted an account when he proposes that either an answer to prayer must be miraculous, or it must be such that the same event would have happened even if the prayer had not been offered (Penelhum 1971: ch.20). If one sees the world as a continuous series of Divine acts of creation and sustenance, many possibilities of non-miraculous Divine action exist, though many natural factors will constrain these possibilities. Creaturely responses to God will modify these factors both for good and ill. My prayer cannot be considered in isolation, but will be part of a complex of mental or spiritual factors which operate upon particular physical events. If God answers my prayer, his answer will be constrained by these factors, which are necessarily unknown to me. So the answer may take a form I do not expect, and be an answer, a responsive Divine action, nonetheless.

It is entirely reasonable to think that, as God responds to my actions by reformulating future possibilities within the structural limits he has determined, so he can respond to my prayers (a species of personal action) in similar ways. In so far as God is personal, we may expect that he will answer prayer. There can be good reasons for why God answers some prayers and not others. But those reasons are unobtainable by us, in any specific case. If they were obtainable, if we knew exactly why God answered particular prayers, then prayer would become a means of manipulating God, which would be self-defeating. So one cannot ever answer the question, "Why did God not answer my prayer?" But one can answer the question, "Why does God answer some, but not all, prayers?" And one can see very good reasons why the former question should remain forever unanswerable by us.

One should add that, although God cannot answer all our prayers in the way we should like, it still remains a duty to pray; and he may answer our prayers, in that he uses them for good in ways we have not considered. If, for instance, we ask God for something silly, he may not give it. But the fact of our having made that sincere request will draw a responsive action from God which is more appropriate to the problems of the world. In this way, we may believe that even ill-considered prayers will be a means of increasing Divine action for good in the world.

Prayer is not a question of reminding God of things he

has overlooked, and ought to be doing (healing the sick, for instance). It is part of establishing a fully personal relationship with God, of asking him to act to realize particular goods, and thus of responsibly using our God-given capacity to channel responsive Divine action in particular ways. Prayer will always make a difference to the world. It will sometimes make precisely the difference we desire. For it is part of the way in which God decrees that his creative and redemptive action in the world should be given a particular shape and form.

In a world in which there is no such thing as "the best" action for God to do, he is creatively free to act in a number of ways. It is his will that, in such action, he is at least in part responsive to human decisions. Since, moreover, part of what he wills is fully personal relationship with human persons, his response will often be to their overt requests, as they bring before him their deepest desires in the context of worship. He responds in love to what they ask of him, just as he wishes them to respond in obedience to what he asks of them. In this way, intercessory prayer is an important part of a fully personal relationship to God. Scepticism about it grows in proportion to scepticism about the possibility of a real personal relationship to a living, active God. Yet such a possibility is involved in the very idea of creation, as the bringing to be of a world of finite persons, whose true fulfilment is to be found precisely by conscious relation to the creator. In this sense, intercessory prayer is a necessary implication of a fully reflective theism.

10

Miracles as Epiphanies of the Spirit

There is no insuperable theoretical problem about God acting in the world, though he will do so under a set of constraints which are not known to us in any detail, which are implicit in the structure of the world-system he has willed. God cannot will such a structure, and then countermand it whenever it suits him. Yet he may act in ways which the structure itself does not explain. In a sense, as we have seen, any basic particular Divine act is a causal influence not wholly explicable by the physical structure alone. It is possible to say that "a miracle occurs when the world is not left to itself, when something distinct from the natural order as a whole intrudes into it" (Mackie 1982:20). In that case, any Divine act, properly speaking, as an event brought about by a being beyond the natural order as a whole, would be a miracle. Yet we do not speak of all Divine acts as miracles, for they normally work within the parameters of the physical structure, determining events which would otherwise be undetermined, or which would have been determined in other ways. Normal Divine agency works within the possibilities inherent in the physical structure, even when it causes events which are relatively improbably within that structure (these improbabilities being balanced elsewhere in the system).

A miraculous action, in the strict sense, would be an event which is outside the possibilities of the structure, a highly improbable event upsetting the conservation of probability laws, since it is not "balanced" elsewhere. It would be, in David Hume's famous definition, "a violation of the laws of nature" (Hume 1902: Section 10, Part 1). There is a logical space for such miraculous events. Any general structure can stand some exceptions, without being destroyed as a structure.

But such exceptions must be rare. From the point of view of the structure, they will be anomalies which can be safely ignored in setting up the "laws" which govern the working of the system.

In a probabilistic universe, it will not be easy to detect when such anomalous events occur; it may even be impossible. The difference between a highly improbable event which is allowed by the structure and one which is not may well be undetectable by a finite intelligence, with its limited range of knowledge. Still, it is possible that an event, or a series of events, could be so improbable that even a specific set of probabilistic laws could not be formulated to include it. At the level of common sense observation, rare events which seem to be well beyond the possibilities of natural explanation available to us will be candidates for miraculous action. They may not be truly miraculous, since there may be physical principles unknown to us which do explain them. But it is logically possible that truly anomalous events could occur; and if they do, strictly scientific explanation will simply have to ignore them or set them on one side for the moment at least. This may be rather upsetting for a scientist, who would like to bring all events under one set of known laws. An editorial in the scientific journal, *Nature*, in 1984, stated that miracles were impossible by definition. For no event could happen which was inexplicable by science. A version of this view is defended by Alastair MacKinnon, who holds that "the idea of a suspension of natural law is self-contradictory" (MacKinnon 1967:309). For anything that happens, he claims, does so in accordance with a law of nature. We might not at present know what the law is. But the scientist may hope to explain all apparently anomalous events in future, with a rich enough set of laws. As Richard Swinburne has pointed out, however, events could occur which are not subsumable under any general law of nature. "Laws of nature ... describe what happens in a regular and predictable way", he writes. "When what happens is entirely irregular and unpredictable, its occurrence is not something describable by natural laws" (Swinburne 1970: ch.3). It is logically and indeed physically possible that events occur which are never repeated and which are not connected by any natural process to other events, so that no law can be found to connect them with other events. If that is the case, we will have to say that some events are beyond the possibility of explanation by the physical sciences. If they are extremely rare, however, they will not impugn the acceptability of scientific explanations.

Thus far, a miracle may be characterized as an event beyond the possibility of physical law-like explanation. This is in line with Aquinas' conception of miracle as an event beyond the powers of the natural order, that is, the order which is "generally followed in things" (Aquinas 1975:3.101.1). Natural laws tell us how things operate according to the exercise of their natural powers or capacities. They cannot tell us how things generally operate beyond their natural powers, since they do not generally do so. The notion of an event beyond the natural powers of objects is more satisfactory than Hume's idea of the violation of a law, since it does not carry the connotation of arbitrary interference, but rather of a temporary elevation of powers beyond the natural. Aquinas distinguishes three degrees of miracle. First, there are events which nature could never bring about by its own power – like the sun standing still. Second, the events which nature could do, but not in the order in which they happen – for example, the coming to life of a person after death. And third, are things that nature can do, but does not in this case – like the coming of rain after a drought. Especially in the case of the higher degrees of miraculous action, the stress is on God bringing about something which "nature does not or could never do". Since all creatures are parts of the natural or created order, Aquinas holds that "whatever is done by the power of any creature cannot be called a miracle properly" (ibid.:3.102.3). So "God alone can work miracles" (ibid.:3.102.1).

Aquinas is working with a concept of the natural order as consisting of objects with specific powers which are proper to them and defined by their essential forms, or natures. So he can distinguish events which are beyond the powers of a created agent from events which are within its powers (e.g. coming to life), though not within the normal ordering of those powers (coming to life at a certain time and in a specific manner). Created spirits may have much greater powers than human beings; yet the exercise of these powers is not miraculous, since those powers have been created by God. A miracle proper cannot be brought about by any created power, however great.

None of this helps us to identify a miracle, since we cannot know for certain when an event is brought about by a spiritual being or indeed a holy person of very great natural (though very unusual) powers, and when it is brought about by God. Yet there can be events which occur which it is beyond the unaided powers of any created being involved in the event to bring about. Whether we talk of "natural powers" or of "laws of nature", one can conceive of there being events which are inexplicable by recourse to descriptions of such powers or laws. In this sense, miracles proper are quite distinct from the exercise of paranormal powers by human beings – which are, after all, powers of such beings, however amazing and unusual. For Aquinas, talk of miracles is conceptually distinct from talk of highly developed psychical abilities, however much the two may result in events which seem to be very similar.

At this point, however, one may pause to ask if this view of miracle has not quite unintentionally helped to make Divine miraculous actions seem arbitrary and irrational interruptions into a closed physical order. In Hume, this is fairly clear in the very use of terms like "violation" and "transgression". But even in Aquinas, the normal powers of objects seem to be so fixed that only God could alter them. The picture of a fixed natural order with some remarkable intrusions into it by God is logically possible; but hardly seems an adequate account of the very complex and widely alleged phenomena, closely connected with religious faith and practice, which would commonly be called miraculous. The Bible itself does not take the view that only God can perform miracles. In the Book of Revelation, the "Beast of the Earth" "performed great and miraculous signs ... because of the signs ... he deceived the inhabitants of the earth" (Rev. 13:13–14). The spirits of demons perform miraculous signs, and so does the false prophet of the beast (Rev. 19:20). The magicians of ancient Egypt were said to conjure up frogs "by their secret arts" (Exodus 8:7). And Jesus himself said that there would be miracle-workers who were evil-doers (Matt.7:22). Miracles are closely associated with magic, and seem to be morally (and therefore perhaps doctrinally) neutral.

In the contemporary world there are many well-attested claims to the occurrence of miracles. The novelist Christopher Isherwood claims to have seen Ramakrishna walk across the Ganges. The Indian guru Sai Baba is alleged to materialize objects out of thin air and heal people in full view of thousands of devotees. There is no shortage of claims to miracle; and one can only think that those theologians who thought that "modern man" can no longer believe in miracles must have had a remarkably limited range of acquaintances. Of course, these claims may all be false. But many of them are as well attested as anything in the Bible, and what is irrational is to accept all Biblical testimonies and reject all others out of hand. If this is so, however, it seems that miracles are not totally unique types of occurrence. They are a sub-set of a widely attested class of paranormal phenomena, associated with special spiritual gifts or altered states of human consciousness. In many Buddhist traditions, the practice of meditation is often associated with the development of such paranormal powers, exhibiting the power of mind over matter, and usually regarded as by-products of the real aim of meditation, which is to escape from the thrall of desire, hatred and greed. Far from all miracles being performed by God, it seems that amazing miracles can occur even where no belief in God exists.

One can still speak of miracles as occurrences beyond the normal or usual powers of objects. For a miracle will be an event brought about intentionally in a manner which is beyond the physical capacities of normal individuals. Some human beings, it seems, can possess such abnormal powers. It is not so much that no law could ever be provided to describe their working, as that we have no idea of what such laws of abnormal mental causality are like. In general, we have no laws relating mental states to bodily or physical events, even in normal cases. Our physical laws relate physical events to one another, and we are very unclear how mental states might fit into such accounts. Truly paranormal mental powers might therefore simply transcend any set of physical laws we could construct. On the physical level, they would remain anomalous, in not falling under any general law formulable by us. Yet such powers are not unlimited – or they would indeed by Divine. So there must presumably be laws of some sort, at least setting out the limits of abnormal mental powers and the conditions under which they could be acquired and exercised.

It therefore seems likely that what on the physical level is simply anomalous could, in principle, be brought under some higher type of law governing the exercise of developed mental or spiritual powers. More clearly than in the physical case, however, such laws would only set the forms and limits of the acquisition and exercise of such powers. One would be much less tempted to suppose that they somehow themselves determine exactly what will happen and when. That will be decided by the spiritual agents in question, which might, it seems, be good or evil, enlightened or deluded, demonic or Divine. God will differ from such spiritual agents in alone possessing unlimited power – though my suggestion has been that he will normally act under self-imposed constraints for the sake of the goods of the relative autonomy which he grants to rational and partly rational creatures.

What is required is not that Aquinas' view should be wholly renounced, but that is should be extended from its rather narrow focus on Divine action to confirm the Catholic faith or specifically Catholic saints. Instead, one can speak, in a more Biblical way, of spiritual agency which transcends the normal physical powers of objects, and which does indeed express forms of human consciousness altered and heightened by their contact with higher non-physical realms of being. It is not God alone who will intrude miraculously upon the physical system which is the basis of human existence. Without being destroyed, that system can be interpenetrated and re-ordered by spiritual agencies, which may, on exceptional occasions, act in ways transcending all formulable laws of the physical order. Since such occurrences are closely associated with the aims and intentions of particular human beings to develop their spiritual powers or to relate to higher spiritual powers, either by prayer or by magical manipulation, one will expect miracle and religious aspiration to go together. And as God interacts with creatures in a personal way, one will expect that those who worship God and seek to follow him truly will sometimes become the focal points of miraculous action, as God responds to their desire to be united with him. We may then think of Divine miracles as a sub-set of paranormal events which are brought about by God in response to the prayer and faith of those who seek him with all their hearts. It is quite unsatisfactory to think of miracles as just rare, highly improbable and physically inexplicable events. The theist has no interest in the claim that anomalous physical events occur. The events in which the theist is interested are acts of God; and Divine acts do not occur arbitrarily, or just as anomalous and wholly inexplicable changes in the world. They have a rationale; and that rationale must be connected with the purposes of God for the world.

For the theist, the physical universe cannot be considered solely as an autonomous system. It has a relative autonomy; it has principles of change which are ordered and intelligible. But, most importantly, it is related to God, its ultimate source, who is an infinite and perfect wisdom. Physical structures, I have argued, have a purpose, which is that they shall produce rational creatures capable of conscious relation to God and of sharing to some extent in his wisdom and power. We might say that the physical universe is inherently orientated towards God. Its structures point beyond themselves to the spiritual reality which underlies and gives form to them. A normal act of God is a physical process which is directed towards increasing such a strictly supernatural orientation. For the theist, the material world is meant to be, or to become, a sacrament of spirit, to be transparent to its spiritual foundation.

One might expect, from such a theistic point of view, that material structures would not be wholly self-explanatory. They would find their fullest and most proper form of being in orientation to a transcendent spiritual reality. One might expect, therefore, that events would occur which would point to the fulfilment of the material in a transcendent spiritual realm. This thought prompts a much fuller conception of the miraculous, as a sequence of events which takes physical objects beyond their normal physical realizations, and displays their relation to their spiritual origin and goal. The miraculous is the transformation of the material to become the vehicle of the spiritual.

It is an essential part of the concept of Divine miracle (and I shall speak from this point of "miracle" as an act of God, not just a paranormal act) – a part which David Hume unsurprisingly overlooks – that it should be closely connected with revelation, in the sense of showing the true origin, basis and goal of the physical order. It should have what Swinburne calls "religious significance". Many twentieth century theologians, realizing the importance of this fact, have defined miracle almost wholly in terms of it. Thus Paul Tillich writes that "a genuine miracle is ... an event which is astonishing, unusual, shaking ... which points to the mystery of being, expressing its relation to us ... which is received as a sign-event in an ecstatic experience" (Tillich 1951: vol.1,116). For Tillich, the three essential marks of a miracle are that it must astonish us. It must somehow manifest "the depth of reason and the ground of being", pointing to the mystery of our existence and our ultimate concern. And it must be apprehended by the faith of those who commit themselves to the disclosure of meaning they receive.

What must be noted is that these three marks all stress the subjective element of the apprehension of miracle, rather than the objective nature of the event itself. That something astonishes me, that it discloses to me the ultimate mystery of my being, and that it is received by me in a commitment of faith – these are all in the end remarks about me and my reactions. If we ask about the nature of the event itself, Tillich is quite explicit that "miracles cannot be interpreted in terms of a supranatural interference in natural processes". Such a thing would destroy the natural structure of events, and it is reminiscent, he thinks, of superstitious beliefs in demonism and sorcery. Tillich wishes to keep the seamless causal robe of nature intact. So miracles become patches of that robe which astonish me and cause me to re-envision and re-establish my inner relation to the ground of my being. The robe remains intact; the miracle is mainly in my mind.

The two major difficulties with such an account are closely inter-related. First, the whole "seamless robe" picture of nature as a closed causal system is much less compelling than it once may have seemed. If nature is an open, emergent and transcendently orientated set of physical systems, there is little reason to exclude the activity of God as a positive causal factor in the way things go. Perhaps in this respect, Tillich is more influenced by a rather restricted neo-Hegelian interpretation of nature as a rational system than by any particular Christian insights. Second, while Tillich stresses the experiential aspect of miracle as having revelatory and commissive force, he construes this in a rather impersonal way. What is discerned is the meaning of being. What one commits oneself to is a new way of being in relation to one's ultimate concern. The event itself is more like a remarkable pattern in a piece of material than it is like a personal action of self-disclosure and an invitation to a new personal commitment. For Tillich, a miracle is a special point which causes one to relate oneself to being in a new way. But might God not be a personal agent who specifically intends to bring about some state of affairs in order that creatures may come to know him more clearly and enter into a more personal way of relating to his mind and will? If so, a miracle could be more than a part of the natural process which happens to point to its transcendent source. It could be a special act of a personal and transcendent God, revealing the fulfilment for the natural order which he plans and which he calls creatures to co-operate in realizing. Some such revelation would be needed in any universe in which creatures do not clearly discern the nature of the personal reality by relation to which alone their true fulfilment will be found. A personal God will wish to show his nature and purpose sufficiently clearly for those who so desire to be able to relate to him appropriately.

On rare occasions, then, material objects may transcend their natural powers so as to become awe-inspiring sacraments and vehicles of the Divine. They will thus be, not mere anomalies in an autonomous nature, but epiphanies of the spirit, showing the underlying nature and the final destiny and purpose of the material order. We might say that what is improbable from a purely physical point of view, is quite probable and only to be expected from a point of view which sees the whole material order as directed towards the full manifestation of the spirit. On this account, miracles have a specific purpose, which is to manifest the inner nature and final destiny of the material. They prefigure and manifest the eternal in time. What they show, primarily, is the true nature of the physical in its relation to spiritual.

The sceptical eighteenth century philosopher David Hume performed a great disservice to religion (as he intended to) when he defined a miracle as "a transgression of a law of nature by a particular volition of the Deity, or by the interposition of some invisible agent" (Hume 1902: pt.1, n.3). He thereby presents us with the picture of a clockwork universe, a closed physical system working in a wholly deterministic and regular way. God can only act in such a system by breaking some of its laws and interfering with it. And the implication is that such interferences are quite irrational, or occur in an arbitrary fashion, in accordance simply with the whim of some extra-clockwork being. Or, equally absurdly, they are needed to correct some defect that has developed in the machinery. It was largely because of such a conception that the eighteenth century deists argued that miracles were absurd and unnecessary for a perfect creator, capable of designing non-defective clocks.

It is a great pity that Hume's definition has become widely accepted, for it is misleading in almost every respect. Physicists know that the universe is not clockwork; but more importantly, for a theist the physical universe is not a closed system. Having its origin in God, it is always orientated towards God, finding its true fulfilment in relation to him. Moreover, the universe does not act only in regular, repetitive ways. It contains unique events and processes, emergent states and surprising sequences of probabilistic causal interconnections. The universe stands to God more as a body does to its controlling self than as a machine stands to its maker – though one must be careful not to let this analogy blur the distinctness and freedom of finite persons. God is present throughout the universe, as the overall purposing field which guides its development and shapes particular sequences towards realizing that general purpose in new, imaginative and particular ways. One might better think of God as the purposive causal basis of the universe itself than as the watchmaker tinkering with his artefacts.

With this rather different picture, God's acts need not be seen as interferences with a regular mechanism. They will be expressed in the purposive direction of the physical processes themselves. They will not be arbitrary – God deciding to interfere here but not there – for God will be involved in every part of the structure, as its purposive ground. A miracle will be an extraordinary event, improbable in terms of the physical system considered in itself, but fairly probable in the wider context of a spiritual purpose for the whole system. For it is probable that a created universe will exhibit particular processes which establish or develop a conscious relation to the supernatural basis of the physical system. In such processes, the physical will not be contradicted; it will be perfected beyond its normal temporal state by becoming transparent to the eternal. What is beyond the powers of nature, considered in itself, becomes a natural endowment of creatures which are infused with Divine wisdom and power, and which thereby become vehicles of infinite Spirit and foreshadowings of the Divinely willed fulfilment of all things.

Miracles are not just anomalous events which interrupt the seamless processes of nature. They are events transfigured by the active spiritual reality which discloses its presence and purpose in them. They are not merely physically inexplicable events, but astonishing and spiritually transforming signs of Divine presence, purpose and power. God brings such miracles about by a special intention to enable creatures to come to a more conscious and dynamic relation with him. At this point, David Hume's definition of miracles misses out precisely the most important thing: that they are intended to be disclosures of the Divine presence and foreshadowings of the Divine purpose for creation. Objects are not at all "violated" in their proper natures. They are, perhaps for one transfiguring moment, taken beyond their natural powers in order to foreshadow their supernatural meaning and destiny. A miracle, as an extraordinary act of God, essentially has the character of a communication, possessing an intended meaning which is to be discerned by those who apprehend it in faith.

Miracles have a semiotic dimension; that is, they are intended by God to convey a meaning of great importance for the human spiritual quest. In a universe created by God to realize his purpose of bringing into being a community of rational creatures attaining eternal bliss by knowing and loving him, it would be strange indeed if no miracles occurred. For in this universe, creation by its nature finds fulfilment in a reality beyond and undergirding it. A miracle is an event which provides a vital clue to the nature of that fulfilment, to the means of achieving it, and to the character of the one who makes it possible. If there really is a God, the occurrence of some such physically highly improbable events becomes overall highly probable. A miracle is not adequately characterized as a transgression of a law of nature by a God or spirit. It is the raising of an object beyond its natural powers of operation, so as to show its supernatural origin, foundation and goal.

In the history of religions, miracles are very often claimed to occur around the founding teachers and saints of a tradition. When persons of deep faith establish a close relation to God, or a high state of spiritual awareness, paranormal events seem to cluster around them. Such people become vehicles of the spirit, and open the physical world to the influence of spiritual powers. So, in the Biblical tradition, the great prophets – Moses, Elijah and Elisha – become transformative points in the world. By the closeness of their relation to God, the power of the spirit breaks in, showing the purpose of God to heal and make whole, or to liberate from oppression those who trust in him. It is their faith or holiness which enables God to manifest his power in extraordinary ways, showing the real basis of the world to lie in his being. Thus Pope Benedict XIV amended Aquinas' stipulation that only God could work miracles by adding that humans could work miracles if God temporarily gave them powers beyond their nature (Benedict XIV 1738: Pt.4). As I have noted, even this is too restrictive, since human paranormal powers can be acquired in the name of evil and falsehood, too. One must be careful, as Jesus seems to have taught, not to use miracle as an independent proof of the correctness of doctrine. It is not the case that, if a religious teacher performs a miracle, then his doctrine must be correct. But it is likely that if an alleged revelation of the nature of God is correct (and if he is indeed a living and active God), then the teacher of that revelation is likely to become a focus for miraculous action. It follows that if the propounder of a theistic revelation does not perform miracles, it is less likely that his doctrine is correct. Benedict's intuition is surely right, that God would wish sometimes to infuse his wisdom and power into the lives of those who love him, and especially into the lives of those who disclose important new truths about his nature. Then they will acquire power which arise from closeness of relation to God; and it is that which makes them extraordinary channels of the Divine power and love.

It is in this sense that exceptional manifestations of Divine power, opened up by faith, disclose God's particular purposes, vindicating the words of the prophets and confirming their witness. Thus the paradigm Christian miracle, the resurrection of Jesus, disclosed the purpose of God to unite human creatures to himself in glory; it vindicated Jesus as the uniquely chosen Son of God, showing that he was not a false prophet – which his death as an alleged criminal might have suggested; it confirmed his testimony to the rule of God which came in his own person; and it challenged those who saw and heard to accept his Lordship over their lives. That miracle might not have been strictly necessary to the realization of God's purpose – who knows what else God may have done? But it is a deeply appropriate as well as astonishing Divine act of power; and its transcendence of the ordinary laws of physical decay and death is precisely what gives it a deep intelligibility, as showing the eternal life which is promised to all human beings who unite their lives with Christ.

Such miracles are not, however, events which compel the assent of all who experience them. Because they have a dimension of meaning and challenge to commitment, they can be disclosures of God only for those who are prepared to conform their lives to the purpose God discloses. To others they must remain simply inexplicable events, or delusions and impostures. Miracles, properly speaking, spring from faith and they speak to faith. God acts in response to the prayer and faith of creatures, as that opens up new possibilities of transforming the everyday to enable it to show the Divine purpose. And this purpose is shown to those who are prepared to embrace it in faith, by commitment to following the Divine will. Thus miracles are not clear and indisputable proofs of God and his purpose. But, for those who live in relation to God, they clarify the nature of his activity in the world, being particular paradigms of his action and purpose for all humanity.

The arguments that have been presented by philosophers against the very possibility of miracle are very weak. Such strength as they have rests almost wholly on making it seem irrational of God not to remove all human suffering miraculously – as Brian Hebblethwaite puts it, "If it really is God's way to intervene miraculously to bring about his purposes ... then why does he not do so more often and to greater effect?" (Hebblethwaite 1976:89). But this, when it is properly thought through, entails the demand that God should make miracles happen all the time. Miracles must be rare, however, by definition. And the reason for their occurrence will not be to remove human suffering as such. It will be to reveal and effect God's purpose in history; and that must be given by consideration of how God wills to make his purpose for the world known and how to effect it without compromising the relative autonomy of rational creatures. At this point one must turn from the conceptual consideration of the notion of miracle to the available evidence for miraculous Divine activity. Only then can one complete the attempt to see the rationale of miracle, and ensure that one is not building a fantasy that does not relate to the real processes of history.

First of all, however, notice must be taken of David Hume's strongest arguments on the subject of miracles – that, even if they happen, we can never be justified in believing that they happen, so there can never be good evidence for them; and that, even if there were such evidence, we could never be certain enough of the occurrence of miracles to make them "the just foundation for any (such) system of religion" (Hume 1902: pt.2). If Hume is right, God could not perform miracles to disclose his purpose to us, since it would never be rational for us to accept that he had done so. And the resurrection could never be, as it seems to be for Christians, the foundation for Christian belief.

Hume's main argument, however, turns on a point the theist has no reason to accept – namely, that a miracle is a maximally improbable event. He argues that we should only believe a report of an event if the falsity of the report is more improbable than the occurrence of the event. Since that can never happen, in the case of a *maximally* improbable event, we should never believe reports that miracles have occurred. Even in the unlikely case where the probable falsity of a report is nil (perhaps because I see the event myself in ideal circumstances and in the company of many honest people), the probabilities will be equal, and I must remain agnostic. Is this a sensible principle?

When I call the occurrence of an event highly improbable, I mean that, on known causal laws and by reference to my own past experience, the event is of a type which has never occurred before, and which cannot be explained by the laws I am familiar with. Assessments of probability in this area depend on two main factors – my own past experiences and my knowledge of the causal basis of nature. Since miracles are rare by definition, I am unlikely to have experienced them before. Since they are physically inexplicable, they will be causally anomalous. So they are highly improbable, relative to my past experience and my understanding of the physical laws of nature. It is not true, however, that they are maximally improbable *per se*. That would only be so if I knew all the physical laws of nature, and knew that there were no other operative causal factors in the whole universe. Then, of course, they would be impossible. It is quite clear that we do not know all the laws of nature; and that we cannot be certain that no other causal factors exist. So it is always possible that an inexplicable event, unique in my experience, could occur. It is even quite likely, if my knowledge of natural laws is very limited, and if there is a God, who is a non-physical cause of change.

There must be specifiable circumstances in which an event cannot be brought under any known law of nature (any principle of regularity among natural occurrences), and in which it is more likely that the event occurred than that the testimony is mistaken. If there are not, nothing that ever happened could falsify an alleged law of nature; and we need not bother to try to falsify such laws. Not only atheism, but the hypothesis that all events fall under universally determining laws, could never be falsified; nor could belief in it ever be reasonably weakened by what actually happens. But in fact the theory that all events fall under a closed set of universal laws is such a wide-ranging and underdetermined theory that the occurrence of counter-instances to it must be not wholly improbable.

One problem here is that the word "improbable" can be taken in two senses. In the first, it means "rare and unexpected". It is in this sense that the occurrence of physically anomalous events will be highly improbable. If and whenever they occur, they will be both rare and unexpected. In a second sense, the word "improbable" means "unlikely to happen at all". Whereas a rare and unexpected event is indeed unlikely to happen on any specific and predictable occasion (by definition), it is not at all true that such events are unlikely to happen at all. It might be quite likely (quite probable) that rare and inexplicable events should happen. Naturally, they will do so rarely and inexplicably. That is hardly surprising. The probability of the anomalous will increase in proportion to the limitedness of my experience and my understanding of the causal bases of the natural order. The probability of the miraculous will increase in proportion to the probability of there being a causally efficacious God who may wish to act in extraordinary ways to reveal himself and his purposes for the world. So it is highly misleading to speak of miracles as maximally improbable. Even if there is no God, anomalous events are only fairly improbable in general, though any specific such event will be highly improbable, in being rare and unexpected. If there is a God, then miracles are quite probable in general. They are only improbable with reference to the physical order alone, interpreted as a completely closed causal system (which, for the theist, and even for many atheists, it is not).

Accordingly, I am wholly justified in believing that a rare and unexpected or physically inexplicable event has occurred if it is observed in good conditions, by honest and reliable observers with no reason to lie. In the case of miracle, it is also important to take into account the religious context of the alleged occurrence. When a miracle is claimed to occur in a context of prayer and attention to God, when it seems to disclose the Divine presence and purpose in a startling yet illuminating way, and when it can intelligibly be interpreted as effecting that purpose in particular historical events, then the believer in God is wholly justified in accepting its occurrence as a miracle, if it is testified to by reliable and honest witnesses.

But what of Hume's point that a miracle cannot be so established as to serve as the rational basis of a system of faith? Again, the objection only seems to succeed because of its vagueness. It is true that one could hardly found a whole religious system, with all its body of truths and practices, its rituals and forms of prayer and worship, upon the occurrence of some alleged miraculous event. As has just been observed, miracles have their proper and important place within a framework of existing theistic belief, prayer and conscious seeking for the Divine will. They arise from faith, within a context of faith, and confirm for faith the character of God and his particular purposes. The Biblical miracles, for instance, are grouped around the great prophets, as they consciously relate to God and seek to pursue his will in their own situations. The prophets do not believe in God because miracles take place. They believe in miracles because the God whom they worship declares his nature and purpose in such extraordinary acts, which are definitive of his universal purposes for the human race. A system of religion must exist within which miracles can have a transforming effect on human insight and response to God. But, within such a system, miracles properly have the function of manifesting clearly and normatively the character and purpose of the God who is in general known so fitfully and ambiguously in human experience. A believer in God may expect a God who is actively concerned that we should know his purposes to act miraculously. When he does, new particular truths of faith may properly be formulated as a consequence. Miracles are important to theism, as normative disclosures of the objective character and purposes of God, which do not simply arise from human imagination and reflection, but which exercise an objective constraint on the riotous energy of the human religious imagination. I may dream and imagine many things about God. But if he confronts humanity with objective acts of astounding power – such as the raising from death of his chosen servant

– then a normative revelation will exist which resists all attempts to replace it or explain it away.

Contemporary Christians cannot, of course, experience such miraculous and absolutely unique events as the resurrection. But if the believer claims to experience within the Christian community, at least to some degree, a sense of the presence of a loving and forgiving God, it will be entirely reasonable to accept the testimony of the founders of that community to past signs of God's saving presence and action, even where it transcends the normal powers of objects. It would indeed be quite unreasonable to reject all such testimony, or to regard it with a high degree of scepticism, or accept it only tentatively or provisionally. For upon that testimony is built our present knowledge of and relationship to God. To the extent that we doubt it, we deprive our present faith of reasonable grounding and confirmation.

We may say, then, that a miracle is a physically improbable event, which is a member of a class of events, the instantiation of some members of which is quite probable, if there is a personal God. The occurrence of miracles will provide important confirming evidence for the belief that there exists a God of a certain character, with specific purposes in creation. Their non-occurrence would tend to disconfirm the existence of a God who is in any sense a personal or causal agent. There will rarely be agreement on the rationality of accepting testimonies to miraculous occurrences, because of background disagreements about whether there is a God at all, whether God discloses his being in natural events, and whether God acts to redeem human lives from sin and unite them to himself. But even for atheists, the existence of well-attested testimony by a sufficient number of people of undoubted integrity, with a great deal to lose if they persist in their testimony, provides a good reason for re-examining carefully one's basic background view of the world. For a theist, such testimony will confirm the general hypothesis of the existence of a personal creator God, will provide good evidence for the particular character and purpose of God, and will provide objective backing for one's description of the present object of faith. Careful investigation of claims to the occurrence of miracles is therefore a rational and necessary part of any assessment of the existence and nature of God.

Bearing these considerations in mind, one can look to the religious experience of humanity for *prima facie* claims to Divine miraculous action. Where they exist, one may hope to find evidence for an objective self-disclosure of the Divine being, which can guide human searches for and responses to the Divine basis of all being. David Hume, as one would expect, holds that we can confidently discount all such claims. First, no miracle is attested to by a sufficient number of men of education and integrity to give us complete confidence. Second, people so love the curious and marvellous that they will invent fables wherever they can, and such tales are never to be trusted. Third, claims to the miraculous "are observed chiefly to abound among ignorant and barbarous nations". And fourth, many diverse religions have miracles claimed for them, and since they all contradict one another, all such evidence is rendered null and void.

Strangely, Hume himself destroys these arguments by citing a number of cases of strong testimony to miracles, including one wherein judges of unquestioned integrity, in a learned country (France) testified to healing miracles at the tomb of Abbé Paris. He then says, "What have we to oppose to such a cloud of witnesses, but the absolute impossibility ... of the events which they relate?" If that is all he has to oppose to such testimony, and if miracles are not absolutely impossible at all, then it turns out that it is Hume, not his opponents, who is irrational in not taking such evidence much more seriously than he did. But one point remains. If many conflicting religions claim miracles, and if only God or his appointed servants perform miracles, how are we to account for that? Pope Benedict XIV held that a miracle must "serve to confirm The Catholic Faith, or to demonstrate the sanctity of some man" (ibid.:1:4.6). Must we then say that Hindu miracles do not happen, but Catholic ones do? I have already argued that such a definition is much too restrictive, and that the occurrence of miracles, though it may confirm a previously held belief in specific respects, does not of itself establish the truth of a whole set of doctrines. Miracles, in the broader sense, are paranormal events strongly suggesting the activity of spiritual powers, both good and bad. It is not surprising that many faiths within which humans strive for spiritual pre-eminence or sanctity make good claim to miracles. One cannot use the occurrence of miracles as a sole and sufficient truth of a religious doctrine; but one might well look to the realm of the miraculous to find evidence of a normative revelation from a personal God. For if such a God exists, he will surely make his power known in those paranormal occurrences which occur around those who seek his presence. The fact that many paranormal phenomena do not show such evidence is only to be expected, given the great diversity of human beliefs and practices. The question for the theist is whether, amid the great diversity of human spiritual experience, there is any evidence of one developing personal self-disclosure of the Divine.

It is at once unequivocally clear that the Hebrew Bible is a unique source of claims that one personal and morally demanding God has acted decisively and miraculously to reveal one coherent set of purposes in a historical and develop-ing way. The religious experience of humanity in general can by no means be set aside. Yet the Bible has a unique claim to enshrine a tradition of Divine self-disclosure to a whole succession of prophets who declare his will. It is therefore to the Bible that we must turn if we wish to assess the possibi-lity that God has acted decisively in history to reveal his will and bring humans into a conscious and loving relationship to himself.

11

Pictures of the Divine

A perfect self-existent being who creates a contingent universe containing free rational agents might be expected to communicate his nature and his purpose to such creatures. Divine action in relation to such agents, I have suggested (chapter 8), will take three main forms – a revelatory form, in which he discloses himself to creatures; an interior form, in which he empowers them for closer relationship with himself and for expressing his purpose more fully; and a responsive form, in which he shapes the world in response to the decisions and attitudes of creatures. But his acts will be persuasive and co-operative rather than all-determining, if his creatures are to have real freedom and autonomy, not just in morality but in every aspect of their personal lives.

If this account is right, there must obviously be places in the world wherein the activity of God can be discerned. There may be no absolutely incontestable discernments; and many mistakes may be made about knowledge of God, just as they may be made in all areas of human knowledge. But one would expect to find claims to discern Divine action at certain points in human history. If part of Divine perfection is love, then a God who loves and wishes to unite creatures to himself must actually do something to show his love and effect that unity, within history.

When will he do so? A first reaction might be to say that a God of universal love will be active in the same sort of way always and everywhere to bring creatures to greater love and knowledge of himself. Thus Maurice Wiles writes that, in talking of special acts of God, "We would not be implying that there was any fundamental difference in the relation of the divine action to the particular worldly occurrences of their situation" (Wiles 1976:141). God does not act in different ways at different times; for this, Wiles holds, would be arbitrary and unjust. All the differences lie in our perception of that constant action. But is it really reasonable to think that God will continue to act in precisely the same way, whatever humans do or however they respond to him? Human beings are free to do evil as well as good; and many events in history show human hatred and destructiveness. To put it at its most brutal, Auschwitz does not show the active love of God; it shows the terrible hatred of men and women. That is not to say that God is absent at such times. But the forms his persuasive power takes, when the strongest human wills resolutely oppose and reject him, will be very different from the forms it can take when people accept and trust in him. It is not just that people do not see God's love so well in Auschwitz, though it remains precisely the same. The way God causally interacts with the world is radically modified by the evil actions of human beings; so that God even seems to be held at bay, his power frustrated, by such terrible evil. God still loves, and his power is not destroyed; but the forms that love and power take are radically modified by human responses. If they were not, if human acts could make no difference to God, if he remained sublimely unmoved by whatever happens, would he be aptly characterized as a God of love? If love is concern for the good of unique individuals, then it must interact in quite specific ways with those individuals. It will accordingly be specifically different in every case. The universal love of God is necessarily particular and diverse in its operations. As Vernon White puts it, "If love is genuinely seeking the best for the other . . . love must include the capacity to order right conditions for the beloved" (White 1985:92). It must also include the "withdrawal" which permits sinful freedom to flourish but which will prevent its triumph and finally shape that evil to a good end. And that entails a responsive and particular ordering of conditions which will vary from case to case.

The active power of God will appear most clearly when human wills are open to his influence and welcoming of his love. If God stands always ready to redeem, where people turn to him in penitence and trust, his action will have most scope for taking positive effect in and around the lives of the great saints, whose lives are wholly centred on God, or at least on the search for inner truth and perfection. As we look at the history of the world, we find, in almost every human society, a record of men and women who claim to discern a deeper spiritual reality, drawing them towards a more perfect life. Among such people are the founders or reformers of the great religious traditions which draw inspiration from their discernments. It is there that we might look for revelations of the Divine being and purpose. But what meets us is a bewildering variety of beliefs and practices.

Religions take many forms, from the unwritten stories and dances of tribal peoples to the great Scriptural faiths of Christianity and Islam; from the performance of rituals for obtaining good fortune to the pursuit of total non-attachment and selflessness. But they are mostly concerned with the right orientation of human life to some supra-human reality which sets the correct goals of human striving. And most of them have some concern with outlining and encouraging a holy life, a life of special relationship to the gods or the supra-human realm. "What the great religions claim, against radically secular ideologies, is that there is a Beyond or an Unborn, and this is somehow accessible to the religious experience of the human race" (Smart 1981:178). Early religion will, no doubt, contain many errors of fact about the physical universe; many relatively crude moral notions and attempts to control the realm of spirits by means of sympathetic or imitative magic. But the theist may hope to find, in its gradual development, a growing sense of God's action, seeking to bring humans closer to himself in knowledge and love.

To a great extent this does happen. But one also finds the growth of atheistic traditions which deny all sense of God, and the growth of a number of competing claims to Divine revelation, which contradict one another at quite important points. It is clear that God does not disclose himself in the same way to all people and cultures. It seems that the way God is seen depends very much on the cultural background and temperament of those who pursue the religious life. That is what we may expect, if we are fully to accept the extent to which God's action will be co-operative with human wills, not just overruling them by omnipotent *fiat*. The particular ways in which God is conceived will naturally vary, as the cultural interests and values of those who respond to him vary. Yet some explanation needs to be sought by the theist for the oppositions which often exist between religious traditions, and the existence of atheistic traditions too.

Among all the traditions, there is one which expresses a distinctive form of apprehension of Divine action; one which sees God as acting in a public, moral and social way for the transformation of the physical world. This is the tradition of the Hebrew Bible, represented in a rather different way within Christianity and Islam, which have both sprung from it. In the Bible, the notion of God as making rigorous moral demands for social justice and as promising a fulfilment of his purposes on earth, or at least within his creation, is developed in a form which is found in no other religious tradition. It can fairly be said that an ethical monotheism which hopes for a this-worldly consummation of the Divine purpose is the distinctive contribution of the Hebrew Bible to the religious life of this world.

The study of the Bible has been revolutionized in the last hundred years; and we are now much more clearly aware of the many strands which have gone into its composition, and the complex editorial process which has brought it to its present state. Most scholars would say that many of the Biblical accounts of ancient historical events are related in a mythologized form. That is, they do not state exactly what happened in history. The flood at the time of Noah did not really cover the whole earth. The ten plagues at the time of the Exodus were not so dramatic, drastic and neatly systematic as they are said to have been. The sun did not actually stand still in the sky to allow Joshua to rout his enemies. And so on. Standard works of scholarship like Alberto Soggin's "History of Israel" (Soggin 1984) show how the Biblical records, especially the early Deuteronomic history and the Priestly writings, present narratives which give a cosmic dimension to the events of earthly history; which speak of mighty acts and wonders in the physical world, when they mean to express important spiritual experiences of the prophets and saints of ancient Israel. The narratives seek to bring out the spiritual meaning of events which are far in the past, and have been recalled through long oral traditions and re-enacted in generations of ritual celebrations. They thus reflect the sorts of relation to God which the community of the final writers and editors felt themselves to have, inextricably intertwined with and projected back on to memories of far distant events which had been treasured as founding-events of the Israelite community.

This does not mean that what actually happened in history is irrelevant. But we cannot ever get back to establish a correspondence between some Biblical account and the facts. What we might naturally expect from studies in the history of religions will be that significant events, like the exodus of the Hebrew slaves from Egypt, would be recounted in religious ceremonies, and would gradually come to accumulate features expressive of the meaning successive generations of worshippers find in them. The final account will be a sort of superposition of spiritual symbols upon an irrecoverable core of historical memory. It remains vitally important that God has acted in the history of Israel, and has been discerned at different times working out his purpose for the world. The Bible is a record of witness to the pressure of the Divine action on human minds and hearts. But the forms in which his action has been understood, and the symbols in which the perception of his action has been interpreted, are many-layered conceptual frameworks of spiritual meaning, which reflect the culture and interests of those to whom that revelation came, and of those who later reflected upon it and found in it the basis of their way of life. The great prophets of Israel find and proclaim God to be judging and saving in the events of their lives. They then interpret and recount the past in terms of this perception. The patriarchal narratives of the Hebrew Bible are past events perceived through the prism of present experience, whose recounting is intended to convey an understanding of the God who lives and acts in the life of those who hear or read them.

It would be a misunderstanding of this process to think that God only really acts in private or inner experiences, that he does not act on the physical universe at all. The prophets experienced God, not just in the privacy of their rooms, but in their social and everyday lives. They discerned his hand in the happenings of their history; and that is what they proclaim. History is important to the Hebrew Bible, because it is a record of what God has done, and it helps us to interpret the ways in which he may be acting in the present. But the business of interpreting the acts of God is not a one-way process, which runs from a definitive past to a present which must simply be interpreted in the same terms. Present experience may bring new insights and correct old prejudices and partialities. Since it is reasonable to think that God acted in the past roughly in the same ways as he acts in the present, these insights may reflect back onto the past records, and lead us to see various emphases in them which we would wish to put differently.

For example, God's reported command to exterminate the Amalekites (Deut. 25:19) would strike most people with horror today; and few would be convinced by the traditional gloss that God can exterminate whomsoever he wishes, since he made them in the first place. We have learned from the Bible itself that we are to love our neighbours and show mercy to all. Subsequent reflection on the character of God, and successive disclosures of his nature to the prophets, lead us to see that he does not command genocide; so that passage must reflect a misperception of God's will, even though it has got into the Biblical text. Here is an example of how subsequent discernments of God and reflection on his nature might lead us to re-interpret the accounts of past history which we have, and acknowledge that each discernment of God is inextricably bound up with the frailties of our own mental processes.

In a similar way, most Biblical scholars would see the accounts of the definitive Divine act in the Hebrew Bible, the exodus from Egypt, as written and edited to express certain current concerns of the Jewish people. In an age of exile in Babylon and of return to Canaan, the chroniclers looked back to the exodus as a symbolic representation of all their hopes for a new future and their reliance on God to liberate them from slavery into the freedom of their own land. The forms in which they wrote incorporated what we might call symbolic accretion or retrojective description, intended to bring out the significance of these events in Israel's history. But the belief that God had acted to liberate from slavery was fundamental to this process; as was the belief that God laid moral demands on his people which they continually failed to meet.

Thus Biblical scholars generally agree that, in the Hebrew Bible, we do not possess an exact historical record of events just as they might have been recorded by a camera. We have a highly dramatized account of formative past events, recounted in a way which expresses the accumulated spiritual experience of generations, as they reflected on those events and saw the present in terms of God's decisive action to call, liberate, command and promise hope for a future kingdom of justice and peace. Nevertheless, the witness of the Bible to the acts of God is quite distinctive; and, whatever the symbolic or dramatic forms of the narrative, we possess here an impressive testimony to discerned acts of God in particular historical events. Here, we can reasonably say, God has disclosed himself as active in judgment and liberation; and has been apprehended through a long and continuing process of prophetic inspiration and priestly devotion.

The Christian Church, again in a very distinctive way, has seen in the life of one man, Jesus of Nazareth, the culmination and fulfilment of this long tradition. This human life becomes for Christians God's definitive self-disclosure; the nature of Divine action is normatively expressed in a human life of service, humiliation and exaltation beyond death. Jesus preached the kingdom of God, healed and forgave sins, taught with astonishing authority, suffered and died. The apostles were convinced that he was thereafter exalted to the glory of the Divine presence, appearing to them after his death, and sending the Holy Spirit upon them with power. Filled with excitement and joy, they proclaimed him as Saviour and Lord of all. In these events originated a unique perception of God as taking upon himself human nature, suffering and dying to reconcile human creatures to himself. For Christians, God's act can be definitively and uniquely identified in the life of Jesus. That life provides the clue to interpreting his actions everywhere for human salvation; but the precise form of his action in the person of Jesus is not repeated anywhere in history.

This particularity and unrepeatability of the Divine action in Jesus is often regarded as a stumbling-block. How could this one human being, in the whole history of the world, be the only Son of God and Saviour of all humanity, when the vast majority of humans have not even heard of him? Would not a God of universal love act everywhere? And would he not be seen in many holy lives? Would it not be better to admit many manifestations of the infinite Divine nature, each reflecting, perhaps, some aspect of his nature, but none of them wholly superior to the others? Would it not be more tolerant to see Gautama, Mohammed, Jesus and Krishna as all servants of God, proclaiming the Divine nature in different ways? This is the suggestion that John Hick makes. He argues that unless we regard all religious experiences as illusory, or regard all experiences as illusory except those in our own tradition, "the pluralistic affirmation becomes inevitable" (Hick 1989:249), that all traditions may be "equally appropriate" ways of responding to one Divine reality.

However, Professor Hick places before us a false dichotomy (or trichotomy). We need not say, "Either all experiences are illusory but mine; or all experiences are equally appropriate". It is obvious that people's experiences of God, even within the Christian tradition, are more or less appropriate. Some are very inadequate; some are wholly misconceived – as when people believe God condemns them to Hell for ever, without hope, as they sometimes do; and some are much more sensitive and morally ennobling. So what one should say is: "Some experiences are more appropriate than others; I try to ensure that mine are as appropriate as I possibly can, and I must claim that they are more appropriate than any which seem to conflict with them". As with individuals, so with religious traditions. Some culturally patterned ways of experiencing the Divine reality may be more appropriate than others. In fact, some must be, since some traditions see the supernatural as malevolent or morally arbitrary, while others do not. So one need not say all other traditions than one's own are "illusory"; but one must say that, where others conflict basically with one's own, they are to that extent not as appropriate to the truth.

Professor Hick's response is to suggest that at least the great religious traditions teach ways of relating to the one Real, seen in different ways. He distinguishes the "Real *an sich*" from its phenomenal appearances, which may be either impersonal, as with the Buddhist Nirvana, or personal, as with the Christian God. This neglects the point that many schools of Buddhism, for example, Tibetan Buddhism, deny outright that there is any Real, or "absolute reality", to relate to (see Williams 1989:60ff.). The attempt to make all traditions aim at one thing is doomed to failure. However, if one confines oneself to traditions which are prepared to speak of "one Real", pluralism may be defended. Contradictions do exist between phenomenal apprehensions; but once they are all seen to be appearances, their character determined largely by our cultural preconceptions, one can see that none of them represent the Real in itself; so that all of them can be seen as partial insights into an ineffable Reality (Hick 1989: ch.14).

This bold hypothesis is not as tolerant as it sounds at first. For what is being proposed is that the Real, with which I aim to have a saving relationship, is totally unknowable – so it is highly doubtful whether any relationship with it can be established at all. How can I know whether humans can relate to it, or in what way? Not only that; but, since all great traditions are equally authentic ways to the Real, it is clear that the Real cannot be as I apprehend it (which would exclude the truth of those competing views). So my view is actually false. How, then, since my view is known to be false, can I be sure mine is an authentic way to salvation? I conceive salvation as knowledge of the Real (of God); but the Real is unknowable; so I must be mistaken. If I am wrong about what salvation is, how can I coherently claim to achieve it by the path I follow?

Even more basically, the idea of a wholly unknowable Real is incoherent, in a fairly obvious way, which critics of Kant have always stressed. The fact is that if something is wholly unknowable, nothing can be said of it, not even that it exists, or is one rather than many. Professor Hick, however, makes very definite claims about the Real – that it is "that than which no greater can be conceived" (246); that it is "an ultimate unity of reality and value" (36); and that it is "the final ground or nature of everything" (248). The Real is perfect, self-existent and unitary; upon it all things depend. These are very substantive doctrines. The suspicion looms that "the

Real" is not a noumenal thing in itself, so much as the vaguest abstraction from a selection of religious doctrines which have the idea of one perfect reality, which humans can experience. The assertion that "only the vague is really true" seems highly dubious; but even if it is made, one is making a selection from a wider range of competing truths in religion. In this sense, all serious claims to truth are exclusive, and there is no escape from judging between them, while realizing the very limited and partial criteria that we have. It transpires that Professor Hick is making a selection from a range of religious truths, and commending it, largely on the ground that it will enable adherents of diverse traditions to relate more easily to one another. But it will only do so if these adherents agree to accept Hick's selection and renounce some of their own previous views. So, though Hick's proposal is indeed important and illuminating in its detailed working out, in the end it represents no advance upon the non-pluralist understanding that some truth-selections (whether they be Hick's or those of some major tradition) are more appropriate to the Real than others.

The proposal that the major faiths provide equally appropriate vehicles of knowledge of God cannot survive a close inspection of the various candidates offered for Divine self-disclosure. Gautama Buddha is proclaimed, for example in the *Lotus Sutra* among many others, as Lord of the universe, Saviour of the world and Teacher of the ultimate truth. But his Lordship is not an intimate union of will with the Divine will; for there is no personal God in his teaching. His salvation is salvation from the wheel of rebirth, and not the transformation of human individuality into a more glorious and deathless form. His ultimate truth, which includes the cessation of human personality and the radical imperfection of the world, which denies creation and hope for eternal life, is radically incompatible with the teaching of Jesus. Though Christians may confess Gautama as a great saint and teacher, he cannot be seen as a manifestation of the very God whose existence he denies. He has to be seen by theists as mistaken in many of his claims; so that he cannot at the same time be identified as a revelation of final truth.

Mohammed proclaims the judgment and mercy of God,

and he can be seen by Christians as a great prophet. But his claim to have a final revelation, in the Koran, infallibly dictated by the Archangel Gabriel, is uncompromising and is again incompatible with many features of the revelation perceived in the person of Christ. One may see both Jesus and Mohammed as mistaken on many points; but one cannot see them both as having a correct insight into the nature of God. The personal God and Father of all, who suffers and dies for his creatures and incorporates them into his own Divine life through Christ, the Son of God, is not identical in all respects with the transcendent and all-determining God of the Koran, who is specifically said to have no Son (Koran 112, 1: "Allah is One, the Eternal God. He begot none"), and who is is utterly distinct from every creature.

Again, the avatars of India teach a rather different doctrine from Jesus. They have no particular interest in history or the future of earthly society, and teach an endless series of rebirths, without goal or purpose, unless one can achieve a non-attachment which ideally releases one from the earth for ever, never to return. While there may be many manifestations of an infinite God, it is not reasonable to suppose that they actually contradict one another on many points. Either all these traditions are substantially wrong; or one, and only one, of them is substantially correct in its view of the character of God and his purpose for the world.

It may sound more tolerant to say that all are substantially wrong. For then some truths can be seen in each tradition, as well as many falsehoods, particularly in the claims they each make to finality and truth. But the appearance of tolerance is an illusion. It is not intellectually tolerant to say that I can see much truth in your tradition, although, of course, its most important claims are false. What I am in fact claiming is that my own view is substantially true, and ought to replace all previous religious traditions. My view is the most adequately true; yours contains many helpful insights, and may even have helped me to form parts of my view; but it must finally be rejected as containing substantial falsehood. In other words, I am in exactly the same position, *vis-à-vis* all religious traditions, as each of them is in regard to the others. Each may find many helpful insights in the others, which may help it to form a more adequate view. But each must logically claim to have the most adequate approach to truth. It may sound arrogant to say that a particular view, which I happen to hold, is more adequate than any other; but it is an inescapable claim for anyone who reflects on what truth-claims logically require.

The only real question at issue, therefore, is whether any of the existing religious traditions is defensible in some form, as giving an adequate, if not finally complete, view of God and his purposes; or whether one needs to devise a new faith for a new age. There is no way of answering that question except by honest and diligent enquiry and argument, using the best moral, intellectual and affective criteria one has. It is clearly in the theistic traditions that one finds claims to discern Divine action in the world. The more specific claim that such actions disclose a God of love, who wills to unite human persons to himself, narrows the field of alleged revelation even further. It will not be surprising if many traditions contain such signs; indeed, it is more surprising to find that many (like Buddhism) do not, at least in many of their forms. But if we are looking for signs of the action of one loving and morally demanding creator with a purpose for creation, there is no doubt that it is the Biblical tradition to which we shall turn. It might then seem rather odd to say that this tradition is no more adequate than others, which lack such a perception of the Divine action. The distinctiveness of the Biblical tradition of revelation must, it seems, be accepted (or rejected) as a fundamental datum of faith.

Indian theistic traditions do speak of a God of love and grace; the picture of Krishna with the cowgirls expresses a belief in a god who can be approached with affection and love. But the central determining image of God in such traditions remains that of God as the unchanging Self of all, who makes no moral demands and offers no promises of earthly transformation. This is an important insight into the omnipresence of God; but it does tend to downgrade the elements of Divine creativity, purpose and interpersonal relationship which are characteristic of the Hebrew tradition. It means that what actually happens in history is of only secondary importance for the believer. Real relationship with God is within the secret cave of the heart, not in the events of publicly observable social life. Of course, metaphor and analogy are always present in such pictures of God; and traditions can contain many diverse strands within themselves. They should not be opposed to one another as monolithic blocks of accepted and clearly conflicting doctrines. We should be glad to acknowledge that God reveals himself in Indian traditions as well as in the Hebrew. Yet it is undeniable that his self-disclosure in the Bible is quite distinctive. In the Biblical revelation, things are said about the character and purpose of God which are not found in the same form anywhere else.

Why should this be? Why did God not reveal himself in much the same way everywhere? One reason is that, since God's self-disclosure is co-operative and persuasive, what he reveals will depend partly on what human minds are capable of understanding. God does not blast through our minds with a clear truth out of the blue. He gently shapes and guides our thoughts, in so far as we are open to his influence; but our human interests and pre-occupations can determine the sorts of disclosures of God we are able to have. To use a rather crude example, if I am a timid aesthete, I may tend to discern God in the beauty of nature, in order and harmony and as a principle of inspiring creativeness. If I am a warrior, I may see him as a principle of heroic courage and resilience. If I am poor and oppressed and a temperamental pessimist, I am likely to discover the Divine either in extreme negation of the world or perhaps, if I am less pessimistic, in calls to liberation. A cynic may say that, in any case, I am simply projecting a God in my own image, or to objectify my own desires. A theist cannot accept that. But the theist can accept that what we discern of God's actions, in a very complex and confusing world, will largely depend upon our personal orientation and temperament. Not all discernments of God will be equally valid, by any means. But one reason for the variety of Divine discernments will be found in the differing temperaments of those who seek to relate to God.

Another important factor is that human beings are not all ready and willing to love God and do his will. Many people, and perhaps most to some extent, reject God in favour of egoism and self-concern. These factors will distort and impede discernments of Divine action. God may guide us to a sense of his almighty power. But our distorted vision may see that as a terrifying, even oppressive, force before which we can only tremble in fear, or which we may use to tyrannize others. God may lead us to believe in his compassion and love. But we may one-sidedly see that as an indulgent indifferentism which ceases to make real moral demands upon us. The possibilities for human misunderstanding are endless. A look at the history of Christianity shows that even the teaching of a God of all-embracing love can be interpreted as compatible with burning heretics to death. In such a world, it will not be true that God is able to reveal himself equally clearly to everyone. Disclosures will centre around holy people, who may be to some extent free from the worst corrupting influences of their cultures.

But even holy people cannot be free of all influence of culture. Indeed, holiness itself needs to be supported (or suppressed) by the character of a culture, a view notably argued for by Alasdair MacIntyre (1985) which stresses the necessity of forming communities in which specific virtues can grow. So the history of a culture may make it able to support a certain view of holiness and encourage certain practices of holiness, which may develop very differently in other cultures. For instance, a powerful and imperialistic culture may make it difficult for the practice of the virtues of holiness and compassion to be valued and encouraged. So one might expect traditions of holiness to grow up in small communities which share in the poverty, suffering and injustice from which faith seeks liberation. Semitic traditions of prophetic holiness and inspiration in a tribal association of liberated slaves and desert nomads, surrounded by violent and aggressive powers, are significantly different from Indian traditions of the *sanyassin*, who renounces all worldly activities in his quest for the unchanging Self of all. Again, God will disclose himself differently to those who seek him, as their culture and history directs and shapes their distinctive practices of sanctity. Even though I have criticized Hick's "pluralist hypotheses" as incoherent, his masterly survey of the way in which culture and temperament affect one's discernment of the Divine is a fruitful extension of his general view of faith as a mode of experiencing-as

(Hick 1957). I do not see that one should, or can, shrink from the conclusion that some cultures, with their characteristic conceptual schemes, make possible a clearer discernment of the character of the Divine and of how humans should relate to it.

Not only do different cultures enable different ways of pursuing virtue, they also have different sets of interests; they tend to encourage and cultivate different sorts of skills. Thus philosophy reached its first period of greatness in southern Italy and in Athens. It is very difficult to say why this should be, but it may involve such factors as the existence of a leisured elite, the development over generations of an interest in physical forms and intellectual enquiry, or the development of democratic processes which led to a stress on argument and skill in oratory. Whatever the reasons, the philosophical tradition developed in one cultural milieu; and, once established, it became a central and accepted feature of Athenian culture.

Similarly, natural science developed in seventeenth-century western Europe, not everywhere at once. No doubt many factors came together to make it possible; among them, the reaction against Scholastic "word-chopping", the development of new technology of lens-making and weapons of war, and a background set of beliefs which enabled people like Isaac Newton to think of the world as a vast rational structure, designed by a mathematical God. Stanley Jaki, in a series of works, has argued for the centrality of Christian faith to the rise of modern science. While his conclusions are disputed, there is little doubt that a revolution in human understanding of the world developed in one particular culture, and from there spread throughout the world. For a whole set of converging reasons, one particular culture comes to have a central, well-favoured and encouraged tradition of interest in a particular form of human activity.

It happens to have been the ancient Hebrews who developed an interest in history, as the arena of the acts of their God; and in social morality, seen as commanded by a holy, all-powerful and gracious Will. Just as the laws of nature existed always and everywhere, but only Newton discovered them; so we may think that God is active everywhere and always, but only the prophets of Israel lived in a society which had

developed the conceptual resources and the interest to interpret history in terms of his action. As that tradition continued
over generations, so the Hebraic apprehension of God became
more reflective and subtle. The idea of a dynamically active,
personal and morally demanding God became their contribution to human knowledge of the world.

The Jew and the Christian will see this idea as developing
in response to the guiding pressure of Divine reality, as it
gradually and responsively discloses itself to the prophets and
empowers them to arrive at a deeper insight into the Divine
nature. The idea did not develop in the same way elsewhere,
because no other culture developed and encouraged quite that
set of interests. In India, for example, the god Varuna seems
to have expressed the idea of a moral high god. But an interest
in history, as opposed to an interest in story-telling and myth-
making, simply did not develop in that culture. Varuna
became less and less important, and was eventually eclipsed
by Indra, Vishnu and Siva, gods whose exploits belong to
the mythic-cosmic order, and who are not seen as importantly
active in historical events. The Indian tradition developed an
interest of its own, in meditation and ascetic practice; in the
cultivation of the forest-traditions of individual Enlightenment and disengagement from the world. What they saw of
God was governed by those interests. So the Indian notion
of God tends to be much more one of a changeless, inactive
pure Intelligence and Bliss than of an active personal God.

Here one reason for religious plurality becomes clear.
People will see what their cultural background and interests
enable them to see. First of all they will see things differently;
and in time they will begin to see different things. Different
religious traditions may embody different perceptions of God,
and they may often be complementary rather than just contradictory. This is difficult to say of Buddhism, it may seem,
which denies God altogether. But even there, one may find
a reason for the rejection of, or extreme disinterest in, God,
as a reaction against superstitious and reactionary practices
which were associated with the Brahmin sacrificial system.
There is a firm stress on personal holiness, on the overcoming
of greed and hatred, and a search for a bliss which, while
indescribable, is certainly not caused by any worldly objects.

The theist must see the rejection of God as mistaken; but may well acknowledge that Buddhist interest in meditation, stress on personal perfection and the rejection of ritual sacrifice carries a legitimate insight into the heart of religious faith. Large parts of the traditions may be complementary, and in this way the different traditions may need to meet if they are to progress towards a fullness of truth. But not all the claims of every tradition can be true.

So the fact that only the Hebrews came to see God as one personal and moral God, acting in history, does not mean that he only acted in the ancient Near East. But we must still ask, did he not act in a special way in regard to the Hebrew prophets? Was this not more than a difference of discernment? Was it not also a difference in the mode of God's action? It seems clear that it was, if the prophets were correct in their discernments. God elected Israel to be his own people, bound in covenant and set apart to keep his teaching and worship him. Again, we may see the way in which Divine initiative, human response, and Divine co-operation interweave. God may call many to respond to him in love; but only those can discern his call who have come to believe at least in the possibility of such a God, a personal God who can so call, through the events of history and personal experience. Perhaps many people, long ago, formed such a concept and did respond to God. But it was in the Hebrew culture that events so co-operated and reasons so converged that the whole people were able to build up a developing tradition of personal response to God's guidance, and to find in God the Liberator and Saviour who took them out of slavery to a special destiny. What is unique about ancient Jewish history is the long succession of great prophets who built on the tradition of the "God of Abraham, Isaac and Jacob", to develop a distinctive, lovingly remembered, history of personal relationship to the one holy creator of all things. As R.H. King points out, a fully personal God can only be known by his actions, and "if God is identified by what he does, it is important to keep alive the memory of his actions" (King 1974:47).

God did act in a special way in this tradition; judging, exhorting, revealing and promising to the prophets whom he called as they responded to him. The deepest reason for this particularity of the Divine action becomes apparent as that tradition develops – namely, that love is, by its nature, responsive to the particular. Divine love, as it is disclosed in the Bible, is the choice of the weak to confound the strong, the poor to confound the rich, and of sinners to carry out his purposes of love. It is not possible to love in general; to have a sort of universal undifferentiated benevolence which wills exactly the same thing to all, whatever their circumstances. I may in one sense will the same thing to all – that is, I may will their well-being and eternal happiness. But if that is to be more than an idle wish, what I must do to help bring that about will vary from one case to another. Each person's experiences must be taken and woven in a unique way into a pattern which will fulfil that particular set of experiences. So if God loves everyone truly, he will have to love each individual in a different and unique way.

God chooses for each individual a unique path to fulfilment. Thus he will act in different particular ways towards each individual. But God does not act towards individuals in isolation. Human wills interact with one another continually; what each does affects the others. So how God acts towards me will effect you, even if only indirectly. Since persons are called, not only to union with God, but to imitate him by loving one another, God will often act in one person, empowering that person to help others more effectively. In this way, God may form particular purposes which require some people to help others in special ways. Those people will have a special vocation or calling, to implement a special purpose of God. Just as one individual may have a vocation to help others in particular ways; so some communities may come to have a special calling in the developing purposes of God. It was such a special vocation that the prophets believed the people of Israel had been given, so that they would be a kingdom of priests, to serve and show God's glory to the world. Thus it is entirely reasonable to look for "the meaning of love in the history of a people who have been called into an intimate, personal relationship with God" (Williams 1968:22).

When God "chose" the children of Abraham, he called them to a special vocation, in working out his purpose for the world. The way in which the prophets responded to him, and in which they continued and extended the tradition of personal relationship with him, enabled him to continue acting in particular and distinctive ways, so that his universal love could be made known by means of a particular choice of a people to realize his purpose. Followers of Christ believe that this calling was brought to a particular fulfilment in the person of Jesus, whose human life was so open to God's calling and presence that his acts are wholly transparent to God. God acts in him to reconcile the world to himself, to be the glory of Israel and a light for all the world. Those who object to this particularity may be failing to take account of the way in which God reveals himself through a long preparation, in a particular culture, at a historically unique point in time. He may reveal himself in other ways at other times. But the life of Jesus is a quite distinctive form of Divine action, made possible only by its placing in a long tradition of the discernment of such action, which created the possibility of his life and vocation. Followers of Christ can thus reasonably (but always contestably) claim that at this unique and unrepeatable point in human history a normative picture of God is given.

If God is really a God of love, then he must act in the world in a loving way. If he acts in the world, then he must do so in particular ways, which will be different for different individuals. History is a concatenation of particularities; and so, if we ask why God acts as he does, much must be ascribed to the creative personal unpredictable choices God makes, taking the unique opportunities that the complex chains of historical causality throw up, which provide unrepeatable opportunities for distinctive sorts of action. If the Christian claim is not to be rejected as mistaken, we must therefore say that at this point in human history, God acted so perfectly in a human life that the will of Jesus and the will of God were wholly congruent. By Jesus' humiliation and exaltation, God showed at one point in history the character of his patient, suffering and ultimately triumphant love. Those who believe that God can act, cannot ignore this distinctive testimony to the character of God's action.

But the question may still be pressed: why does not God act at many times? And why cannot many wills be identical with God's? Can there not be many avatars or "incarnations"? The question still embodies a misunderstanding of the particularity of history, and the uniqueness of each historical event, in its context, within a continuing process of socially appropriated experience. God does act at many times and in many lives. But in each he acts in an appropriately different way. He acts co-operatively with human response and understanding; and his particular acts will be consonant with the sorts of historical opportunities which occur. In the Indian traditions, there is little concern with history; there is no sense of a pilgrim people called to establish a priestly community of their own. These elements are missing in Indian culture. Other elements are present, of course – the stress on the interior life and on ascetic practice; a sense of the immanence of the Divine and a unity with it which transcends action and desire. So a quite proper awareness of God develops which is unconcerned with historical action and seeks the changeless Self within the cave of the heart. We may suppose that God is active in encouraging such a tradition; but it is a tradition which is relatively unconcerned with the acts of God in history for human redemption.

Once one understands this, one can see that the concept of incarnation in Christianity, and the concept of avatar in Hinduism, are importantly different (cf. Parrinder 1983). In Christianity, it is the historical life and activity of a person, summing up a whole prophetic tradition and giving it a new direction, which is the perfect vehicle of the Divine activity. The classical Hindu avatars are not historical, in any important sense. They are symbols of Divine concern to release humans from ignorance. The historical avatars, like Ramakrishna, are great saints and teachers with a strong sense of unity with God and the claimed possession of many psychic powers. But they do not fit into or sum up any continuing prophetic tradition; they do not suffer and die for human sin; they do not rise from death to show the coming transfiguration of all flesh; and they do not inaugurate a new historical phenomenon (the church) which mediates their personal life to others. Their particular placing in history is not relevant to their mission, which is simply to proclaim an eternal truth. Jesus is not, like them, a great spiritual teacher who brings his followers to enlightenment. For his disciples, he is the liberating act of God, giving eternal life to those who live in union with him. The uniqueness of his person, which depends upon the uniqueness of his whole cultural and historical context, cannot be assimilated to a general type of "Divine manifestation", which may occur in any holy man or woman.

Thus we may say that many religions convey pictures of the Divine which form part of the rich spiritual treasury of humanity, and need to be incorporated into a wider vision of God still to be attained. Yet it is inescapably true that, either all religious traditions as we have them are false; or that one of them carries a more truthful, adequate conception of the one true God. It is not intolerant or absurd to claim that in the life, death and resurrection of Jesus of Nazareth, there exists a definitive embodiment of God's own activity for human redemption, which is the matrix for interpreting the Divine activity everywhere. Its very particularity is the mark of its authenticity, since all truly personal acts must be particular and embody particular purposes whose consequences may spread out to embrace the whole world. What those consequences may ultimately be, we cannot yet tell. But Christians believe that the cosmic Lord who is the eternal mediator between God and human lives will be one who has been truly discerned dying on a cross outside Jerusalem.

12

Divine Nature and Human Nature

Theists do not generally believe that they work out all their beliefs about God for themselves, by pure reflection. It would be very odd to think that there is a personal God, who is concerned that persons should achieve a vitally important goal; that this goal involves personal relationship with him; but who does nothing in particular to tell them what this goal is or to help them achieve it. We need to know the truth about the Divine nature; about what true human life is; and we need to find some appropriate way of establishing a personal relation to God. God might reveal these things in many ways; but it would seem to be deeply appropriate for such a God to disclose his personal character in a personal life, which would also show a perfectly fulfilled human life and would establish a way of relating to God through that person. "A genuine incarnation, revelatory of God's essence and his very self in an actual human life, goes beyond any other kind of divine self-manifestation" (Hebblethwaite 1988:125). For if the essential being of God is personal, it can be best manifested in the life of a person. This is the core of the idea of incarnation; and it is an appropriate mode of revelation for a personal God who wills personal relationship with rational creatures.

In putting it like this, it may sound as though I am arriving at the idea of incarnation *a priori*, saying that a personal God of love must become incarnate. That would be disingenuous; for of course I heard of the incarnation long before I developed this view of God. Indeed, it is probably true that I view God as a loving personal God only because I came to accept the incarnation in Jesus of Nazareth, which normatively showed God to be fully personal, redemptively loving and active through the Spirit to unite human nature to himself. What I am suggesting is not that one can deduce an incarnation from a loving God; but that there is a deep consonance between the idea of a loving God and of an incarnation. If an incarnation is reliably claimed to occur, that raises the probability that there is a loving God, who really acts in the world to unite human persons to himself. And when one sees that God is love, the idea of incarnation becomes, not an absurd contradiction, but a natural form of his self-revelation.

Religious traditions which do not believe in a personal God, like Buddhism, can have no concept of incarnation – though they can and often have developed the concept of a perfect human life which expresses the character of the Ultimately Real and which can become an object of reverence and imitation. Thus the Amida Buddha of the Pure Land school is an object of personal faith, and assures one of personal companionship with him in the Western Paradise if one calls upon his name (cf. the Lotus Sutra, ch.24). Most orthodox Buddhists would regard this as a skilful means to help devotees at a relatively primitive stage of development; but from the Christian viewpoint, one has here an example of the way in which God works even in non-theistic traditions, to provide a way to enter into his presence and loving compassion.

A fact more difficult for the Christian to explain is the existence of the semitic theistic traditions of Judaism and Islam which have encountered the idea of incarnation, yet find it deeply abhorrent. One reason for this is their desire to emphasize the utter unity of God, and his difference from all finite created things ("Allah is One, the Eternal God. He begot none, nor was He begotten. None is equal to Him", Koran 112). From that viewpoint, it seems to be idolatry to identify any finite thing with God, any creature with the Creator, much less a mere human being. It may also seem contradictory to identify a creature and the Creator of all; so that the idea of worshipping Jesus Christ seems both idolatrous and intellectually absurd.

Both Judaism and Islam find Divine revelation to be embodied in a body of living law – Torah and Sharia – of commands and guidance which lay down a right code of life for societies as well as for individuals. We can call them faiths of Divine Teaching, to which one should humbly submit. That Teaching is Divinely revealed; and it mediates the presence of God, the Law-giver. It is not just a legalistic set of rules; it is more like a set of guidelines laying down the ways in which one should relate to the incomprehensible Creator of all.

Yet, from the Christian perspective, there does remain something impersonal and external about a law-based faith. Might God not disclose himself in a truly personal life and place that personal presence within our hearts to unite us to him in an intimately loving way? I am not at all trying to "prove" that Judaism and Islam are inferior to Christianity. I merely wish to see why the idea of incarnation seems abhorrent to them, and what overcomes that sense of horror, for disciples of Christ. The horror is at the thought of identifying Creator and any creature. That horror may be overcome if one can see a way in which the Creator can be truly mediated in the finite. And it should be noted that there are tendencies towards a quasi-incarnational doctrine even in Islam, in the works of the Sufis. The statement of al-Hallaj, *"Ana l'haqq"* – "I am the Real" – for which he was admittedly put to death, may nevertheless be seen as an extreme form of that mystical strain in Islam for which the human person can become wholly transparent to God, the only finally real being. The thirteenth-century saint Jalal al-Din Rumi wrote, "No one will find his way to the Court of Magnificence until he is annihilated" (Chittick 1983:193). There is here at least a hint of the possibility that a finite person may be a vehicle of the infinite God. Of course an infinite reality can never be contained in any finite reality. It will always have some – indeed, an infinite number – of properties which any finite object lacks. So the sense in which a creature can be identical with the Creator cannot be the sense of complete quantitative identity of properties. It cannot be that strict Leibnizian sense that, if A is identical to B, then A and B possess all their properties in common. But that strict sense of identity is hardly ever used anyway; it does not even apply to the identity of persons who, while being the same person at birth and death, have very different actual properties at birth than they do at maturity and again at death.

One may suggest that idolatry is the sin of giving complete submission to what is of less than unlimited value. It implies the view that some finite object is, just as it is given, the sum totality of all that God is. But if one stresses fully the infinity of the Divine nature, it seems that there may be no way in which we can come to be acquainted with it at all. One might be tempted to say that we can be acquainted with part of the Infinite. Yet, even if the classical doctrine of Divine simplicity stands in need of qualification, it represents the insight that the Infinite cannot be divided into parts. What possible relation can there be, then, between finite and infinite? This is not just a problem for Christian theology, but for any adequate form of theism. What needs to be said is that some finite reality can mediate the infinite; can come to stand for it or to stand in its place or to represent what it is, at least in relation to us. Now one might say that what mediates God to us need not be identical with God. It could be a messenger, an angel or a message. A message may tell us the mind or will of God. God could speak directly to us, through prophets whom he raises up. The semitic traditions all believe that he does so. Then words mediate the reality of God. The words are not identical with God; yet they convey to us his thoughts. If they do so adequately, then they convey a meaning which acquaints us, however indirectly, with the mind of God. We might not worship the words. But we might worship the God who speaks them, and worship him *as* the speaker of these words, as the one whom these words express.

It is no accident, then, that Jesus is spoken of in the Gospel of John as the word or wisdom of God (John 1:14). We might not worship the flesh and blood of Jesus; but we might worship God as the Father of Jesus, as the one who speaks his word to us in the life of Jesus, the one whom Jesus expresses, in the course of his life, as well as in his explicit teachings. Yet the relation of Jesus to the Father is closer than that of words to their speaker; and it is precisely in this greater intimacy that the Christian would see the glory and uniqueness of the doctrine of incarnation. Words are clearly distinct from their utterer. They can be separated, recorded and repeated, in the absence of the one who first uttered them. Can the human person of Jesus be separated from God, and exist in his absence? His words can; but Christians believe that his person is inseparably united to God, from first to last. Here is a form of mediation which makes a human person the inseparable vehicle of the presence and action of God. It is more like the way in which my tears express my sorrow than it is like the way in which these written words convey my thoughts. The sorrow is embodied in my physical gestures; whereas the words are in the end conventional tools which I use well or badly. I do not decide to show my sorrow by weeping. My weeping *is* my sorrow, though it does not exhaust the reality of it, and it would be wrong to say that my sorrow is nothing but my weeping, as some behaviourists do.

Weeping is the form my sorrow takes, in the social context of human life. Could the human life of Jesus be the form the love of God takes, in the historical context of human life? We could then say that Jesus does not only tell us about God's love or even act out a living parable for the distinctly existing love of God. Rather, what he enacts is the very love of God itself, as embodied in this human world and for us human beings. As God is truly personal, so he can manifest his true being in a personal life, under the forms of space and time. What we see in the life of the historical Jesus is not the totality of Divine love; the infinite love of God is not exhausted by one short human life. But a human life could be an embodiment, an enfleshing, of the love of God. That is the possibility incarnation presents. If it is a possibility, then it would not be wrong to worship Jesus as God in finite form. It would not be incoherent to say that a finite person could be identical with the infinite Creator, even though that person would not share all its properties with God. This would be a form of possible Divine self-disclosure which would be more intimate and adequate than any other we can conceive.

God's love might, then, be embodied in the life of a human person. We must at once be careful to add that "embodiment" is itself an inadequate concept, since it suggests that only a human body is filled with the mind of God. Whereas it must be a complete human person, body and soul, that is the form of Divine love. For that unique relation of identity, only the term "incarnation" will suffice. Since we cannot, as humans, know the essential nature of God, we can have no idea of what it is like to be God. Consequently, it is necessarily beyond human comprehension what it is like for God to be incarnate, to take true human form. We can speak only in partial images. Yet we can see that incarnation is not a contradictory idea; and that it is well fitted to express the fullest possible form of Divine self-revelation in the finite world.

But are human persons not essentially distinct from God, as autonomous centres of will and moral striving? Is incarnation really a possibility, if every properly human will is free to accept or reject God's love? This is perhaps the central philosophical problem with the idea of incarnation. The classical doctrine of incarnation holds that the human will of Jesus was necessarily and fully subordinate to the will of God (thus the Sixth Ecumenical Council at Constantinople in 681: *"Humanum voluntatem ... subjectam divinae eius atque omnipotenti voluntati"* Denzinger 1960:556). If Jesus is the Divine love itself, it hardly makes sense to say that he might have chosen to reject Divine love. Was his human will, then, devoid of real choice? The puzzle arises from thinking of Jesus as a distinct human person, who is capable of choosing to obey or to disobey God, who decides to trust God and who thenceforward is wholly faithful to God. This is precisely what the idea of incarnation denies; God incarnate cannot ever be a distinct and separate human person. Jesus must have been, from the first, inseparably and necessarily united to the Divine love and will, as its true and adequate enfleshment. The precise form this "unity" takes is what is beyond our comprehension. The resolution of the puzzle lies in stressing the uniqueness of Jesus, as not being a *distinct* human person, but as being a human person nonetheless, body and soul, inseparably united to God in an utterly distinctive way. If a human soul can be united to God, then it will be incapable of falling from God. It seems a coherent thought that a human soul could be so united from the first moment of its existence.

But could Jesus ever really have been tempted, if he could never fall from God? If so, is he really like us at all? We might suggest that Jesus could be tempted (his temptations are recorded in the synoptic gospels), in that he could know what it feels like to have human desires, even though these desires could never overpower the strength of Divine love in him. He could never have been free, in the sense of being peccable, of being able to reject God, though he could experience the desires and inclinations which lead human persons to do so. This is no defect in Jesus, any more than it is a defect in me that I could never bring myself to murder anyone, though I can understand what leads people to it. It follows that it is not essential to human nature that it should be free to reject God in fact. Hebblethwaite remarks, "It is sheer romanticism to suppose that 'peccability' is of the essence of human nature" (Hebblethwaite 1987:72). After all, we hope that in heaven we shall be no longer free to reject God, though we shall be essentially human. Jesus is at least as unlike us as the perfected saints are. Unlike them, he did not have to become perfected through grace and through contingent choice, but was indissolubly united to God from the first. This makes him unique in an important sense; nevertheless, he possesses all that is essential to human nature.

This, however, raises a second problem. Why could God not have united all human souls to himself, and so have prevented any evil from arising in the first place? The reason Christian theists usually give is that a fully interpersonal relationship of love between distinct beings is only possible where created beings can reject love and choose self. It may not be an essential defining characteristic of human nature as such that a human will should be able to reject Divine love. But it may be essential to *independent* souls that they should be so able. This entails making a distinction between human souls, as such, and independent human souls. One could have properly human souls which are not independent of God, which have an intellect and a will, but which do not have the capacity to choose in opposition to the Divine will (though they may still be creative, in forming options left open by the Divine will). Such souls would be parts of God, in the sense that one might properly call their acts the acts of God, in the form of finite wills; they would never commit evil, and their knowledge, while it would be subject to the limitations of their senses and intellects, would not be subject to culpable ignorance or misleading passion.

The sort of love that is possible between distinct souls and God is different from the sort of love that will exist between souls which are parts of God and the Divine being which is their inmost reality. Each distinct soul loves God as another. Jesus loves God as his true self. This would make the relationship between Jesus and God quite unique; not a relationship of two distinct beings, one human and one Divine, but a relationship of a finite human will to an infinite Divine will with which it is essentially one. That is precisely what the classical doctrine of Incarnation asserts. It means that Jesus may possess a human nature (a finite embodied intellect and will) without being a distinct human being, capable of loving or rejecting God (the Council of Chalcedon of AD 451, described Christ as "one and the same" person in two natures, Divine and human, Denzinger 1960).

Why, then, should not all humans have been parts of God? Precisely because they would not then be distinct beings, capable of determining their own existences to good or evil. It was God's will that there should be such distinct souls. If Jesus is God incarnate, he clearly lacks the property of "being a distinct being, capable of determining his existence to good or evil". Is this an essential property of being human, without which one could not be truly a member of the class of human beings? If so, the classical idea of incarnation is incoherent. Compare the case of humans having animal bodies. Clearly, humans are animals; they possess animal natures. But those natures are transformed by being possessed by rational persons. It would be misleading to say, "I, Fred, am an animal", though in one way it would be true; that is, I belong to an animal species. I am an animal and more; and the more affects my animal nature. I am not an animal just like all others; but I may possess many properly animal attributes. So the eternal Son of God may possess a human nature, which will be transformed by being possessed by God. It would be misleading to say, "Jesus is a human being", though in one way it is true. He is human and more, possessing many human attributes, but also possessing all Divine attributes. One could make it definitive of being an animal that it does not possess a rational soul. Then humans would not be animals. So one could make it definitive of being a human being that one is distinct from God and peccable, able to sin. Then Jesus would not be a human being. Yet he may possess importantly human properties – perhaps all those essential properties which are not entailed by possessing the properties of distinctness from God and peccability. It does not seem incoherent to suppose that there could be someone who was impeccable and one with God, and yet possessed a finite rational soul and will, an embodied intelligence and subject of action and awareness. It is in this sense that the claim that God is incarnate in Jesus is the claim that he shares our nature; but he is not, and could never be, a distinct and separated soul.

Thomas Morris has explored this possibility in *The Logic of God Incarnate* (1986). He distinguishes between being "merely human" (i.e. no more than human) and being "fully human" (being properly human, but perhaps being more as well), in rather the way that I have distinguished between being an animal (being "merely animal") and being a rational animal (possessing animal properties but being a rational person). He then suggests that Jesus had all the properties essential to human nature, but that he was not merely human, since he possessed Divine properties as well. "Such properties as that of possibly coming into existence, coming to be at some time, being a contingent creation, and being such as to possibly cease to exist are, although common human properties, not essential to being human. They, or some of them, may be essential to being merely human" (ibid.:67). We are merely human; quite properly human but no more than that. Our human nature is possessed by peccable and distinct subjects of intellect and will, largely ignorant of the nature and presence of God. But a fully human nature, with all its essential properties – basically, those of being an embodied subject of knowledge and agency – is capable of manifesting the Divine nature, without any loss of humanity, but with an access of Divine knowledge and purpose, in so far as that can be manifested in a properly human nature. What is being claimed is that an embodied subject of consciousness, a human soul and body, can properly manifest the Divine nature in a particular finite form. The human does not intrinsically exclude the Divine, but is, as it were, intrinsically fitted to express the Divine. If it does so, of course, it is not "merely human", though it is certainly "fully human". And it is not distinct from God, as we are. There thus seems no logical

219

H

barrier to God becoming incarnate in a fully human form; but such an incarnate being, while being fully human, would also, and necessarily, be quite distinct in very important ways from any merely human being. The trend in much modern theology is to make Jesus merely human, on the ground that only so can he be sufficiently like us. If what I have said is correct, this is a fundamental error; since, while Jesus must be fully human, he must be very unlike us indeed if he alone is to be the Saviour of the world.

Since human nature is intrinsically fitted to express the Divine, God could unite many human souls to himself, in principle. Brian Hebblethwaite does not seem to be correct in saying that "Only one man can actually *be* God to us, if God himself is one" (Hebblethwaite 1987:50). For God is also infinite, and could surely express that infinity in many different limited forms. Logically speaking, it seems that there could be many incarnations of the Divine in the human world – and Indian Vishnaism comes close to asserting that there have been, in its doctrine of the avatars of Vishnu. However, most of these "incarnations" are obviously mythical, and one of them – Gautama Buddha – virtually never spoke of God, and certainly never spoke of himself as an incarnation of a personal God. It therefore transpires that there are very few realistic claimants to incarnation in history. One must consider further that each human person is unique in temperament and social context; one cannot consider the possibility of incarnation without looking at the whole cultural context in which it might occur. When one does so, the Jewish context in which Jesus was born is seen to be historically unique and unrepeatable. Jesus' life is shaped by that whole prophetic tradition, as its claimed fulfilment and renewal. The idea of multiple incarnations is superficially attractive, because it seems much less restrictive than having only one. But when one examines carefully the religious traditions of the world, the supposition of multiple incarnations becomes quite unrealistic. It turns out that claimed incarnations are so rare – Vishnaism generally supposes that only one avatar exists in many thousands of years – that they are in practice as restrictive as the Christian one; that most of them deny that the others are incarnations at all; and that the lives and teachings of the "avatars" are not in substantial agreement with each other or with the whole Jewish tradition which shaped the life of Jesus. Perhaps one incarnation is in order after all, as long as it can be plausibly seen as the focal point of a general historical process which permeates the whole world and aims at a future universal goal for the whole human species.

One way to bring out the plausibility of one unique incarnation of God in history is to recall the centrality of the idea of atonement for the Christian notion of incarnation. God did not in the Christian view assume human nature only to teach us the truth, or to show us what he is truly like. The avatars of Vishnaism come to teach the way to overcome self and attain unity with the Absolute Self of all. They are primarily *educators*, in a spiritual sense. They bring us to knowledge of the spiritual basis of all reality, and the profound unity of the self and Absolute Reality (Brahman). Even at this level, it must be emphasized that this teaching is not identical with the Christian view of the human soul and its destiny. Christ comes to bring each uniquely individual soul to its fullest personal fulfilment. The liberated soul will not cast aside its personality, its particular agency and unique experience. Though there are teachings similar to this, even in Vedanta, the avataric tradition stresses to a much greater degree the necessity to leave behind individual personality (*jiva*) and enter into a state of pure intelligence and bliss (cf. Sankara 1962:37). Jesus' teachings are not identical with those of the avatars.

There is, however, a much more profound distinction. Jesus is not primarily an educator, who comes to bring salvation through knowledge, achieved in meditation and stilling of the individual mind. He is primarily a saviour, redeeming humanity from the rule of sin by his sacrificial life and death. It is that redemptive act which occurs only once in the history of the world; for when redemption is won, it does not need to be won again and again. Christ died "once, for all"; and to think that such a sacrifice could or should be repeated detracts from the power and efficacy of this act of God. This idea is alien to the Indian tradition of spirituality. It has no place in the Upanishads – though ironically the notion of sacrifice is central to Brahmin religion itself. The idea of God taking human personhood so that he can redeem humanity by his own sacrifice is distinctive to the Christian doctrine of incarnation. It distinguishes it from all avataric doctrines, and makes it quite impossible to view Jesus as one among many avatars – who are often taken to include tortoises, dwarves, the Buddha, Krishna the warrior-king and one of hundreds of present-day claimants to omnipotence and omniscience.

What is this unique Divine act of redemption? How can we understand its necessity and its nature? Let me say at once that I disclaim any pretence of being able to propound an adequate theory of the atonement – a doctrine upon which the Christian Church has made few dogmatic utterances, even though it is the foundation of its life. Of the importance of the belief I am in no doubt; but all I can do is to make some suggestions about why it may seem to have such importance, and to be such a distinctive religious doctrine. To understand it, perhaps one first has to be convinced of the radical nature of evil; the way in which it cuts people off from God and renders them unable to return to him by their own strength. There is no returning to God by any set of human practices or acts. It is not surprising, if this is so, that asceticism and meditation can bring one rather to a state of emptiness or complete quiescence than to the presence of a living personal God. God may be absent to the most determined spiritual search; for he cannot be found by human efforts to eliminate the grip of sin. The life of Jesus, which ends in his judicial murder, shows us that all of us kill God in our hearts. Without his gracious love transforming us, there is nothing we can do to take that murderous intent from our deepest selves.

What can even God do in such a situation of despair? He cannot simply forgive us, while we are unable to turn from our sin – that would be to say that it does not really matter; that somehow we can love God while at the same time continuing to hate him! He cannot compel us to love him, without depriving us of the very freedom that has cost so much to give us. He cannot leave us in sin; for then his purpose in creation would be wholly frustrated. What the New Testament suggests is that God, taking a human form, gives his life as a ransom for our sin, as a price paid to buy us back from sin; even that he "becomes sin" for us (2 Corinthians 5:21).

God does not leave us alone; he does not compel us to love him; he does not forgive us, just as we are. He takes upon himself the consequence of our sin, the agony and despair of sin. In human nature, he reforms the human heart in the image of love, so that by our becoming sharers in his uncorrupted life, he might begin, in each one of us, to change our nature from within.

How can his life pay a price that releases us from sin? The price is that he enters into human suffering; he even shares in the experience of desolation and death; he penetrates to the heart of the abyss of sin. This is a price that none but God could pay. To enter into the heart of the horror that is evil, but to remain unflawed by it, to go through it and leave it powerless, is something we could not have the courage, even if we had the will, to do. He pays the price of our sin, taking its worst consequences upon himself in an ultimate sharing in spiritual suffering that none of us can begin to imagine.

But how can that price ransom and release us from the power of sin? Precisely because he, and he alone, remains untouched by evil. He takes human nature through the valley of the shadow of death, and in him alone that nature is not corrupted. He is the one victor over evil; he has experienced the worst it can do, and he has overcome it. But we remain in evil, haters of God and helpless to change ourselves. How can this victorious Christ help us? He helps us because he has remade human nature in an uncorrupted form. We are all sharers in corrupted human nature; that is what makes it impossible for us truly to turn to God. At every turn, our corruption perverts our deepest intentions. Now, however, God has made it possible for us to become sharers, by adoption, in a renewed human nature, the nature established uniquely in Christ ("Just as through the disobedience of one man the many were made sinners, so also through the obedience of the one man the many will be made righteous" Romans 5:19). I may hate God in my heart; but is it possible that God could place a new heart within me? Could he renew the nature that I have? Could my heart of stone be replaced by a spirit-filled heart of love? Could he place his own love within me, and rebuild my whole nature from its foundations?

This, the Gospel proclaims, is how Christ's victory redeems us – by placing the new victorious humanity established by Jesus within our hearts, by making us sharers in the perfected nature of Christ.

Does this talk of sharing in a renewed human nature make sense? It may seem to be primitively Platonic, and incomprehensible to our nominalist age. It is not absurd, however, to speak of sharing in human nature. As individuals, we belong to a species to which it is proper to think, to choose and to be embodied in a particular animal form. To state what our nature is, is to state the properties which are either essential or natural and proper to members of such a species. To "share in a nature" is to possess the properties essential to that nature. According to Christian tradition, the human nature in which we share is "fallen". This means that, while it is not essential to full human nature to be fallen, or even to be distinct from the Divine nature or to be peccable (to be capable of falling), there is at least one essential property of "merely human-ness", the property of being a distinct and peccable moral agent, which is defective in every distinct individual of the species. Every human moral agent inclines to the lesser and more selfish good, and is attracted to power, desire and hatred to such an extent that it is "naturally" unable to escape their force. It is not essential to the will as such to be so inclined to evil. In heaven, the saints will be free but will have mastered such inclinations. Christ was free, but because of his indivisible unity with God, he had total mastery of his inclinations from the beginning and at all times. The Christian view is that every distinct and merely human person is born with a defective moral will (apart, perhaps, from Mary, mother of God, who was, according to the doctrine of the Immaculate Conception, miraculously preserved from such defect by the grace of Christ). This is that solidarity in sin of which the New Testament speaks so forcefully ("There is no one righteous, not even one", Romans 3:10). It is a defect of human nature, and not proper to it. Yet every distinct and merely human individual is born with that defect.

Why should this be? The Bible seems to regard it as a defect inherent in the human race, passed on from parents to children inevitably, rather in the way that we pass on physical characteristics. It is, of course, not a physical but a spiritual characteristic. Yet the estrangement of the human world from God may lead to the created soul being deprived of that unitive power which orients it properly to God as its source and sustenance. When the interior link which binds the soul to God is broken, then the will is radically disorientated, and inclines to finite goods. Each human soul should be united to God by a natural knowledge and love. But, because of human sin, knowledge of God is remote and one can hardly love what one barely and imperfectly knows. Lacking this knowledge and love, which should have been naturally infused into each soul as its proper fulfilment and perfection, transfiguring the merely human into the fully human, souls incline to the evil which surround them, without sufficient power to withstand the attractions of temptation.

It is into such a corporately sinful or estranged human world that Christ is born, having a nature bearing every property essential to full humanity, but preserved from this defect of the will by his unique unity with, his full knowledge and love of, the Father. He is like us in nature; but unlike us in being without defect. How can that nature replace our own? What is required is that the natural but improper inclination of our wills to finite goods should be corrected by a re-orientation of the will to the infinite good of God. As an individual, I possess a defective moral will. Jesus possessed a will fully united to God in knowledge and love. No human person can replace my will with theirs; nor would it be right to do so, as it would infringe my autonomy and distinctness as an individual. But could I, through my own assenting choice, receive an access of knowledge and love which would bind my will to God, despite its continual turning away? Could God place his own love within us, as the vehicles of his life? The gospel is that this is precisely what Christ offers, in the gift of the spirit, bringing me to a new spiritual birth. To be made fully human is, as the Cappadocian Fathers saw, to have human nature enriched and transformed by its inner relation to the divine, "to have the divine as the determining element of our being. It is for God to be, in an active and not merely in a passive manner, the source, the inmost centre of our reality" (Sherrard 1987:119). If I die to self, to the old defective merely human nature, Christ, who establishes full humanity in himself, can progressively establish his life in me, until at last I "become mature, attaining to the whole measure of the fullness of Christ" (Ephesians 4:13).

So the Christian gospel is that human persons are reborn by the spirit of God; the Christian life consists in letting this reborn nature come to fruition in human nature: "Christ in you, the hope of glory" (Colossians 1:27). That happens within the community of the Church, by means of which the new nature, established in Christ, is spread throughout the whole of humanity. This is why it is not ridiculously exclusive to say that Jesus is the only means to relate all creatures truly to God ("There is no other name under heaven given to men by which we must be saved" Acts 4:12). Though Jesus was only one human being, living at a particular place and time, the Church, which is his body, the continuation of his incarnation in the world, spreads throughout the world to bring his risen life to all. The incarnation is not simply over and done with; it is represented at every moment all over the planet through the sacraments of the Church. One may say that God could just have given us a new nature anyway, without the bother of incarnation and sacrifice. But that would fail to take note of just what this new nature is. The nature that we receive from God is a human nature that has triumphed over evil, that has entered into its heart and remained uncorrupted. It is not that God simply creates a new nature in us when we ask; but that he takes human nature to himself, shows what it truly is and what its destiny is and shows that it cannot be conquered by sin and death. That is the nature he places within us, making us sons by adoption, taken into the life of the Son.

But how, it may be asked, can the one individual perfect will of Christ be placed within innumerable other individuals? It is not the will of another individual, Jesus, that is placed within me. What is given to me is a new capacity for knowing and loving God, a new orientation of life to be nurtured within the community of the Church. This is a capacity that was realized in the life of Jesus, and that realization was lived out in one individual person. God recreates it within me as I place complete trust in Jesus Christ. God acts in us, though incompletely because of our defective response, as he acted fully in Jesus. I cannot have a capacity to know and love God, or at least I cannot begin to realize such a capacity at all, unless God makes himself known to me and gives me a power of loving truly. It is in the life of Jesus that he shows what he is; it is in the death of Jesus that the power of love is fully established in a human life. That power is the power of the Word of God; it is the Word, who was manifested in Christ, who also works in us. It is the Word who was in Christ, who *was* and is Christ, who creates the new capacity for supernatural life in us. The Word can work outside the Church, of course. But he is declared to be what he is in Christ; so if I am to know and recognize the Word which creates a new capacity for eternal life in me, I only do so when I recognize him in the person of Christ, as the one who has suffered and died that I might be freed from sin for eternal life.

The capacity to know and love God must be freely appropriated by human wills. So they must first know what sort of capacity it is; how it might be properly exercised; and they need a supportive community in which it can grow and flourish. For all these reasons, God's re-creation of human nature is accomplished by a life of perfect love, which shares in human suffering and takes on itself the cost of human sin, and which founds a new community, moved and enlivened by the Spirit of love. Thereafter, my truest willing lies in becoming more and more fully the vehicle of the action of the Spirit in me. The new capacity of the perfected will is not only modelled upon, but also moulded by, the Word of God whose nature is normatively expressed in Jesus Christ. Incarnation, sacrifice and redemption go together, as a complex of ideas which give the person of Jesus a unique and unrepeatable place in the history of this planet. He is the one in whose life God acts to re-unite an estranged world to himself, as the focal point of an historical process which needed long preparation and which needs to be worked out to completion over many generations.

This is the Christian picture of how God acts in the world. So if we are prepared to believe in a God who acts, this is a testimony to his acts which needs to be very carefully considered. At first, it may seem that God will act in the same manner everywhere, so that we may find similar traces of his action in all societies and at all times. But the Bible speaks of a God who prepares for and executes a unique and distinctive action to reveal his nature definitively in a human life and redeem estranged humanity by a sacrificial death. Of course, God will be active in some way at all times and places; but, if the New Testament witness is true, there is only one normative revelation of his nature which is at the same time the definitive matrix for the realization of his redemptive purpose.

The "scandal of particularity" is only a scandal if one thinks that all things should show God's nature and realize his purpose equally well. But that thought is itself absurd, given the extent and depth of human evil. Perhaps one thinks it more charitable to see all faiths as converging to a future agreed goal. There is much truth in this view, in so far as human understanding of faith surely stands in need of continual development; but what will they converge on? There is a danger that faiths will find themselves coming to agreement only as they lose their own most distinctive emphases, and accept a highest common factor view. But there is a deeper objection to this proposal of universal convergence. Since it must be thought of as a convergence towards a truth as yet unattained, it follows that nearly all present religious views are false. However, since one must have some idea of what one is converging towards, one in fact selects one's own preferred views as nearest the truth. This view is not tolerant at all, theoretically speaking, since it denies almost all actual religious traditions, and selects as "most nearly true" a particular set of beliefs which are as disputable and unsettlable as those of the rejected traditions. Is it more scandalous to think that God will leave all religions to grope slowly towards him, or to think that he will reveal his purpose in a definitive way? One does not have to suppose that one historic faith contains the *whole* truth about God. But, if God acts to reveal at all, it is reasonable to think that at least one tradition will contain a normative truth about God; and, where traditions conflict, only one of the conflicting traditions can do so. This may sound like intolerance; but two things should be remembered. First, one can emphasize our very limited understanding of the normative tradition we may have. And second, to hold to the exclusive truth of one belief, against those which conflict with it, by no means entails that one must eliminate the others by force. In fact, the danger of such a course might lead one to think that the normative tradition is likely to be one which prohibits the use of force or repression against others. Jesus quite un-ambiguously does that, in commanding his followers to pray for their enemies and to love them; the tragedy is that his followers have often denied his teachings. But he can hardly be blamed for that. The fact is that all truths are particular; they all exclude innumerable possibilities of error; and one cannot avoid this situation by calling one's preferred options "nearly true" instead of just "true"! In any case, the wise believer will fully understand that his basic beliefs may be unequivocally true, while yet his particular interpretation and understanding of them may be very far from adequate. Parti-cularity is no scandal, but a condition of historical truth. If God acts at all, then he must act in history; and presumably accounts of his action will be both true and particular.

Those who object to a historical revelation are discounting the possibility that God might really act. They probably think that knowledge of God should be available to all people at all times, by direct personal intuition. Nobody will be in a privileged position with regard to Divine truth; it will be equally available to all; and everyone can be their own judge of it. All these assertions – that God is directly accessible by personal experience; that he is equally accessible to every-one; and that everyone can be the judge of Divine truth – are highly dubious; indeed, they all seem to me to be clearly false. Inward personal experience does not lead everyone to God. It can lead to atheistic Buddhism, to Advaitic monism, or to demonic possession. How people interpret their experi-ence depends very much on the concepts available to them in their culture, and on the sort of being they think God might be. From the Christian viewpoint, of course, God's revelation is in the person of Jesus, not in any set of personal experiences; that is, it consists in bringing about sets of straightforwardly observable physical events by direct Divine intention.

Nor is there any reason why God should be directly accessible to everyone, whatever their temperament, ability, practice or cultural background. Knowledge of truths in almost any area depends on appropriate training, circumstance and ability. So in religion, one would expect that there will be people of a certain temperament, who have trained themselves in prayer and who grow up in a tradition of worship, who will be in a better position to know God. The Biblical prophets are, for reasons like this (but also because God calls them) in a privileged position with regard to knowledge of God's purposes. It is reasonable that they should be taken as authorities in such matters.

It follows that it is silly to encourage everyone to be the judge of religious truth, to believe what appeals to them and reject what does not. Naturally, one can decide whether to accept a tradition or not; but once one believes that God has really revealed something, one is bound to believe it on simple authority. A belief that there are genuine Divine acts leads one naturally to seek authoritative testimony to acts revelatory of the Divine purpose. This is not to say that a Divine revelation gives a way of resolving disagreements. It does not; since people will unfortunately continue to disagree about what precisely is revealed. Yet the claim that God has revealed something in a set of historical events is one that challenges any belief that everyone is in an equally good position to work Divine truth out for themselves. It challenges us to believe certain truths on the ground that they are revealed in a Divinely inspired historical process. While one must carefully sift all claims to have discerned such a process, it seems irrational to reject all such testimony and to continue to believe in real Divine action in the world.

13

The Witness of the Past

Reasons have been suggested why it should be extremely hard, if not impossible, to identify particular Divine actions in the world. Yet if the notion is to have any purchase on reality, one must know what sort of actions they are, and where they are likely to be found. One must know the nature of Divine action; and I have suggested that if God is a personal agent who wishes human creatures to enter into conscious relation to him, he will disclose this nature in an appropriate way. Further, this is not simply an *a priori* speculation, since the whole idea of God as a personal agent arose primarily in the Biblical tradition. That tradition claims that God reveals his nature and purpose in a series of historical acts, interpreted by the prophets as acts of moral calling, judgment and liberation. Christianity finds a culmination of such a historical process of revelation in the life of Jesus. Here one can find testimony to a historical life which declares in a normative manner the character and final purpose of God. For Christians, the life of Jesus is the normative act of God, both because of its placing in a history of developing revelation and because of its intrinsic character as a unique raising of human nature to unity with the Divine.

The notion of such a unique unity of Divine and human nature in Jesus is the doctrine of the Incarnation. I have defended that doctrine as a coherent and intelligible one. But it may be objected that such a doctrine is not in fact to be found in the New Testament, that it is a fourth-century Greek invention quite foreign to the writers of the gospels. Even the Regius Professor of Divinity at the University of Oxford has held that the whole thing was a mistake: "Christology arose because it was not unnaturally, *yet none the less mistakenly*, felt that the full divine character of redemption in Christ could only be maintained if the person and act of the redeemer

were understood to be divine in a direct and special sense"
(Wiles 1976:127; my italics). Even if some such doctrine was
to be found in the Scriptures, it may be argued that the New
Testament documents cannot be taken as a trustworthy record
of Divine revelation in the life of Jesus, as they are replete
with legend, myth and error. Clearly these are very serious
objections, since if the incarnation has no secure grounding
in the historical sources it is no more than a chimera of metaphysical speculation of the worst sort; and if the historical
sources are unreliable anyway the whole idea of an objectively
self-disclosing act of God in history collapses. There is little
point in a self-disclosing act which is not reliably recorded.
And there is even less point in such an act, if it gives rise
to a wholly fantastic metaphysical doctrine which has minimal
relation to the initial act, whatever it was. It is therefore necessary to examine, first, the whole issue of the rationality of
placing one's ultimate trust in historical records of a highly
disputed nature; and second, the question of whether the doctrine of incarnation is consonant with the New Testament
records, such as they are. There can be no doubt that the
historicity of the gospels is widely disputed. Some scholars,
though admittedly very few, like G.A. Wells, of Birkbeck College, London (Wells 1975), deny that Jesus ever existed. Others
hold that we can know virtually nothing about him ("The
Gospels tell us more about the early church than they do
about Jesus" Knox 1958:39). Some, on the other hand, believe
that the gospels provide virtually firsthand and highly reliable
records of Jesus' life. Is the philosopher forced by Biblical
colleagues to be agnostic in his historical beliefs, since the
nature of the evidence is so disputed by the experts?

In general, one cannot defend the view that no commitment
is rational if the object of the commitment is disputed. John
Bowden comes near to such a view in his very readable and
iconoclastic book, *Jesus: The Unanswered Questions* (Bowden
1988). He writes: "Where there are two rival options with
no universally compelling grounds for choosing one over the
other, the only truthful answer anyone can make about what
can authoritatively be said ... must be, "In the end, we really
do not *know*" (ibid.:45). He is correct, if he means to assert
that where two equally rational and informed people cannot

settle a dispute, neither of them can claim objective certainty for the view they hold. Objective certainty leaves no room for rational doubt; that is a matter of definition. Nevertheless, each disputant may justifiably assert a view; and may *have* to take some view, if it is a matter of extreme importance. It is not the case that I am only justified in holding a view if I have complete theoretical certainty about it. A much lower degree of evidence and argument is usually acceptable; so that two conflicting views may both be justifiably assertible, where they are not settlable by observation or argument.

In justifiably asserting such a view, I cannot reasonably claim that it is the only possible view. But I may sincerely claim that the arguments seem to me to support it more strongly. And I may commit myself to its truth without hesitation. This is hardly adequately characterized as saying, "I do not really know" – as though I was just making a shot in the dark. I can commit myself to the truth of a view, while not denying the right of others to hold different views; and this is very different from complete agnosticism. The Biblical scholar should neither say, "There is no question at all that this view is true"; nor should she say, "I just do not know what is true". The rational course is to say, "I commit myself to this view, as the one that seems to me best established, or that best accords with an authority I accept on other grounds". Such commitments to truth accord well with the nature of faith, and their rationality is compatible, in appropriate circumstances, with the fact that others dispute them. In fact, many commitments will be such that the more important they are the more disputed they will be. If I commit myself to the view that abortion is wrong, my view will be highly disputed; but that will not impugn the necessity of making some commitment on the issue, and of sticking to it (unless it comes to seem irrational to do so). Similarly, I may commit myself to an assessment of some historical situation (e.g. the likelihood that Russia will attack Europe; or the right of Argentina to sovereignty of the Falkland Islands) where there is deep dispute. On many important matters of life, and not just in religion, we simply have to make decisive commitments on evidence which is highly disputable, and which there is no neutral method of resolving. There is nothing irrational, then, in committing oneself to a particular interpretation of the gospels. But how can one decide what sort of interpretation to commit oneself to?

Some disputes about the historicity of the gospels spring from variant accounts of the possibility of Divine action. It is clear that, since belief in God is itself widely disputed, any allegedly historical accounts of Divine action will be inherently problematic. Historians who do not believe in God will have to interpret narratives of Divine acts in some other way, as due to combinations of various natural causes. Critics who do not allow the possibility of real physical changes, brought about by God, will discount stories of the miraculous, of mighty acts and wonders wrought by God. These are underlying philosophical disputes, which help to determine the interpretation one will take. Sometimes a scholar may propose that we should take a minimal view of historicity, since that has the least chance of being in error. However, that proposal is wholly mistaken. The view that very little of the gospel material is historical is logically on all fours with the view that most of it is historical. It would be as great an error to suppose that nothing happened, when it did, as it would be to suppose that lots of things happened which never did. In any case, the believer certainly cannot allow his view of the evidence to be determined by any minimalist or "highest common factors" view, since such a view will rule out the possibility of Divine action in principle. The minimal view is that the whole thing is legend; and then, of course, there will be no records of real historical Divine action at all. To rule out such a thing by definition is highly arbitrary.

Very often, the criteria of historical authenticity proposed by Ernst Troeltsch are accepted by scholars in some form (Troeltsch 1913:729–53). There are three main such criteria. First, the principle of criticism requires one to treat all historical accounts critically (or even sceptically); not taking them at face value, but looking for hidden motives, legendary accretion and so on, being aware of the tendencies to exaggerate, stylize and embroider which are characteristic of most ancient religious writings. Second, the principle of analogy requires one to interpret past events as being similar in kind to presently experience events. And third, the principle of correlation requires one to interpret accounts in the same way as one interprets other, competing, accounts from a similar age and culture, like the Homeric poems of Babylonian epics; realizing that early historical writing was used more to teach social or spiritual truths than to provide a strictly neutral account of what happened.

Using these principles, the critical historian will look at an ancient document, expecting to find elements of myth, hyperbole, propaganda and rhetoric. She will assume that the events recorded are similar in kind to events that occur in history today. And she will be careful to stress the very different and often quite alien world–views and beliefs which underlie the narratives. Finally, she will insist that belief should be proportioned to the strength of the evidence, so that after all these investigations, one can only come to a provisional and tentative view about what really happened in history.

The use of these critical historical methods is bound to result in a discounting of most of the Biblical narratives as history. The events recorded are many years prior to the writing of the records, and the records are written by prejudiced observers (e.g. believers in Jesus as Lord). The miracles recorded in the texts are unlike anything that happens in the world today. And other documents of a similar age are largely mythic accounts in support of some political doctrine or other. The result is that one must be agnostic about almost all the historical parts of the Bible, and tentative even about the rest. Surely no faith can be founded upon such an insecure base!

It is acceptance of the propriety of such methods that has led some theologians to regard history as unimportant to faith. Thus Rudolf Bultmann writes, "The real Easter faith is faith in the word of preaching" (Bultmann 1953:42). For him, what is important is not something that happened in the past, about which we can know virtually nothing. It is a present challenge to existential commitment. A hint of historicity remains, in the proclamation of the resurrection of Jesus, though this itself exists only in a mythologized, legendary set of stories. The American theologian Schubert Ogden was only being consistent when he eradicated the *kerygma* as well as the myth from Christian faith, and left it entirely as a way of present self-understanding, expressed in legendary forms whose historicity is quite unimportant. Consistent though it may be, that is a truly extraordinary step to take with a form of religion whose chief claim to distinctiveness has been that it believes in a historically acting God. This might lead one to ask again whether these methods are as compelling as they may at first seem. Or are they ruling out authentic testimony to Divine acts in history by definition?

Suppose (to take a case which is much more problematic than the gospels, since the events it records happened many centuries before the records were finally written down) that God did act uniquely to liberate the Israelites from Egypt. This would be passed on by oral tradition, celebrated in ritual, and written down many years later. However accurate the account, the critical historian would have to distrust it, because of the long gap of time between the event and the written records; because of its importance to the self-image of the Israelites; and because of the (quite unsurprising) lack of Egyptian corroboration. Further, nothing like it happens now, or happened elsewhere in the ancient world. So this event fails all the critical tests; the critical historian must be wholly agnostic about whether it ever occurred. Yet on the hypothesis we are considering, God did act; and the Israelites are right to see this as an authentic revelation of God's will to them, and to celebrate its memory as a continuing expression of God's relation to them.

The critical historian could only be satisfied if overwhelming testimony to a Divine act existed. But this is virtually impossible, since God is not said to act in such an unambiguous way that even unbelievers will be convinced. As Pascal put it, "Willing to appear openly to those who seek Him with all their heart ... He has given signs of Himself, visible to those who seek Him, and not to those who seek Him not" (Pascal 1966:427). Divine acts, though real, are discerned by faith. To others, they remain at best as puzzles or unexplained oddities. Faith can never be "proved" either by history or by argument. So asking for an incontestable historical record is like asking for a conclusive proof of God. There is no such thing; though there are good reasons for believing in God, which the believer may find convincing. So there may be reliable (sincere and sober) historical testimonies, which only the believer may find convincing.

What is missing in the critical historian's account is an acknowledgement that the Bible is the book of a believing community. It is not written as "objective history". It is written as testimony, in order to evoke praise and thanksgiving and to disclose God to his people. It says: "These events disclosed God to us; we now recount them so that you too can come to discern God". In the process of repeated recounting, the community may come to discern new depths of significance, as new events place this original testimony in an ever-widening perspective of faith; and these insights may be written into the accounts. If someone gives a testimony of faith, it is no use saying, "That does not prove the event happened". The response desired is a joyful affirmation of that faith as one's own. But of course, without that personal sharing in faith, all one can do is be sceptical of the interpretation and even of the occurrence of the alleged event.

Does this mean that critical historians cannot be people of faith? No; it means that the limits of critical history should be clearly perceived and stated. Those are: that the critical historian is concerned with the attempt to state what can be said from an "objective", neutral, uncommitted viewpoint. The task is the impossible one of attempting a neutral observer's view of history. The Biblical writers were completely unconcerned with any such enterprise. They cannot be taken as witnesses to neutral history. The neutral observer can only say of them that they claimed certain things. As a historian, he should not even say that these things are probable or improbable. For once one asks about probability, one must ask, "Probable from the standpoint of faith? Or from the standpoint of atheism?" What is likely to happen if there is a God is quite different from what is likely to happen if there is not.

The question is: can it ever be part of religious faith to affirm that a certain historical event occurred? The thought behind the question is that, since history is always uncertain, and faith should never go beyond the evidence, such faith would be left uncertain and permanently vacillating with the latest historical researches. "Accidental truths of history can never become the proof of necessary truths of reason", wrote the eighteenth-century German philosopher G.E. Lessing (Lessing 1956:53). There is an "ugly, broad ditch" between contingent and uncertain truths of history and necessary and certain truths of reason. However, it is not at all clear that Christian faith lies in embracing any necessary truths of reason. It may lie precisely in faithful response to contingent acts of God, which must occur in history if they occur anywhere. But can a believer reasonably be more certain of a historical event than a competent professional historian? This difficulty is mitigated when one considers that critical history is methodologically uncertain, confining itself to recording claims and assuming only normal, well-attested, probabilities. Faith is, on the other hand, in its prophetic inception, a disclosure of God in a certain situation, and the responsive commitment to the God who is disclosed there. Faith is essentially a wholehearted commitment, in response to a personal disclosure. It naturally seeks to evoke this disclosure in others. It does not do this by recounting a piece of objective history. It does so by telling the story of personal encounter which evoked one's total commitment. When this story is received in faith, it is received as evoking a corresponding disclosure in the hearer, who takes that story as his own. As I. T. Ramsey puts it, "Empirical criteria are relevant, but these criteria are organized by, and are never exhaustive evidence for the loyalties they name" (Ramsey 1957:129). The story never becomes non-historical, for it is founded upon a historical occasion of discernment. But it possesses an additional dimension, which affects the way the story is presented and which grows with repeated recounting – a semiotic dimension, enshrining, preserving and seeking to evoke new levels of meaning which the community discerns in its originative narrative.

Personal faith is not assent to evidence which is so strong as to be beyond reasonable doubt. It is assent to a discernment of God which is personally overwhelming but not objectively testable. This is not discernment of a historical God, timeless and unchanging. It is discernment of an active, loving God, making himself known in personal lives at specific points which become the matrix of a communal response to his will. The semiotic dimension is in principle beyond the reach of the critical historian. He must register its presence, while refraining from commenting on its truth. The critical historian can help to make the historical context clearer, and thus help greatly to see the meanings the original texts may have had. He can rule out some interpretations as highly improbable, because of anachronism or lack of attention to the detail and complexity of the texts. But he can never claim to have uncovered "the truth" behind the testimony.

Quite a good parallel, already briefly referred to, can be made with the philosophical "proofs of God". The philosopher will attempt to marshal arguments for and against God with neutrality; she will probably end with methodological scepticism, since no proof is overwhelmingly compelling. Yet in the context of participation in a worshipping community, with its characteristic types of personal experience, the proofs may make an impressive rational articulation of a world – view one is disposed to accept. So with the Biblical accounts of Divine acts in history. The neutral historian is bound to marshal various probabilities, and no overwhelmingly compelling account of what actually happened will be available. Yet, in Brian Hebblethwaite's words, "historical evidence together with the data of experiential participation in the living Church and rational reflection on the Church's doctrine from within" will make a vital difference to one's assessment of the situation (Hebblethwaite 1987:82). If one is a member of the community which is built upon the testimony of Divine action, and within which experiences of a God of the character testified to do occur, then a more positive assessment of historicity becomes possible. Where the dispassionate observer can remain agnostic, the one who has committed her life in trust to the God revealed in this tradition is bound to trust the foundation documents of her faith. She may not claim for them clear historical provability. But she may claim that they provide a trustworthy testimony to discernments of the God now experienced in the community of faith. Present belief in a God of redeeming love requires me to trust in the future, to hope that all will be brought to fulfilment in his love. So present belief in such a God requires me to trust in the past, to hope that the Biblical narratives are reliable records of discernments of the God whom they have taught us to worship. It may seem odd to speak of hope for past reliability; but when one commits oneself to their veracity one assumes that such veracity is possible, even likely on certain assumptions, but one cannot be theoretically certain of it. In such a situation, it is entirely in order to speak of hope; and it may be helpful to bring out the connection of present commitment to a historically acting God with a reasonable and hopeful trust both in the records of his past acts and in the promises (contained in the same records) of his future purposes.

Members of a community of faith which receives the Biblical documents as testimonies to the original disclosures upon which the faith itself is founded must commit themselves to the essential correctness of those testimonies. The onus of disproof is upon the sceptic. Troeltsch's methods can be used to show how pious legends do build up quickly in religion in general; to draw parallels from the cultural context of the original documents to illuminate their meaning; and to insist that the subsequent history of the tradition, including especially our contemporary insights from that tradition, can be usefully used as a corrective or yardstick in assessing the earliest stages of the tradition's existence. It would be absurd and irresponsible to ignore such scholarly tasks. What must be rejected is the view that historical agnosticism is the only rational response to make to the Biblical accounts, or any suggestion that our own rather limited religious experiences can be used to discount the testimonies of the great prophets and saints of other times and places.

In the final analysis, historians seek to provide an account of what happened which creates a likely and illuminating pattern. It must be a pattern which coheres with our general beliefs about the structure of things, and which gives an acceptable account of why certain beliefs or practices arose. History is a creative as well as a critical discipline. There is no evading the primary subjective element of personal creativity in history. Each good historian recreates the past in his own image. So if we read history critically, we must evaluate the writer as well as his preferred account. We can never get back to an uninterpreted past. We only have access to interpretations of what happened, which in the case of religion especially have always been disputed and diverse. Accordingly, it is rational to let our interpretation be led by the community and tradition of which we are part. As W.J. Abraham argues (Abraham 1982), the intelligible pattern of events which a Christian or Jewish historian will discern in the history of Israel is different from the pattern available to an atheist. For there is good reason to think that a God who desires to make his saving will known to humanity in the community of Israel or of the Church will ensure that this tradition enshrines and preserves the truth which he desires to be made known through it to all the world.

Something really happened in the past; some accounts are nearer the truth than others. But we have no neutral way of saying which these are. We cannot fail to belong to one tradition of interpretation; our intellectual responsibility is not to leave that tradition and pretend to an impossible neutrality; but to be conscious of its particularity, to remain true to it but allow our understanding of it to grow by being challenged by others, and to help to develop it by internal reflection. Hans-Georg Gadamer has said, rather provocatively, that "It is not so much our judgments as it is our prejudices that constitute our being" (Gadamer 1960:261). The point is not that we should be content to remain with our cultural pre-orientations and starting points of thinking; but that we should recognize them as both partial and as ineluctably ours. It is ironic that the very same writers who often insist so much on cultural relativism will often assume the absolute correctness of their own liberal secular views of history, as though they were beyond the general relativity of knowledge. We all belong to a tradition; but traditions are not sealed off from each other; they can interact. There is, quite properly, a Christian tradition of interpretation, which patterns its primal historical documents in accordance with basic insights focussed on the person of Jesus. Commitment to trust in the God whose nature is disclosed in the preaching and life of the Church will naturally place high reliability on the gospel interpretations of the life of Jesus, and therefore on the Biblical records of the historical disclosures of God to the Jewish people.

Thus if it is said that "we can never get back to the historical

Jesus", the conclusion may be drawn that we must, if we are honest, be agnostic about him. This is a conclusion invalidly drawn from a half-truth. It is a half-truth, because we can never get back to exactly what happened at any time in the past (we can very rarely establish exactly what happened even in the next room an hour ago). In the gospels, we have interpretations, in the form of testimonies that God has been disclosed as active in history; and that is as much as we usually have in history. We have access to many testimonies of faith to the historical acts of God. Certainly, their historical value varies, but it would be a vast exaggeration to say that we had no challenging testimonies to the immense impact of Jesus on his contemporaries.

The invalid argument is that, if we cannot establish the historical facts with certainty, then we cannot commit ourselves to the truth of any historical accounts. Such an argument would make it impossible for me even to believe that I dreamed of an elephant last night – I could not establish that fact to anyone else's satisfaction; and I cannot even *establish* it to myself, otherwise than by simply believing it. In general, I can commit myself to a belief which cannot be established with certainty, under conditions which have been summarized by William James as presenting me with a "vital, living and forced option" (James 1896). I am entitled to adopt a belief if the option between it and its contrary is "forced" – if I have to come to some decision at least in practice about it (I have to worship a personal, and therefore historically active, God or not). I am entitled to adopt a belief if it is a matter of my vital interests; if, for instance, my eternal destiny may depend upon it, or if it is morally better and psychologically more healthy for me that I do so. And I am entitled to adopt a belief if it presents me with a living option – if it is not merely an intellectual possibility, but if it seems to be a presupposition, or at least the basis, of other beliefs which I find confirmed in my experience. It may be said that talk of "adopting" a belief is rather unrealistic, since we do not choose our basic religious beliefs. The point is, however, that we need assurance that our beliefs are not irrational, that they can be justifiably held. James' analysis is helpful in pointing to factors which justify me acting irrevocably on beliefs which are uncertain, from a purely theoretical point of view.

In the normal Christian case it is not that I come across the Bible in a history class; rather, I participate in a worshipping community. This community builds its life in response to a God who judges, forgives, loves and acts to reconcile us to himself. The character and quality of many of my experiences confirms the presence of such a God. Perhaps my life is transformed by what I believe to be his power. In such a community, the Bible is a primary witness to the self-revealing acts of God upon which the Church was founded. It provides the canonical matrix which defines this concept of God. I receive it as an expression of a set of responses to primary disclosures of the God on whom I base my whole life, expressions which are determinative of my own self-understanding. I cannot, at the same time, distance myself from them as some sort of objective investigator, sceptical of all unusual or paranormal claims.

To do that would be to remove myself from the community of faith. And it would undermine the very basis of the documents, which is to testify precisely to paranormal events – events brought about by the agency of a supernatural being, God. I approach the gospels with initial trust, because they testify to the origin of the idea of God in whom I trust. At this point, the ideal of the critical scholar, viewing all things with rational detachment, stands in contrast to the ideal of the worshipper of God, who seeks spiritual illumination through the words of Holy Scripture. Of course, the believer can be a scholar; but she cannot be agnostic, as the critical historian must be, about the fact that God discloses his being in historical events recorded in these documents. If such disclosure is accepted in faith, then one necessarily commits oneself to the occurrence of appropriately disclosive events.

What is historically acceptable depends, ultimately, upon whether one's view of the world is materialist or spiritual; whether one regards the material realm as one of purely quasi-mechanistic processes or as the manifestation of an underlying spiritual, purposing reality. The Biblical view is undoubtedly the latter; and for Christians the life of Jesus is seen as the supreme and definitive case of the sacramental character of the material world, wherein a perfected human nature openly manifests the infinite spiritual reality which is its true basis and goal. How very odd it would be for a Christian to expound the Bible as though from a virtually materialist viewpoint, thereby rendering its own testimony false and delusory.

One may therefore accept a tradition of interpretation by a commitment of faith to that tradition, founded on a present response to God as experienced within it, which renders its interpretation canonical for one's own faith. For its primary documents are worshipping responses to perceived acts of God. And if those responses, which form the pattern of our present responses, are appropriate, then the perceptions they record must be accurate. My present faith in the God they describe must give those documents a special authority, as records of discernments of a reality I am not free to invent or control. "If God has acted decisively in the past, then that past history, however hard to recapture, is bound, ever and again, to constitute a check and a control on our understanding and expression of divine truth" (Hebblethwaite 1987:107). It is reasonable, therefore, to take the gospels as a trustworthy record of the life and teachings of Jesus. This view can take account of all the valuable contributions of scholarship about the diversity of sources, the variety of viewpoints and the subtlety of the symbolism used in the texts. But it can remain firmly committed to the essential historicity of the documents, as testimonies to real acts of God.

Now, however, we must face the objection that the Jesus recorded in the synoptic gospels, if not in John, is very far from being an incarnation of God. Such an idea, it is sometimes said, would have been quite inconceivable either to Jesus or to the apostles. Even Brian Hebblethwaite, who defends a strong doctrine of the incarnation, holds that "it is highly implausible for us ... to suppose that Jesus knew himself to be or thought of himself as divine" (Hebblethwaite 1987:67). I have to say that it is the idea of unconscious divinity that strikes me as highly implausible; I do not find it at all odd that a human person should believe himself to be a finite embodiment of God. It is not, after all, a very unusual claim. Nevertheless, if gospel criticism forces one admit that Jesus never made such claims, so be it. Is there any sense in which the synoptic gospels testify to a unique incarnation of the infinite God in the person of a particular Jewish man?

It is generally agreed that the earliest gospel is that of Mark. It is in many ways the least theologically developed, the one which has the most straightforward, almost brusque, narrative. How does this gospel see Jesus, with regard to a doctrine of incarnation? There are a number of possibilities. Its account may be incompatible with the view that Jesus is God incarnate. It may be compatible with it, but completely innocent of any suggestion of the doctrine's truth. It may contain beliefs which, when they are fully thought out and developed, give rise to a doctrine of incarnation. Or it may state that in Jesus, human and Divine natures are uniquely united. We may say at once that at least the latter view is not found in Mark. But that is hardly surprising, given the strict monotheism of Judaism, which would make such a blunt statement almost unintelligible to many of those hearing the earliest preaching of the gospel. Nevertheless, what Mark says about Jesus goes well beyond the bounds of what one would regard as proper for even a prophet. Does it present a doctrine of incarnation in embryo? Three elements must, I think, be present in a doctrine of incarnation. Jesus must be truly human. He must fully manifest the Divine nature. And this manifestation must be unique. If, in Mark, we find Jesus presented as being human, as being uniquely related to God, and as being a full manifestation of the Divine nature and activity, then it is reasonable to say that the doctrine of incarnation is already present, even if not explicitly formulated. What, then, does Mark say?

According to Mark, Jesus thought of himself as "Son of Man", serving mankind and giving his life as a "ransom for many" (10:45). He knew he would rise and be seen by the apostles (9:30); that he would come in glory, and that men would be judged by their attitude to him (8:38–9:1). He claims supreme authority over all men, over the elements and spirits. He is declared to be God's dear son. He sits at the right hand of God. Yet he has certain human limitations and characteristics. He is hungry; he weeps and he is tired. He prays to the Father, and asserts that the time and exact nature of the final Kingdom are known only to the Father (so he is not omniscient) (10:39; 13:32). Overall, he is presented as a man with Divine authority, the saviour and proclaimer of the Kingdom, the bridegroom of the Kingdom Feast, the son, who is contrasted with the servants, of God (12:6).

Matthew's gospel agrees with this general picture of Jesus, but adds the significant statement, "My Father has given me all things. No one knows the Son except the Father, and no one knows the Father except the Son and those to whom the Son chooses to reveal him" (11:27). The use of *my* father shows an exclusive relationship between Father and Son, and the Son as the only one able to show the Father as he is. Jesus is shown as King of the Judgment Day (Matt. 25), sitting in the place of God, disposing final judgment on all men. He stresses that Jesus' blood is poured out for many for the forgiveness of sins (26:28). And the gospel ends with the statement, "I have been given all authority in heaven and on earth" (28:18). Matthew tones down Jesus' ignorance about the time of the End and the place of the apostles in the Kingdom. For Matthew, Jesus' authority is absolute; his relation to the Father personal and unique. The Father may be different from the Son; but the Son, as man, acts as or in place of God; and he knows God in a unique way.

It is clear that in both gospels Jesus is presented as human, and that he is given a unique relation to God. The first two elements of a doctrine of incarnation are unequivocally present. What of his being a "full manifestation of the Divine"? Though not so unequivocal, the more one reflects on what it is for the Son to act in the place of God, with God's authority and with such a total and undeviating obedience to the Divine will that the will of the Son can be said to be the will of the Father also, the more plausible does the view become that he expressed the Divine nature in human form. Indeed, no other view adequately accounts for the uniqueness of his vocation, so astonishingly vindicated by his resurrection. Many theologians, wishing to distance themselves from asserting a straight identity of God and man in Jesus, nevertheless assert that the man Jesus had a uniquely close relation to God. Apart from the fact that it seems arbitrary to accept evidence for such a unique closeness while rejecting the much greater amount of evidence about Jesus' miraculous powers, there is, as Hebblethwaite remarks, a "general weakness regarding the sense that can be made of the idea that God was able at one point in time to win the pure and unbroken response of a particular individual man two thousand years ago, and nowhere else before or since" (Hebblethwaite 1967:62). How, indeed, can one account for such a unique purity of response, except by supposing that Jesus' nature, in which that response was grounded, was itself unique in an important way? And does that not point to the necessity of further reflection to determine in what precisely this uniqueness could consist?

The gospels do not contain such reflections. But they do clearly claim for Jesus an ultimate authority over all human beings, born of unique relationship to God. Yet, it may be said, is there not a gulf, at first a hairline crack, suddenly widening into a chasm, between following a man with Divine authority and believing in a God who takes on human properties? There is no doubt that Mark's gospel starts from the humanity of Jesus, not from some theory about the Divine nature. Jesus is a man, but no ordinary man: "What manner of man is this, that even the wind and waves obey him?" (Mark 4:41). In forgiving sins and assuming authority over Sabbath and food laws, he acts in the place of God. In teaching about the coming Kingdom and the way to it, he assumes unique insight into the mind and will of God. In seeing his death as a ransom for sin, he gives it a causal efficacy that no human life can easily bear. And in rising from death, he shows that his humanity is uncorrupted by sin. This is a perfect man, related to God in a quite unique way.

It has sometimes been suggested that Jesus' uniqueness might lie, not in his personal nature, but in his function, in the role he plays within the economy of salvation. But this view seems to divorce nature and function in an implausible way. Jesus is not a man who bears the office of Messiah and Lord, like an earthly King, who might be quite an ordinary person, fulfilling an exalted social role. In Jesus' case, the role and the person are inseparable. He mediates Divine authority precisely because his person is such as to be wholly transparent to the Divine action. His will is perfectly conformed to the will of the Father in love, and his mind is suffused with the wisdom and knowledge of the Father, at least so far as it concerns human salvation. So he can, according to the synoptic gospels, see his life as a showing of Divine love, he can interpret his death as a ransom for sin and he can foresee his rising from death as a consequence of his uncorrupted human life. Is it not a virtually inevitable consequence of this view that one must think of Jesus' humanity as raised to a unique status by its identification with the mind and will of God? And is this not already the core of the doctrine of incarnation?

Why should a man who had a uniquely close consciousness of God and a uniquely perfect obedience of the will to God, who knew the tradition of the Suffering Servant of God, of the expected Messiah of God and of the triumphant coming of God's Kingdom, not see himself as called to a unique vocation to serve, to suffer, to die, to rise in glory and to return in the power of the Kingdom of God? Such a thing is conceivable. And if it turns out that this self-interpretation is correct – that he does suffer, die and rise again – then one must surely accept that his understanding of God's purpose and his obedience to the Divine will was indeed uniquely perfect.

So Jesus has a uniquely intimate knowledge of the Father; he conforms to the Divine will so closely that he acts in place of the Father (e.g. in judging and forgiving sin); and he has a unique vocation, as King of the Jews and Light of the Gentiles, suffering and redeeming King of all humanity. Moreover, the great unspoken theme of the gospels is Jesus' redeeming death for the forgiveness of sins, mysteriously presented at the Last Supper, and commemorated in the early Church community.

How is it possible for a man to have such a unique knowledge and love of God, to be the redeemer and judge of all other men and women? That is the question with which the early Church wrestled. The Church saw, surely correctly, that Jesus could not be just a man who happened to know more about God than anyone else; a man in whom others saw the nature of God; or by means of whom a new knowledge of God came to others. He must have been united to God, in knowledge and love, in a distinctive and unrepeatable way.

The saints can show the love of God in their lives and obey his will with heroic steadfastness. Yet even the greatest saint lacks that inner knowledge of the Divine mind and that indefectibly obedient love which Jesus possessed. The conclusion seems inescapable, that if the earliest gospel is reliable in its account of Jesus' life, he had, while being truly and fully human, an inner unity of mind and will with God which raised his humanity to a new dimension. He was a man but also more than a man. He is a man made fit to know and express the mind of God, to be transparent to the Divine mind and will. We may thus say that he is the full manifestation of God in a human person. His humanity is always wholly open to God. He was, by his nature, one with God. He is the enfleshment, in a human mind and will, of the mind and will of God. His whole life is the conscious and intentional act of God; the act of God mediated in a human mind and will. It is not that God uses a human body and soul to do whatever he wants, as a passive automaton or puppet. It is not that a man manages to obey God better than anyone else. It is rather that God transforms a human subject of consciousness and action by uniting it from the first moment of its existence to himself. Then the acts of Jesus are both the acts of a conscious human agent and the acts of God.

There is a great conceptual difference between Jesus perfectly bringing about what God wants, and God bringing something about through Jesus. God cannot properly be said to bring something about by means of Jesus knowing what he wants and freely doing it. Properly described, what God then brings about is that Jesus knows what he wants. It is Jesus who brings the thing about (or who may conceivably not do so). God may intend *that* Jesus does what he wants. But he cannot bring it about that Jesus does so, if Jesus is a being distinct from God. That is because a person can only be said to bring about something that is within his power. Even God cannot intend to bring something about by means of my freely knowing his will and realizing it; since my will, so long as it is truly free, is not wholly in the power of God. For this reason, it is not wholly satisfactory to make the difference between "inspirational" Christologies and "incarnational" Christologies lie in a distinction between God acting "through" Jesus, and Jesus being God's own act, as Hebble-thwaite does (Hebblethwaite 1967:69). For God can only pro-perly act through Jesus if he can bring it about that Jesus freely does what God intends. So he can only act through Jesus if Jesus' acts are themselves the acts of God.

Suppose God intends that Jesus should die and rise again. He can, of course, simply bring that about. But can God bring it about that Jesus knows that he should die and be raised, and that he should freely accept that destiny? God cannot do that, so long as Jesus' will is free, independent of God and thus able to frustrate the intention. Death and resurrec-tion could be God's purpose, but not something he himself could bring about – unless he could know that Jesus' will is *guaranteed* to obey and his knowledge is guaranteed to be correct. Jesus' act can be, at the same time, God's act, only if his human will is necessarily aligned to the Divine will. How can Jesus' will be both fully human (free) and necessarily obedient to God's will? The traditional answer is that Jesus' human will is not the will of a distinct person; but is the mediation, in human nature, of the Divine will itself. It is a will which is human in nature, but which belongs to God. Now the fully-fledged doctrine of incarnation comes into being – not as an abstract conceptual fairy-tale, but as an exploration of the implications of the earliest Christian gospel, and of what it means to regard Jesus as the unique Son of God, the only human person who is by nature inseperable from God, and as such is declared to be the Lord and Redeemer of all. Uniqueness of function is seen to presuppose uniqueness of being, if it is not to be accidental and fortuitous.

Willing is, essentially, causality through intention. It is Div-ine willing if the agent is omniscient and omnipotent, knowing absolutely all possibilities and being able directly to intend any of them. It is human willing if the agent is a human subject of consciousness, having developed in a human body, learned many things by means of the senses while being ignorant of many others, and being able to do a restricted number of things because of its place in a shared environment with other agents of the same sort.

We may say that Jesus was certainly a human subject of consciousness, though one always open to the mind and will of God, which would increase his powers of understanding and willing enormously. His will was human, in being the will of such a human subject. But its unique openness to the Divine reality made it unthinkable that it would ever choose an egoistic good. He had from the first the sort of indefectible will that the saints hope to possess in heaven, the presence of God. From the human point of view, Jesus is a man uniquely open to God. From the Divine point of view, he is the vehicle of the Divine purpose, the act of God in and through a human subject. Here, the personal nature of Divine action is fully disclosed and realized, and the final purpose of God for creation is foreshadowed.

The life of Jesus is certainly extraordinary; but there is a lack of intelligibility if one sees it as simply a suspension of the ordinary processes of nature, the eruption of direct Divine causality into a world wherein his action is normally persuasive and only ambiguously detectible. A more coherent view would be to see the incarnation, the Divine determination of a human nature (a set of essential human properties, as Thomas Morris characterizes it (Morris 1986)), as a perfected example of the general form of Divine action. That action we have seen to be co-operative, revelatory, empowering and responsive. We have also seen that it builds up into a pattern of vocational choice, of prophetic teaching and expectation. Torah, as the living guidance of God, is readily seen as incarnated in the lives of the great sages. As the Jewish scholar Jacob Neusner points out, "In the Talmud of the Land of Israel or Yerushalmi, c. A.D.400, the Torah came to be represented in the person of the sage, who was, in himself, the Torah incarnate" (Neusner 1988:214). The idea of incarnation is not as foreign to Biblical Judaism as has sometimes been suggested. In the history of ancient Israel, it is reasonable to hold that the way is being prepared for the revelation of the empowering and responsive love of God in a human life and person. A finite vehicle is thus created which can normatively express the Divine will. When God takes human nature, he transforms it into something which mediates infinity under the forms of time. Jesus' paranormal wisdom and power is, one might paradoxically say, the result of the raising of human possibilities to their highest level, allowing Divine power to be mediated through him as it was in a lesser and more indirect way through prophets such as Isaiah and Elijah.

If Divine action can include the action of assuming a human nature and uniting individual persons to him by means of that action, then the testimony to this possible act is certainly high enough to found a rational commitment to its reliability. In this sense, the doctrine of the incarnation is well grounded in the New Testament, and it is intellectually vastly preferable to the strange belief that God revealed his nature through a series of unreliable testimonies which attribute legendary and improbably Divine attributes to a person who was, after all, a failed apocalyptic prophet. The intellectual coherence of the doctrine of incarnation, its apparent confirmation by continued experience of the Lordship of Christ in the Church, and its fruitfulness in suggesting illuminating ways of understanding both the nature of God and of human experience in general, all combine to place the gospel accounts within a framework of interpretation which makes them strong enough to bear the doctrine which has historically grown from reflection upon them. But one major problem remains to be faced. The earliest followers of Jesus saw themselves as living in the "last days", and Jesus as the culminating act of God in history. But the world did not end, and the figure of Jesus has now receded into the past. John Bowden writes, "If the world continues to be able to support a human population for further millennia and there are still Christians upon it, the Jesus of two thousand years ago will become the Jesus of a still more distant past and the Palestine of his day will become even more unimaginable" (Bowden 1988:147). With the prospect of millenia of history yet to come, is it any longer plausible to take a freelance Rabbi from the ancient New East as the centre, much less the culmination, of the whole of human history? This question threatens the plausibility of any doctrine of incarnation, and makes it imperative to see whether and how that doctrine can be set into the much expanded view of human history that we now have.

14

The Redemption of Time

If God becomes incarnate, that event will be the central and decisive turning-point of human history. Many early Christians saw it as the end of history, the culmination of the world-process – "the end of all things is near" (1 Peter 4:7). That was a natural assumption, and in one sense it was true; for the incarnation prefigures the destiny which awaits all of us. But in the greatly enlarged perspective we now have, of a hundred thousand year prehistory for human beings and a potentially multimillion year future, we can see how it is more intelligible to view the incarnation as the beginning of a new age of history, rather than as the end of all history. Human beings turn from God to seek the pleasures of self-will. In Christ, God takes upon himself human nature, and thereby perfects it and unites it in the closest possible way to himself. Jesus is not a man, who might have chosen against God or might have been alienated from God. For the classical view, he *is* God; and, though he has a human will, that will can never be alienated from the Divine will. It is indefectible, in rather the way that the wills of the redeemed in heaven will be indefectible. God could not have united all humans to himself in this way; if he had, their freedom to sin would have been abolished, and we would not have been the creatures we are.

Such an incarnation required a long period of preparation. Jesus lived within a specific culture, and his life was the fulfilment of many hopes and prophecies. For a Christian, the successive revelations of God through the prophets of Israel, the very founding of Israel itself, the exodus from Egypt and the giving of Torah, are acts of God preparing the way for the coming of the Lord. This preparation had to be particular and distinctive, if the incarnation was to be unique. So we begin to see why God could not reveal himself everywhere in the same way. He was preparing for a unique event in history; and this could best be done by a long preparation within one culture, which he set apart for himself. Of course God would be active for salvation in all places, in some way. But the particularity of his incarnation entails that he must reveal himself in a quite distinctive way within one tradition. And so it is, since only in the history of Israel do we find God revealed as having one moral, social this-worldly purpose, the purpose of bringing about a moral transformation of the social and physical world, of bringing about the Kingdom of God. He acts elsewhere in inspiration, miracle, providential answer to prayer and guidance. But it is to the prophets of Israel that he begins to reveal his unique purpose of becoming man, for the redemption of the human race. It is not that God is only at work in this tradition. But God is only at work in this way, revealing himself as a morally demanding, world-redeeming Judge and Saviour, within the Biblical tradition of Israel.

Further, the incarnation was not the end of God's action in the world; it was the beginning of a new age, an age when all people could be incorporated into the new humanity of Christ, hallowed by its unity with God. The Church is a distinctive form of religious community, seeking to unite all people in the life of Christ, and so to spread the good news of Divine incarnation throughout the whole world. In the symbolic language of the New Testament, the Son of Man gathers the elect to himself from every corner of the earth, drawing them to be with him in the glory of the presence of God (Mark 13:26–27). This is not to be taken as a literal picture of a man flying by on a cloud, and levitating people up into the sky. Every symbol has a rich meaning, which analytical thought can never fully uncover. We may say, however, that the Son of Man is the new humanity which is transfigured by its union with the Divine nature. The elect are those who respond to God in penitence and faith, and who are incorporated into the new Divine-human community of the Church, the body of Christ. The cloud is the Shekinah, the cloud of the glory and the presence of God. And the ascent into the heavens, the sky, is the transfiguration of time into eternity, the apotheosis of the present moment to find its eternal fulfilment in the Divine Mind. In the Church, eternity is continually brought into time as the Holy Spirit illumines the minds and hearts of human persons; and time is continually "redeemed", by being taken up into the ultimate reconciliation of creature and creator which has been established in Christ. God acts in the pouring out of the Holy Spirit, bringing out the riches of the meaning of the incarnation and its continuing significance for the true understanding of human life and destiny. The activity of the Spirit is the application to every present of the historically particular matrix of Divine action in the world in the life of Jesus. It is to the activity of the Spirit that we must look if we wish to discern God's action in the contemporary world, what he is doing to unite people to himself and realize the Kingdom which Jesus proclaimed.

The person of Jesus will always remain central in the history of humanity's encounter with God. It is not that an itinerant Jewish preacher from an increasingly archaic and alien culture will be the only path to God, however many million years of evolution there may be ahead of us, and however many millions of people have never heard of him. Rather, those who confess Jesus as Lord will look for the activity of the Spirit throughout the whole world, leading them to hope for the personalization of all things in the unity of love. But if one asks what his love is, what is its source and what is the nature of the goal to which it leads, then we shall point to the one on whom the Church was founded, the revelation of the love of God in the life of his Chosen Servant, and the gift of the unending life of God through the obedient death of one in whom the fullness of Godhead dwelt. What Christ shall be, when all are one in him, we cannot yet see. But that God took flesh and dwelt among us, to give us a pattern of salvation which is normative for all ages and cultures, is the faith of those who dare to become his disciples and seek to embody the Spirit of Christ in their own very diverse times and places.

There is, however, still a difficulty about the particularity of Christ, as the normative pattern of Divine action. For the dependence of Christian faith upon the Bible may distract attention from the urgency of the spiritual life, making endless scholarly problems out of what should be the well-spring of eternal life. Does Christianity not all too easily give rise to unsettlable arguments about what happened long ago, or what the truth of the Divine being really is? Concern for the correctness of doctrine displaces concern for spiritual realization. In addition to being historically and metaphysically problematic, Christianity can also seem too restrictive, requiring us to give one human being absolute supremacy over all others, one Scripture absolute supremacy over others, one institution absolute supremacy over others.

Is it not better to concentrate on what really matters – prayer and meditation, the increase of love, understanding and reverence? Should we not let people find their own way to enlightenment, offering help when they ask; not telling them they *must* believe various highly disputed facts if they are to be saved? One might more profitably hold that there is one Mind of Love underlying all things, which is knowable within the self. Salvation lies in realizing unity with this Mind, being its vehicle and sharing its endless bliss. We can do this by way of many images and doctrines, many mythologies which may help people at different stages of development; but the final unity is beyond all our conceptual schemes. "Different mythologies may each be valid as ways of evoking ... human self-transcendence in relation to the Real" (Hick 1989:375). Perhaps many people have realized Enlightenment, and can teach us the way to it. Our concern will be with the present, not with the continuously receding past; with the true Self within, not with arguing about the nature of a man who lived centuries ago, and deciding how unique he might have been. As Professor Hick remarks, "Whereas understood literally the doctrine of an unique divine incarnation in Christ has divided humanity and has shrunk the image of God to that of the tribal deity of the West, understood mythologically it can continue to draw people to God" (ibid.:372). Our goal will be unity with the Self of Love within. We will not have to try to believe that somebody rose from the dead long ago, or even that we will survive death ourselves. We can concentrate on present spiritual experience and self-transformation, not on theoretical disputes beyond human capacity to resolve.

There is much that is attractive and right here. But do the

old problems really disappear? Or will they not soon return in another form? For instance, how do we know that there is a "Self of Love within"? The reply will be: you must experience it. But human experience is infinitely diverse; some (many Buddhists) deny the existence of such a Self; others (like the Indian sage Ramanuja) hold that it is the embodiment of all good qualities; yet others (Sankara and the school of Advaita Vedanta) that it is without duality or qualities at all; which view is authentic? In the end, one must rely upon teachers who, by their superior wisdom, inner calm and moral heroism, may plausibly claim to be enlightened. Almost all religions confess that people are like sheep without a shepherd; they need to be taught, to be shown the way to eternal bliss. And it is not true that they naturally cleave to the inner Self. On the contrary, they are lost in greed and hatred; they are ignorant of the way to bliss, and estranged from the Self of all. Those who seek the Self are few ("The gate is narrow and the way is hard, that leads to life, and those who find it are few", Matt.7:14); and even they must begin by seeking one who can show the way to union, one who can show the way because he has achieved union, and one who can help to overcome greed and passion by his presence and encouragement.

If we are to tread the spiritual path, our first steps must be to find a reliable guide, an Enlightened Teacher of the Way. At once, thousands of candidates present themselves, all claiming our attention. We, or at least most of us, need guidance, strengthening and encouragement. We need to learn, not just to make it all up for ourselves. In this respect, the demand for autonomy, if it takes the form of asking that everyone should begin all over again for themselves in religion, is positively misleading. Where rich traditions of spiritual life exist, and where the way to wisdom is hard to discern and difficult to follow, what is infantile is not obedience to a guide, but the childish insistence that one can do it all on one's own. Of course we need protection from the hacks and charlatans who litter religions like confetti at a wedding. So the question of authority arises: who is the reliable authority and guide, in a world of greed and deception? Seeking, in our new religious quest, for autonomy, we must very soon confess, if we are not blindly arrogant, that we are in need of a reliable authority, of an enlightened teacher who has attained the goal we seek. Seeking to escape from the constraints of an imposed revelation, we find ourselves turning again to seek an authentic revelation, one that will lead us to our true fulfilment.

Who is enlightened? This question cannot be answered without having some view of what enlightenment consists in. Professor Zaehner (Zaehner 1961) distinguishes three main types of mystical thought: one sees enlightenment as consisting in a conscious loving relation to a personal God; a second sees enlightenment as lying in achieved identity with an undifferentiated non-dual reality; and another (exemplified by Samkhya-Yoga) sees it as the achievement of the total isolation of an infinite number of atomistic pure Selves from their material forms. It is not possible to know who is truly enlightened without knowing which of these views is nearer the truth. There is no neutral test of enlightenment. We cannot long suppress the question of what this "reality beyond the finite self" truly is, by relationship to which enlightenment is achieved, and how it relates to our egoistic human world. Is it conscious? Is it capable of action? Does it have a positive goal for the world? Does the world exist independently of it? If so, how does it relate to the world? If it is infinite blissful consciousness, and the world is a plurality of egoistic and conflicting wills, has it any relation to the world at all? The old theological questions are back – and rightly so. For if one is to see the supreme goal of human life as lying in establishing relation (or even union) with a transcending reality, one must have reason to think there is such a reality, that its nature is such that we can be united to it, and that human life is somehow fulfilled by relation to it. But who is to answer these questions? It takes little reflection to see that, if the ultimate reality is a loving, conscious Self of All, it would hardly be compatible with its nature as loving to remain hidden from human knowledge for ever. Love is self-revealing as well as self-giving. So one is led to seek, not only an enlightened human teacher, but a self-revelation of the Self of All, a disclosure of its nature which shows the way to union with it. This prompts the thought that perhaps the Supreme Self will disclose its nature in an enlightened teacher who shares its mind and is the vehicle of its actions in the world. One can indeed search for the Self within; but to know what it truly is one must seek the place of its disclosure, in the lives of the enlightened who mediate its reality, unhampered by selfish passion.

Though it is hard to be sure of who is truly enlightened, perhaps one may suggest certain minimal necessary conditions of enlightenment. An enlightened person must be one who consciously shares in a reality beyond the finite self, without the barriers erected by egoism, prejudice and partiality; one whose life is the vehicle of such a reality, living in love and compassion; one who has entered into eternal joy and communicates it to those around; one who cannot be deflected from the true course by the promises of passion or by threats of suffering. The enlightened one will not point to himself, but to the Self of All. Yet that Self is disclosed in and through him; he is the place of its revelation and of the mediation of its power. There may be many such manifestations of the Supreme Self in human history, many teachers who point the way to the Self of All. But now an awkward yet inescapable question appears: are there many teachers who point to the same Supreme Self? Or do doctrines of the Self and its relation to the world disagree? And the answer is, unfortunate as it may seem to one who wishes to escape from the exclusivity of one religious tradition, that doctrines of the Supreme Self differ. When and in so far as they do so, some of them at least must be mistaken.

We may seem to have let exclusive intolerance back on to the agenda. Have no lessons been learned from the bloody history of religions? Perhaps the most important lesson we could learn is that the beginning of faith is the search for enlightenment, for universal love and compassion, for understanding and wisdom. If we have learned that, our religion can never be used as a defensive ideology, as a weapon of hatred against others, as a body of propositions to test the loyalty of those whom we suspect of deviation. This search has led us to seek enlightened teachers, teachers of love, not hatred. And it has led us to seek for self-disclosures of a Supreme Self of Love, since that is the highest value of which we can conceive. We are compelled by truth to see that a revelation of the Supreme Self necessarily excludes the truth of propositions which deny the content of that revelation. Truth is exclusive, by nature. Not all spiritual teachers proclaim the same message. So a claim to the unique truth of one revelation, or one tradition of revelation, is not a restrictive and intolerant refusal to see any good in others. It is a necessary consequence of taking truth seriously.

Now we must face again the possibility that we cannot, just by looking within ourselves, and out of our own resources, haul ourselves up to enlightenment by our own bootstraps. Perhaps the truth is that there is a supreme spiritual reality which discloses itself in a unique way in one tradition, and which calls for our response in love to a supreme manifestation of love. Once that possibility has been raised, we do not have to go searching through ancient documents for evidence of such a manifestation. For at this point, Christianity, which might have seemed to offer only an ancient, external, dogmatic authority, offers a truly extraordinary possibility. It offers the presence of an Inner Teacher, present, inward and dynamic in power, who mediates to us the enlightened self of Christ, in the community of his disciples – "When he, the Spirit of truth, comes, he will guide you into all truth" (John 16:13). Strangely, this teacher is easier to find and more inward than almost any other one can discover. For, while enlightened humans are rare, and fakes are many, the Spirit, who is the inner teacher of truth, is available to all, wherever the Church exists; and he can never be removed by time or distance from one who turns to him.

Christians will not point simply to a long-dead Jewish teacher and miracle-worker for their spiritual authority. They have the present life of a community which mediates now the presence and power of the Supreme Self, but which does so as a perpetual re-enactment of the foundational disclosive events which lay down its character and the basic truths about the Supreme Self which define its uniqueness. Entering into this community, one accepts in faith the revelation upon which it is founded, and to which it is a continually renewed response. There is much still to learn and much to unlearn, as this community continues its historical exploration of the present reality of God. But the basic nature of that God, and the self-revealing acts which constitute the community as one of responsive, other-regarding and creative love, is given uniquely in the person of the enlightened teacher who was himself the full manifestation of the Supreme Self of Universal Love. If this is how one may come again to accept the uniqueness of Christ, it will no longer seem a problematic and unduly restrictive claim, but a grateful acceptance that God has acted to disclose his nature fully and decisively as the inner reality of Love which is the true Self of all, hidden by human sin but revealed once in the perfected human nature of Jesus and for all time in the renewing activity of the Holy Spirit.

That does not at all mean that other traditions have nothing to teach or to contribute to the search for truth. On the contrary, human minds are so partial and weak that any hope of reaching the fullness of truth will need to take many perspectives into account. We can hardly imagine the developments this will bring about in our understanding of faith. But it could be said that we now live at a time when a closer convergence of the semitic and Indian religious traditions is both possible and necessary. Bede Griffiths, who explores such a convergence in practice at Shantivanam, in South India, writes: "How can we reconcile these two 'myths', these two 'revelations' – the cosmic revelation of the infinite, timeless being manifesting in this world of time and change, but ultimately unaffected by it, with the Christian revelation of God's action in history ... bringing this world of time and change into union with himself? This, it seems to me, is the problem of the modern world" (Griffiths 1982:177). The Indian traditions have helped us to see more clearly that the universal Self of Love is to be found within the heart of each individual; that the way to it, and the fruits of it, are lives of love, compassion, peace and joy. What Christ teaches is that this Self of Love is also the goal of human history; its realization in matter is the reason for human existence; its transformation of the material to become the open manifestation of the spiritual is assured in the objective life of Jesus, which unites the human to the Divine indefectibly. That life is not a secret, kept for the few; it is given to the world through the life of the Church, and extends throughout the whole earth the pattern of redeemed humanity. As creation is logically the first Divine action, so the transfiguration of the creation is in the order of logic the last, its fulfilment in open relation to the creator. Between creation and consummation comes the incarnational process, the long series of patient Divine initiatives in history by which the material is personalized; a process finding its matrix and disclosive paradigm in the life of Jesus, but destined to spread throughout the world, as the rule of God comes near day by day.

Those who believe in Divine action are committed to belief that the purposes of God will be realized. He may permit creaturely freedom to frustrate his will; but not for ever. Evil will be eliminated; the material world will be filled with the glory of God; humanity and Deity will be united in love. How will these things be? When the Bible speaks of the End of all things, it speaks in the same deeply symbolic but mysterious way in which it speaks of creation. It does not in either case provide a timetable of events with an exact specification of the mechanics of the physical processes involved. It relates truths beyond the comprehension of those who hear them, perhaps beyond the capacity of our conceptual thought, adapted to the needs of this present embodiment, to convey; it relates these truths in terms which portray the inner and ultimate relationship of Divine and creaturely reality.

The whole ministry of Jesus was centred on his proclamation of the coming of the Kingdom of God ("From that time on Jesus began to preach, 'Repent, for the kingdom of heaven is near'"; Matt. 4:17). That is the time when God, perceived in his true nature as a God of love, will rule totally in the lives of human persons. Jesus speaks clearly of judgment, of a casting away of evil like chaff to be burned or rubbish to be thrown on the smouldering fires of the rubbish tip of Gehinnon. The apostles still thought of God as "consuming fire", before whom the whole earth rightly trembled in fear. There is a problem in reconciling this view with the total love of God, a problem which Christians have not always resolved very happily. But it reminds us that Divine love is not a sentimental weakness which overlooks all faults. It is a requirement as much as a gift. Those who would enter into the love of God must make themselves ready by entering into the love of their fellows. Those who hate their fellows exclude themselves from the Divine love. And when the restraining influence of that love is withdrawn from the world, then hatred, anger and destruction reign unchecked. That is the judgment; the Divine reflecting back of hatred upon the hearts which have first conceived it.

Much that happens in the world can rightly be seen as a foreshadowing of this judgment. We can say that God acts in judgment, as he causes the evil of human hearts to take shape in the events of human history – "This is the verdict: Light has come into the world, but men loved darkness instead of light" (John 3:19). It is possible that humans may destroy their world, by their own choice – but only if God permits them to do so. And it is quite clear that God will not permit everything to be wholly destroyed. Even at the most fearful time, he begins to create a new heaven and earth, which will endure for ever. When the New Testament apocalypse speaks of the time of great tribulation, of the stars falling from the sky, and the sun and moon being darkened, it relies upon the imagery of the Old Testament prophets, originally used to portray political catastrophe for Israel and Judah. God will not prevent all evil; for he will reflect back upon corrupted human wills the evil which they have perpetrated.

The prophets of Israel do not look for some safe heaven where earthly ills can be simply overlooked. On the contrary, they condemn social abuses of wealth and power as sins against God. What they hope for is not a forgetting of history in a changeless eternity, but the freeing of human society from oppression and injustice. As Reinhold Niebuhr put it, "The eternal can only be fulfilled in the temporal" (Niebuhr 1935:59); the eternal is not an escape from time, but the apotheosis of time into eternity, preserving its real significance and the importance of our historical actions within it. The social and material dimension is distinctive to the Biblical tradition and its successors. It is important for them that God really calls Israel to a special vocation of obedience; that he will establish his Kingdom; that he will eliminate evil from creation. The prophets do not experience God as related only to their own individual and inner lives. They experience him as related to the whole people in judgment and mercy, in ways which radically affect what happens to them in history. God requires of us that we act in history to overcome oppression and exploitation, and to build a society in which the virtues of justice and mercy can flourish.

In the Hebrew Bible, Divine actions call out prophets who proclaim judgment on sin and liberation from oppression for the faithful. God's purpose is to judge sinners and redeem the penitent; and to effect this through particular acts of the prophets and of the covenant community which they lead. The Biblical god is the judge and law-giver as much as the comforter and healer. Liberation, in the Bible, is not accomplished without judgment; and the mercy of God cannot be properly felt until the terror of his judgment has been seen. So it is the prophetic experience of social corruption, of a call to justice and of a hope for a renewed community, which grounds their depiction of God as stern judge and merciful liberator. God calls Israel to holiness and the world to repentance, revealing himself as the Lord of history, the personal judge and deliverer of humanity.

Is this picture changed in the New Testament? The Book of Revelation leaves us in no doubt about the reality of judgment. Nevertheless, there *is* a change; for Jesus, in dying the death of an outcast, dramatically changes the prophetic expectation of a Messiah who will liberate his people in triumph. The resurrection is not a political triumph at all; as far as the community of Israel goes, the crucifixion was a defeat and an end to their hopes for liberation. The destruction of the Temple in Jerusalem, predicted by Jesus, put an end to all hopes of a political triumph for the nation of ancient Israel. So the model of Divine action is changed from that of victory by plague and battle, to that of humble love which endures worldly defeat. True, there is judgment and destruction, the flaming triumph of angels, to come. But in this age, Divine action is to be found in the form of a servant, despised and rejected, mocked and put to death. The paradigm model of God becomes that of the suffering servant, and the community which takes his name must be shaped on that model. From that time on, "man is challenged to participate in the sufferings of God at the hands of a godless world" (Bonhoeffer 1971:361). God is still the judge and deliverer; but he is now also seen as the suffering servant; his judgment is withheld and his deliverance does not take form in the political sphere.

If Christ shows us the form of God's action, then God heals, forgives and inspires; in this world he foreshadows the reality of the Kingdom; but he does not destroy or wholly transform the structures of the world.

Of course, Jesus does not only or even primarily speak of fearful judgment. He preaches a time of liberation, of freedom for the oppressed, healing for the sick and forgiveness for those burdened by guilt (Luke 4:18–19). God's action will be a liberating and reconciling action, creating a reality which will survive judgment and achieve perfect fulfilment. The final redemption is not portrayed as wholly other-worldly, as if this material world would be utterly destroyed and only an immaterial world of disembodied souls left. The resurrection is of the body; it is a refashioning of the physical, transfigured by Divine glory. Counterpointing his view that the eternal must be fulfilled (or, we might say, expressed in its full creative reality) in the temporal, Niebuhr writes that "To believe that the body is resurrected is to say ... that history is fulfilled in eternity" (Niebuhr 1937:302). Historical action is real; but its true fulfilment is found beyond its ephemeral reality. Paul writes of this present age as groaning in expectation of a new birth (Romans 8:13–23). He writes of our present corruptible bodies as seeds which will flower in a spirit-filled, incorruptible form (there will be a *soma pneumatikon*) (1 Cor. 15:35–44). This is certainly a transformation well beyond the limits of present embodiment. But it is a form of embodiment; a new humanity, but still a form of humanity. We can as little conceive of what this will be like in detail as the apostles could. Here, images are our only speech, stammering before our inability to know what a fulfilled relation of our humanity to God will be, or how we might stand in relation to a full manifestation of the Divine glory. Divine action is seen now in all those processes which embody the Spirit in the forms of flesh, and which conserve all that is good in creation for eternity.

How will this take place, and when will it be? As to that, even Jesus professes ignorance (Matt. 24:35–36) – which strongly implies that human minds, as such, cannot or are not permitted to know. Yet one thing is reiterated by Jesus; that we are to watch and be ready, for the Lord will come

"Like a thief in the night", at the time we least expect (Matt. 24: 42–43). The meaning seems to be that, while we are ignorant of how and when God's rule will be fully manifested (by the *par-ousia*, the unveiled immanence of Being, the manifestation of the Ultimately Real), we must not think either that it is so far in the future that we can safely defer consideration of it, or that we will have plenty of time to prepare ourselves later. As Jesus says, "The Kingdom is at hand" (Matt. 4:17). The Eternal is not far off in time; but breaks in now, whether perceived or unperceived. Moment by moment, we define our relation to Eternity; there is no waiting to settle our exact situation later, while we busy ourselves with more pressing worldly concerns. We must look for an eternal fulfilment of every present, by its relation to the Being which Christ brings near. And we must regard each moment with hope, as bearing the presence of Christ. God acts by confronting us when we least expect it, now and not later, with the challenge to respond in trust to his declaration of purpose and fulfilment.

If we ask about the ultimate end of the universe, we are not thinking of many billions of years in the future, when the cosmos will, in accordance with the second law of thermodynamics, have reached a condition of final entropy, of unified non-activity, and when the planet earth will millions of years before have been swallowed up by the exploding sun. We are, in the theistic context, thinking of the endless flourishing of finite persons, made one in the infinite ocean of the Divine love. Clearly, this will not be in the present physical structure of the universe, which, by the presently known laws of physics, is bound to decay and die. Human fulfilment, then, is to be found beyond the boundaries of our presently known physical cosmos. Paul tries to make this clear by contrasting our present bodies of flesh and blood (*soma psychikon*) with the Spirit-filled and incorruptible bodies of the resurrection world. The Apocalyptic images, strange and unfamiliar to us, so that we hardly know how to interpret them, nevertheless speak of the destruction of the stars and the creation of a new heaven and earth. The goal of creation does not lie far in the future, in a physical state within this space-time, however wonderful, in which we shall have no share. All of us, now living, long dead and as yet unborn, are to share in the new creation.

In other words, the consummation of all things will be in God, in the realm of the eternal.

It is obviously inadequate to think of the purpose of the creation as lying in some final temporal state, however perfect. For then all that has gone before will be forgotten and put aside, and we ourselves will have died long before it comes. As David Pailin clearly sees, "the proper goal of divine creativity is not to be envisaged as the attainment of a particular state of affairs but as the continual pursuit of aesthetic enrichment" (Pailin 1989:132). I am uneasy about the restriction of realized values to the category of the aesthetic; but otherwise, the point is well made, that "the end of all things" is not properly conceivable as some last state. It must refer to the nature and value of the whole process. The purpose of creation lies in the continual realization of value. Yet that purpose is hardly realized totally in this ambiguous world of so much suffering and evil. The values of the present must be conserved and transfigured in God; and it must be possible for us all to share in that final indestructible vision of the completed, redeemed pattern of values which has been the history of this world, and to which our lives have contributed, for good or ill. The Biblical view is that such a consummation is not adequately representable in the concepts we have for understanding this world. But it gives us vivid images of the destruction of evil and the transfigured life of our present personalities in full knowledge of the glory of God (the image of "being with Christ in the air"), and in the community of all those who have been made one in Christ ("This plan, which God will complete when the time is right, is to bring all creation together, everything in heaven and on earth, with Christ as head", Ephesians 1:10).

It is not playing fast and loose with the evidence to take Biblical language in a poetic and metaphorical way. In his magisterial study, *The Language and Imagery of the Bible* (Caird 1980), G.B. Caird shows in detail how, throughout the whole Bible, metaphor and imagery, sometimes fantastic in its details, is central to the style of writing. The Biblical writers "regularly used end-of-the-world language metaphorically to refer to that which they well knew was not the end of the world" (ibid.:256). Thus, when Jesus speaks of the Son of Man as coming within a generation, though only God knows its day and hour (Mark 13:39 and 32), "the paratactical Hebrew mind did not need to be told that the two sayings were at different levels: embodied in the historical event which Jesus predicted, the day would come within a generation; in its full final, literal reality its time was known only to God" (ibid.:267). All that is needed to gain a rich spiritual under-standing of Jesus' teaching about "the end" is a sense of the mythical imagery which is essential to speak of human relation to ultimate judgment and salvation at every time. So Caird comments on Weiss and Schweitzer that they "were right in thinking that eschatology was central to the understanding of biblical thought, but wrong in assuming that the biblical writers had minds as pedestrian as their own" (ibid.:271). Eschatology is not literally about the final seconds of time; it is about the consummation in eternity of every temporal moment, a consummation which is represented to humanity under the form of the crucified and risen Christ.

The danger of stressing that the fulfilment of God's purpose lies in the future – perhaps far in the future, as 2 Peter 3:8 implies – is that we shall see our present material existences as unimportant by comparison with the glory to come, or that we shall see our material world and our present actions as insignificant in the perspective of eternity. It is this danger that is counteracted by Jesus' insistence that the Kingdom is even now among or within (*entos*) us (Luke 17:20–21). God begins his rule as we enter the community of his love with child-like faith. As we should see creation as our present total dependence upon God, so we should see the End as our trans-figuration into God's unveiled presence. We must be alert and watchful for the coming of the Kingdom, which will be fully realized in the renewed resurrection world, out of the responses of our present faith, hope and love. It is this life and this world which will be fully redeemed and united to God, by his transforming action. But it will be so transformed beyond the confines of what we now understand as physical reality.

Our hope is wretched if it is for this world only; but it is vain if it is not for this world at all. The perspective of Christian theism delivers us from thinking that if our plans fail now, all is lost. And it prevents us thinking that what we do now does not matter, that all action is vanity, that the material is incompatible with the spiritual. It is our vocation to make the material the sphere of unrestricted Divine action. There is a real goal in history, the establishing of a human community of love. But what happens in the future of this planet earth is not the final goal of creation. The goal must be the integration of every moment into an eternal fulfil-ment. The Kingdom is not an idle dream; it can be brought about, but only by love, never by hatred or violence. The time and manner of its realization are unknowable by us; but God begins to realize it in us as we allow him to do so, and he will fully realize it when the history of the earth has run its course. As long as evil persists, it will be hindered. So praying for its coming is praying for the ending of evil, of selfish egoism, pride and hatred. In moments of pessimism, we cannot see these things passing from human life. But with God all things are possible. So we may hope and pray for it; we must begin by extirpating egoism, pride and hatred from our own lives; and we may be sure that, whatever hap-pens on this planet, our lives will continue for ever far beyond its boundaries. God's ultimate goal will not be defeated; for all the good of this world will be conserved. Having played our parts in the unfolding of the Divine purpose, we shall, in a fully liberated and realized state, experience the completed pattern of values of this world which is eternally conserved in God. What precisely those values will be, and how precisely they will be realized, is, by the free decision and desire of God, a matter for humanity itself to determine. The realization of that goal, however, is the final aim of Divine action in the world; and that aim provides the rationale for all the parti-cular Divine actions which continually shape and direct the temporal process of this universe. Within such a perspective, God has not been driven out beyond the periphery of our scientific and moral concerns; nor has Jesus receded into an ever-more ancient past. God is the goal of truth and goodness; the nature of his love is indefectibly shown in Jesus and is conveyed to humanity through the community of the Church. Divine action, normatively present, though surely not yet openly displayed, in this community, and creatively present throughout the whole universe, is to be discerned in every movement towards the fulfilment of all things in love, which is the final purpose and first motivation of all creation.

Reference Bibliography

Abraham, W. J. (1982) *Divine Revelation and the Limits of Historical Criticism*, Oxford: Clarendon Press.

Anscombe, G. E. M. (1957) *Intention*, Oxford University Press.

Anselm (1965) *Proslogion*, trans. M. J. Charlesworth, Oxford: Clarendon Press.

Aquinas, T. (1964) *Summa Theologiae*, vols. 1–60, Blackfriars ed., London: Eyre and Spottiswoode.

Aquinas, T. (1975) *Summa Contra Gentiles*, trans. A. C. Pegis, Notre Dame: University of Notre Dame Press.

Aristotle (1960) *Metaphysics*, trans. R. Hope, Ann Arbor: University of Michigan Press.

Armstrong, D. (1968) *A Materialist Theory of Mind*, London: Routledge.

Atkins, P. W. (1981) *The Creation*, London: Freeman.

Augustine. (1945) *The City of God*, London: Dent.

Augustine. (1876) *The Confessions*, in Dods M. (ed.) *The Works of Augustine*, Edinburgh: T. & T. Clark.

Bacon, F. (1863) *Of the Proficience and Advancement of Learning*, in *The Works of Francis Bacon*, ed. J. Spedding, R. L. Ellis and D. D. Heath, Boston: Tagard and Thompson.

Baelz, P. (1968) *Prayer and Providence*, London: SPCK.

Barbour, I. G. (1966) *Issues in Science and Religion*, London: SCM Press.

Barrow, J. D. and Tipler, E. J. (1986) *The Anthropic Cosmological Principle*, Oxford: Clarendon Press.

Bartholomew, D. J. (1984) *God of Chance*, London: SCM Press.

Benedict XIV, Pope (1738) *De Servorum Dei Beatificatione et Beatorum Canonizatione*, part 4: 'De Miraculis', Bologna.

Bertocci, P. A. (1951) *Introduction to the Philosophy of Religion*, Englewood Cliffs: Prentice-Hall.

Bohm, D. (1980) *Wholeness and the Implicate Order*, London: Routledge.

Bohr, N. (1958) *Atomic Physics and Human Knowledge*, London: Wiley.

Bonhoeffer, D. (1979) *Letters and Papers from Prison*, London: SCM Press.

Bowden, J. (1988) *Jesus: The Unanswered Questions*, London: SCM Press.

Brummer, V. (1988) *What Are We Doing When We Pray?* London: SCM Press.

Bultmann, R. (1953) 'New Testament and Mythology', in *Kerygma and Myth*, ed. H. W. Bartsch, trans. R. Fuller, London: SPCK.

Butler, Bishop (1906) *The Analogy of Religion*, Plymouth: Brendon and Son.

Caird, G. B. (1980) *The Language and Imagery of the Bible*, London: Duckworth.

Capek, M. (1961) *The Philosophical Impact of Modern Physics*, New Jersey: Princeton.

Capra, F. (1976) *The Tao of Physics*, London: Fontana.

Chittick, W. C. (1983) *The Sufi Path of Love*, Albany: State University of New York Press.

Cupitt, D. (1980) *Taking Leave of God*, London: SCM Press.

Denzinger (1960) *Enchiridion Symbolorum Definitionem*, (3rd. ed.), Freiburg.

Descartes, R. (1966) *Discourse on Method and Meditations*, trans. A. Wollaston, London: Penguin.

Farrer, A. (1967) *Faith and Speculation*, London: A. and C. Black.

Flew, A. and MacIntyre, A. (eds.) (1955) *New Essays in Philosophical Theology*, London: SCM Press.

Gadamer, H.-G. (1960) *Wahrheit und Methode*, Tübingen.

Geach, P. (1969) *God and the Soul*, London: Routledge.

Geach, P. and Anscombe, E. (1961) *Three Philosophers*, Oxford University Press.

Griffiths, B. (1982) *The Marriage of East and West*, London: Fount.

Hartshorne, C. (1953) *Reality as Social Process*, Boston: Beacon Press.

Hebblethwaite, B. (1976) *Evil, Suffering and Religion*, London.

Hebblethwaite, B. (1987) *The Incarnation*, Cambridge University Press.

Hebblethwaite, B. (1988) *The Ocean of Truth*, Cambridge University Press.

Hick, J. (1957) *Faith and Knowledge*, London: Macmillan.

Hick, J. (1971) *Arguments for the Existence of God*, London: Macmillan.

Hick, J. (1989) *An Interpretation of Religion*, London: Macmillan.

Hume, D. (1902) *Enquiry Concerning Human Understanding*, ed. L. A. Selby-Bigge, Oxford University Press.

Hume, D. (1935) *Dialogues Concerning Natural Religion*, ed. N. K. Smith, Oxford: Clarendon Press.

Jaki, S. (1978) *The Road of Science and the Ways to God*, Chicago: University Press.

James, W. (1896) *The Will to Believe*, London: Longmans.

Kant, I. (1952) *Critique of Pure Reason*, trans. N. Kemp-Smith, London: Macmillan.

Kant, I. (1956) *Critique of Practical Reason*, trans. L. W. Beck, Indianapolis: Bobbs-Merrill.

Kaufman, G. (1972) *God the Problem*, Harvard University Press.

Kenny, A. (1969) *The Five Ways*, London: Routledge.

Kenny, A. (1979) *The God of the Philosophers*, Oxford: Clarendon Press.

King, R. H. (1974) *The Meaning of God*, London.

Knox, J. (1958) *The Death of Jesus*, Nashville: Abingdon Press.

Langford, M. (1981) *Providence*, London: SCM Press.

Laplace, S. P. (1951) *A Philosophical Essay on Probabilities*, trans. F. W. Truscott and F. L. Emory, New York: Dover.

Leibniz, G. W. (1973) *On the Ultimate Origin of Things*, in *Philosophical Writings*, trans. M. Morris, London: Dent.

Lessing, G. E. (1956) 'On the Proof of the Spirit and of Power', in H. Chadwick (ed.) *Lessing's Theological Writings*, Edinburgh: A. and C. Black.

Lloyd Morgan, C. (1926) *Life, Mind and Spirit*, London: Williams and Norgate.

Lucas, J. R. (1976) *Freedom and Grace*, London: SPCK.

MacIntyre, A. (1985) *After Virtue*, London: Duckworth.

Mackie, J. L. (1982) *The Miracle of Theism*, Oxford: Clarendon Press.

MacKinnon, A. (1967) 'Of Miracle and Paradox', in the *American Philosophical Quarterly*, 1967, vol. 4.

Mascall, E. L. (1966) *He Who Is*, London: Darton, Longman, Todd.

Mill, J. S. (1969) *Autobiography*, ed. J. Stillinger, Oxford University Press.

Monod, J. (1972) *Chance and Necessity*, London: Collins.

Montefiore, H. (1985) *The Probability of God*, London: SCM Press.

Morris, T. (1986) *The Logic of God Incarnate*, Cornell University Press.

Nagel, E. and Newman, J. R. (1959) *Godel's Proof*, London: Routledge.

Neusner, J. (1988) 'Is the God of Judaism Incarnate?' in *Religious Studies*, vol. 24, 2.

Newton, I. (1952) *Opticks*, New York: Dover.

Newton, I. (1962) *Principia Mathematica*, trans. Motte, Berkeley: University of California Press.

Niebuhr, R. (1935) *An Interpretation of Christian Ethics*, New York: Harper & Row.

Niebuhr, R. (1937) *Beyond Tragedy*, New York: Scribner.

Nietzsche, F. (1972) *Thus Spake Zaracthustra*, London: Penguin.

Pailin, D. A. (1989) *God and the Processes of Reality*, London: Routledge.

Parrinder, G. (1983) *Avatar and Incarnation*, Oxford University Press.

Pascal, B. (1925) *Pensées*, ed. Brunschvigg, Paris: Hachette.

Peacocke, A. R. (1979) *Creation and the World of Science*, Oxford: Clarendon Press.

Peacocke, A. R. (1986) *God and the New Biology*, London: Dent.

Penelhum, T. (1971) *Religion and Rationality*, New York.

Phillips, D. Z. (1965) *The Concept of Prayer*, London: Routledge.

Plantinga, A. (1974) *The Nature of Necessity*, Oxford: Clarendon Press.

Plantinga, A. (1977) *God, Freedom and Evil*, Grand Rapids: Eerdmans.

Plato (1971) *Timaeus*, London: Penguin.

Plato (1982) *Phaedo*, trans. H. N. Fowler, London: Heinemann.

Plotinus (1966) *Enneads*, trans. A. H. Armstrong, London: Heinemann.

Polkinghorne, J. (1979) *The Particle Play*, London: Freeman.

Polkinghorne, J. (1988) *Science and Creation*, London: SPCK.

Polkinghorne, J. (1989) *Science and Providence*, London: SPCK.

Prigogene, I. and Stengers, I. (1984) *Order Out of Chaos* London: Heinemann.

Ramsey, I. T. (1957) *Religious Language*, London: SCM Press.

Sankara (1962) *The Vedanta Sutras*, trans. G. Thibaut, in *Sacred Books of the East*, ed. Max Muller, vols. 34 and 38, Delhi: Motilal Banarsidass.

Sherrard, P. (1987) *The Eclipse of Man and Nature*, Rochester: Lindisfarne Press.

Smart, N. (1981) *Beyond Ideology: Religion and the Future of Western Civilisation*, San Francisco: Harper and Row.

Soggin, A. (1985) *A History of Israel*, London: SCM Press.

Stump, E. (1979) 'Petitionary Prayer', in the *American Philosophical Quarterly*, 1979, 16: 81–91.

Surin, K. (1986) *Theology and the Problem of Evil*, Oxford: Basil Blackwell.

Sutherland, S. R. (1984) *God, Jesus and Belief*, Oxford: Basil Blackwell.

Swinburne, R. (1970) *The Concept of Miracle*, London: Macmillan.

Swinburne, R. (1979) *The Existence of God*, Oxford: Clarendon Press.

Swinburne, R. (1986) *The Evolution of the Soul*, Oxford: Clarendon Press.

Taylor, R. (1966) *Action and Purpose*, Englewood Cliffs: Prentice-Hall.

Tillich, P. (1951) *Systematic Theology*, vol. 1. Chicago: University of Chicago Press.

Torrance, T. F. (1980) *Christian Theology and Scientific Culture*, Belfast: Christian Journals.

Troeltsch, E. (1913) 'Historische und Dogmatische Method in der Theologie', in *Gesammelte Schriften*, vol. 2, Tübingen.

Ward, K. (1982) *Rational Theology and the Creativity of God*, Oxford: Basil Blackwell.

Wells, G. A. (1975) *Did Jesus Exist?*, London: Pemberton.

White, A. R. (1968) *The Philosophy of Action*, Oxford University Press.

White, V. (1985) *The Fall of a Sparrow*, Exeter: Paternoster.

Whitehead, A. N. (1929) *Process and Reality*, Cambridge University Press.

Wiles, M. (1976) *Working Papers in Doctrine*, London: SCM Press.

Wiles, M. (1986) *God's Action in the World*, London: SCM Press.

Williams, D. D. (1968) *The Spirit and the Forms of Love*, Welwyn.

Williams, P. (1989) *Mahayana Buddhism*, London: Routledge.